Rabbits For Dummies®

WITHDRAWN

Cheat Sheet

Emergency Numbers

Contact	Phone Number
Veterinarian	
24-Hour Emergency Pet Hospital	
ASPCA Animal Poison Control Center	888-4ANI-HELP (888-42...
Pet Sitter	
Animal Control	

D0572376

Proactive Ways to Keep Your Rabbit Healthy

- ✔ Feed a proper diet
- ✔ Provide a clean, safe environment (home and hutch)
- ✔ Encourage plenty of exercise
- ✔ Spay or neuter
- ✔ Groom frequently
- ✔ Know your rabbit's normal behavior
- ✔ Maintain a relationship with your rabbit's veterinarian
- ✔ Know the symptoms of common rabbit diseases
- ✔ Keep safe from predators
- ✔ Handle properly

Important Rabbit Organizations

- ✔ **House Rabbit Society:** 148 Broadway, Richmond, CA 94804; (510) 970-7575; Internet: www.rabbit.org
- ✔ **American Rabbit Breeders Association (ARBA):** P.O. Box 426, Bloomington, IL 61702; (309) 664-7500; E-mail: arbapost@aol.com
- ✔ **Humane Society of the United States:** Companion Animals Section: 2100 L St., NW, Washington, DC 20037; (202) 452-1100; Internet: www.hsus.org

For Dummies: Bestselling Book Series for Beginners

Rabbits For Dummies®

Situations That Require a Visit to the Veterinarian

If your rabbit is sick or injured, take him to a veterinarian in a pet carrier. Handle your injured rabbit gently so you don't add to the injury.

Symptom(s)	Possible cause
Bleeding	Injury (Apply pressure to stop the bleeding)
Blood in urine	Severe infection or bladder injury
Inability to stand; staggering	Severe sickness
Paralysis	Injury to the spine
Rapid breathing, raspy breathing, heavy coughing	Illness or infection
Refusal to eat	Serious illness or mild colic
Severe pain indicated by refusal to eat, teeth grinding, and limping	Injury or illness
Straining to defecate or urinate	Intestinal or urethral blockage
Swelling on body part that's hot to the touch	Injury
Teary, closed, red, or cloudy eye	Eye injury or infection
Temperature significantly above or below 101–103ºF	Chill or fever
Tilted head	Injury, bacterial infection

Things to Keep Your Rabbit Away From

Some things are dangerous to a rabbit. Sometimes a rabbit is a danger to something.

- Antifreeze
- Balconies
- Carpet edges
- Cleaning fluids
- Electrical cords
- Heating elements
- Paint fumes
- Stairways
- Telephone wires
- Toxic plants

First-Aid Kit

- Antibacterial cleanser
- Cotton pads
- Eyewash
- Gauze pads
- Heating pad or hot water bottle
- Scissors (to cut the tape)
- Surgical tape
- Thermometer
- K-Y Jelly (to lubricate the thermometer)

For Dummies: Bestselling Book Series for Beginners

Rabbits
FOR
DUMMIES®

by Audrey Pavia

WILEY

Wiley Publishing, Inc.

Rabbits For Dummies®

Published by
Wiley Publishing, Inc.
111 River St.
Hoboken, NJ 07030
www.wiley.com

About the Author

Audrey Pavia is a former pet magazine editor and an award-winning freelance writer specializing in animal subjects. She has authored articles on various rabbit topics in *Rabbits, Critters,* and *Pet Product News* magazines and is a consulting editor for *Rabbits Magazine*. She has authored 12 other animal books besides *Rabbits For Dummies*, including the *Owners Guide to the Rabbit*.

Audrey has been involved with rabbits since the age of 10, when she first joined her local 4-H rabbit project. She currently resides in Santa Ana, California, with her husband and a house full of pets.

Dedication

To Doey and Rusty, who introduced me to the world of rabbits and loved me despite my inexperience.

Author's Acknowledgments

I would like to thank the following people for their assistance with writing this book:

Laura Doering of *Rabbits USA* magazine; Wayne Kopit, DVM, of Brook-Ellis Animal Hospital in Fountain Valley, Calif.; Richard Gehr of the American Rabbit Breeders Association; Linda J. Hoover of the Rabbit Hopping Society; attorney Roberta Kraus; my editors Tonya Maddox Cupp and Tracy Boggier; technical editor Susan Brown, DVM; Dominique DeVito; veterinary technician and future veterinarian Heidi Pavia; Margo DeMello, president of the House Rabbit Society; my always supportive husband Randy Mastronicola; and my very helpful parents, Haydee and John Pavia.

I would also like to thank my animal companions, Simba, Murray, and Nigel, for being so patient with me while I was glued to my desk.

Publisher's Acknowledgments

We're proud of this book; please send us your comments through our Dummies online registration form located at www.dummies.com/register/.

Some of the people who helped bring this book to market include the following:

Acquisitions, Editorial, and Media Development

Project Editor: Tonya Maddox Cupp

Acquisitions Editor: Tracy Boggier

Copy Editor: Esmeralda St. Clair

Acquisitions Coordinator: Holly Grimes

Technical Editor: Susan A. Brown, D.V.M.

Editorial Manager: Jennifer Ehrlich

Editorial Assistant: Elizabeth Rea

Cover Photos: Faith A. Uridel Photography

Cartoons: Rich Tennant, www.the5thwave.com

Production

Project Coordinator: Nancee Reeves

Layout and Graphics: Carrie Foster, Joyce Haughey, Stephanie D. Jumper, Tiffany Muth, Brent Savage

Proofreaders: TECHBOOKS Production Services

Indexer: TECHBOOKS Production Services

Special Help: Beth Adelman, Richard H. Fox

Special Art Illustrations: Sally Brown

Publishing and Editorial for Consumer Dummies

Diane Graves Steele, Vice President and Publisher, Consumer Dummies

Joyce Pepple, Acquisitions Director, Consumer Dummies

Kristin A. Cocks, Product Development Director, Consumer Dummies

Michael Spring, Vice President and Publisher, Travel

Brice Gosnell, Associate Publisher, Travel

Suzanne Jannetta, Editorial Director, Travel

Publishing for Technology Dummies

Andy Cummings, Vice President and Publisher, Dummies Technology/General User

Composition Services

Gerry Fahey, Vice President of Production Services

Debbie Stailey, Director of Composition Services

Contents at a Glance

Table of Contents

Part II: Keeping Your Rabbit Well Fed and Funk Free 59

Chapter 9: Nipping and Gnawing Common Health Problems in the Bud 119

Part III: Holing Up With Your Companion 147

Chapter 10: Reading Your Rabbit 149

Introduction

W elcome to *Rabbits For Dummies,* the one and only book that you need to get started in the wonderful world of rabbit ownership. Of course, when it comes to rabbits, you can never stop discovering. Although they may seem like simple little creatures, rabbits are actually physically and emotionally complex and never cease to amaze those who live with them.

You came to the right book. Whether you're thinking about getting your first rabbit or already have a bunny and want to find out more about how to take care of him, I'm certain this book can be a great help.

Why You Need This Book

Why do you need a book like this? How hard is owning a rabbit? *Rabbits For Dummies* is designed to be a useful reference for those who aren't experts, as well as those who know zero about rabbits. Even people who know a thing or two about bunnies can benefit from this book, as it's a reference for behavior and health.

Actually, rabbits are nothing like cats and dogs, the two most-common pets. The rabbit's digestive system is more akin to a horse than a feline or a canine. And the psychological make up of a bunny is closer to that of a bird than that of a cat or dog.

In order to understand your rabbit and care for him properly, you have to know the details specific to rabbit ownership. By finding out about rabbit psychology, rabbit physiology, and basic rabbit care, you'll have what it takes to take care of a rabbit just right.

So why *do* you need this book? Because it can

- Help you understand rabbits — *your* rabbit.
- Tell you how to communicate with your bunny.
- Show you how to care for this amazing creature, who can prove to you in a short amount of time that you aren't dealing with a cat or a dog!

This book's for you if you

- ✔ Want a rabbit.
- ✔ Think rabbits are cool and want to know more about them.
- ✔ Have a rabbit and are considering getting another.
- ✔ Own a rabbit and are considering breeding or showing it.
- ✔ Have a rabbit (or two) and want to expand your knowledge on how to care for these pets.

About This Book

If *Rabbits For Dummies* is like a department store: You're able to enter on whatever floor you like. You don't have to walk past that smelly perfume counter to get to the housewares section on the third floor. You just walk into the housewares section.

In other words, you don't have start reading this book at the beginning, going through each page until you reach the end. You can turn to any section of the book that interests you and begin reading at that point and not feel lost. You don't have to remember what you read yesterday, and you don't have to read chapters of sections in order. Just find something that interests you, read it, do it, and put the book back on your shelf. (No one expects you to read from cover to cover except maybe your high school English teacher, but you can ignore her this time around.)

Conventions Used in This Book

In this book, I refer to rabbits with the male pronouns (he, his, him) and the female pronouns (she, her). This convention is merely for readability's sake. I don't call rabbits "it" because they're living creatures.

Also, new words that you may not have seen before are in italics, while keywords are listed in bold.

What You're Not to Read

From time to time in this book, I share some information that may be interesting but isn't essential to the complete understanding of the topic at hand. In these cases, I placed the information in a gray box called a *sidebar*. You don't have to read these if you don't want to.

Foolish Assumptions

In this book, I assume you know a rabbit when you see one. And that's about it. Except that I also take for granted that you care about rabbits and want to treat them with kindness. I also assume that you are allowed to keep rabbits in the area where you live.

I also assume that you're no dummy, despite the title of this book. You may not know much about rabbits, but you're sharp enough to develop a little savvy. You also aren't going to pretend to be an expert on a subject that you don't know much about. You know the best way to find out about things is to read about what the experts have to say on the subject. I think you're pretty smart — otherwise, you wouldn't have bought this book.

How This Book Is Organized

Rabbits For Dummies is made up of five parts. That's more than enough parts, but you need plenty of the right information to get started.

Part 1: Bringing on the Bunny Basics

Before you even get a rabbit, you need to know what rabbits are all about. This section can help you figure that out. This part offers information about whether a rabbit is right for your lifestyle; how rabbits are put together; how to go about choosing a rabbit; and the best place to find one.

Part II: Keeping Your Rabbit Well Fed and Funk Free

Housing, cleaning and feeding: Three important elements for keeping a rabbit, all covered in this section of the book. You can find out if you prefer to keep your rabbit indoors or out; why keeping your rabbit clean is important; and how the age-old convention of feeding rabbit pellets is quickly becoming a thing of the past.

Rabbits are prone to illness. In this part, you can find out how to recognize common rabbit illnesses, how to prevent them, and when to go to the vet. You also get help putting together a bunny first-aid kit and discovering how to handle rabbit emergencies.

Part III: Holing Up with Your Companion

Rabbit personality is what makes living with a bunny so much fun. Find out how to understand bunny body language. (They can't speak English.) Discover how to litter box train your rabbit, do some fun tricks, and deal with behavior problems. This part also discusses breeding your rabbit and how to say the final goodbye when that inevitable moment comes.

Part IV: Enjoying Your Fun Bunny

Think rabbits don't do much except sit in a cage all day? Wrong! You can have all kinds of fun with your rabbit. Part IV discusses traveling with your pet, playing with him, and even showing your rabbit. The unique sport of rabbit-hopping is discussed, along with details on how to get involved with rabbit social issues.

Part V: Part of Tens

In the Part of Tens I tackle two different subjects: ways to keep your rabbit healthy and rabbit Web sites. In the health chapter, you'll find an overview of the ten most crucial elements in rabbit care. Follow the advice in the chapter, and your rabbit is likely to live a long, healthy life. Chapter 19 has the best links on the Internet for rabbit lovers.

Appendix

The appendix in this book contains a plethora of rabbit resources, including purebred rabbit clubs and registries, rabbit activity groups, educational organizations, rabbit rescue societies, rabbit publications, and other useful sources for rabbit owners.

Icons Used in This Book

As with all the other books in the *For Dummies* series, this book has little icons in the margins to call your attention to specific types of information. See the following explanations of what each of those icons means:

You'll see this icon throughout this book because when it comes to rabbits, you need to do plenty of remembering. I placed this icon next to important information that you won't want to miss or forget.

When you see this symbol, beware! This icon indicates a serious circumstance to watch out for.

Occasionally, rabbit information gets a bit technical, hence this icon. When you see it, put the left side of your brain in high gear.

This icon alerts you to helpful hints regarding rabbits, pertaining to their care and handling. If you read the information next to this icon, you'll find you have a happier, healthier rabbit.

Where to Go from Here

Go wherever you want. You can start at Chapter 1 and read all the way through to the final Appendix, or you can hop, skip, and jump around — much like a rabbit.

If you're going to do that skipping around thing, can I at least ask you for a favor? Before you start jumping from place to place, take a few moments to read through Chapter 1, which contains the most important questions you want to ask yourself before you embark on the responsibility of rabbit owner-ship. If you

- are considering getting a rabbit, hop over to Chapter 1.
- have decided you're going to buy a rabbit, Chapters 3 and 4 help you find the right one.
- already have a rabbit or two and want to get the latest perspective on a healthy bunny diet, see Chapter 7.
- want to train your rabbit, Chapter 11 will help you out.
- want to participate in rabbit-related activities, Chapter 17 can get you started.

Part I
Bringing on the Bunny Basics

"Oh, it was so cute. He looked at me with those big ears, his nose twitching, and he started hopping up and down. That's when I said, 'Arthur, stop hopping up and down! We'll go pick out a rabbit this afternoon'."

In this part . . .

If you're just starting out with a rabbit, you need the basics. This part gives them to you. You find details on how to tell if a rabbit is the right pet for you, the different breeds and types of rabbits available, and the best places to find a healthy rabbit. You also see details about how the rabbit's body works and receive pointers on how to understand your rabbit's brain.

Chapter 1

Is a Rabbit Right for You?

Rabbits are cute, fuzzy, and make great pets, but these truths alone aren't good enough reasons to own one. If rabbits are so wonderful, why not have one? The answer is simple: Though rabbits are terrific companions for many reasons, they also demand plenty of work and a serious commitment. For example, my friend Sarah (name changed to protect the not-so-innocent) works eight hours a day at an office job and spends another hour a day commuting back and forth to work. So she's gone from her home a good nine hours a day, and that's on the days when she comes right home from work. Often, Sarah, who is single, meets her girlfriends after work for happy hour or heads off to the gym to exercise. On those nights, she doesn't get home until 9 or 10 p.m. Because Sarah's schedule doesn't give her enough time to spend with a dog, she opted for a rabbit. She should have chosen a hermit crab. A rabbit, a very social animal, would be just as unhappy as a dog in this situation.

In addition to the number of hours that you need to spend with a rabbit, also consider the workload and responsibility involved in owning a rabbit and whether you really want to deal with it. A rabbit needs watering, feeding, exercising, and interacting along with having her fresh foods washed and her cage cleaned — all on a daily basis.

If you find yourself with the overpowering urge to be a rabbit owner, it's time to ask yourself some questions before you actually take the plunge. If you take the time to do the soul searching that ultimately comes along with answering these questions — both you and your rabbit will be happy — should you decide to get one.

What happens if you don't ask yourself these questions and just go out and get a rabbit because you *think* you want one? If it turns out that rabbit ownership isn't really right for you, then the rabbit will ultimately suffer. Typically, when people don't want their rabbits, they end up taking them to an animal shelter or turning them loose in the woods in the hopes that the rabbit can get by on its own. Sadly, rabbits are put to death in animal shelters, just like their canine and feline counterparts, and domesticated rabbits that are set free to fend for themselves are rarely capable of doing so. Finding another home for him is an option but not an easy one. Prospective rabbit owners don't grow on trees, as you will quickly find out when you start trying to find another home for your rabbit. So spare yourself and the rabbit all the heartache and probe deep into your psyche before taking the plunge, using the following questions as a guideline to your self-scrutiny.

Why in the World Do 1 Want a Rabbit?

People are drawn to rabbits for different reasons. Most of them think rabbits are cute (and they're right). Others want to breed and show them for enjoyment and prestige. Some are looking for a pet that's less work than a dog yet different from a cat. The fact that rabbits are cute and fuzzy may motivate you to explore the possibility of rabbit ownership. That's okay, but notice that I said *explore,* not *jump into* rabbit ownership. Before you acquire a rabbit, you need to find out as much as you can about rabbits and what's involved. Only then can you have a thorough understanding of rabbit ownership really means. This book can help you do that.

Meanwhile, check out the following few reasons *not* to own a rabbit:

- ✔ It's Easter time, and you think getting a rabbit would be a fun way to celebrate the holiday.

- ✔ You think a rabbit would look good sitting in a hutch outside in your backyard. A bunny in the yard may lend a rural feeling to your garden decor.

- ✔ You want to breed rabbits, so you can make a pile of money.

- ✔ Your child wants one, and you plan to teach him responsibility by making him care for the rabbit.

- ✔ Your dog needs a companion, but you don't want to get another dog.

The only truly legitimate reasons to get a rabbit is for companionship and/or to get seriously involved in the purebred rabbit community. Any other reason bodes trouble — for the rabbit.

Am I Ready for a Rabbit?

Fantasizing about owning a rabbit is quite different from actually being ready to take one on. Think hard about your lifestyle and whether this is the right time to be adding such an animal to your household. Ask yourself these questions:

- **Do I have at least three hours of free time a day?** Your rabbit needs at least two hours of exercise, which is described in Chapters 15 and 17. That leaves another hour to clean his hutch and to groom, feed, and water him, which is described in Chapters 5 and 6. Are you embroiled in something right now that's taking up much of your time or energy? Like the holiday season, a move, or a personal transition, such as a new marriage or divorce? Are you putting in long hours at work on a special project? Do you travel often for work? (If so, see Chapter 16.) Do you have a new baby (as opposed to an old baby)?

  Adding a new pet to the household during an already stressful time can be disastrous for all involved. Wait until things settle down and are back to normal. That's the time to bring a new rabbit into the home.

- **Do I have the space to house a rabbit?** Can I put him in my yard or in my house? Does my apartment complex allow pets? Rabbits require adequate cage space (see Chapters 5 and 6 for more information on this), and you must have the room to accommodate this. You must also do some investigating to find out if you are zoned for rabbit ownership. Rabbits aren't allowed in some residential areas. Check with your local zoning board to find out.

- **Can my kids handle the responsibility?** Kids and rabbits make great companions, providing the children are old enough to respect the rabbit and are properly supervised. Mishandling can result in serious injury or even death of the rabbit. Likewise, rabbits who kick or even bite when held improperly can hurt children. See Chapter 9 for a more detailed discussion of how to properly handle a rabbit.

  Give serious thought to whether your children are old enough to behave properly around a rabbit and whether you have the time to properly supervise their interaction time with the new pet. Children can't be expected to be in sole charge of the rabbit. In fact, an adult must oversee the rabbit-caring tasks that children are given for the sake of the rabbit.

- **How will my other pets get along with a rabbit?** Rabbits can get along with other pets, depending on the type of pet they're being asked to live with. Introducing your pet rabbit to another strange rabbit may jeopardize one or both pets, putting them in serious danger. Rabbits have been known to kill each other, and two male rabbits may try to castrate each other. Cats and rabbits often come to tolerate each other, and cats rarely pose a danger to rabbits. (Although not common, cats can injure rabbits and should be supervised during their initial time together.) Birds and rabbits usually just ignore each other, as long as they're given ample room to stay away from each other. Dogs, on the other hand, can be a real problem for a rabbit. (See Chapter 13 for tips on how to figure out if your pets can get along.)

✔ **Am I willing to alter my lifestyle?** Rabbits are notorious diggers and chewers and can make short work of your backyard or your wooden furniture legs if you don't make certain changes to your home environment. You have to thoroughly rabbit proof your home and/or backyard if you bring a rabbit into your life. And in many cases, the results of your rabbit-proofing won't exactly be an asset to your home decor. (Chapter 6 can help you figure out how to rabbit proof your home, and Chapter 14 supplies the details on how to train your pet.)

✔ **Do I have enough money to set up and sustain my rabbit?** You need cold, hard cash (or a warm credit card) to purchase any rabbit, plus the cage and supplies that your rabbit must have to be comfortable. You should also have money on hand to pay veterinary bills (see Chapter 9) for the annual preventative physical exam, in the event of an illness, and the health difficulties that becomes more likely as the pet ages. (See Chapters 7 and 8 for details on rabbit health.)

✔ **Am I ready for the emotional commitment?** Rabbits are friendly, sociable creatures who need plenty of attention to thrive in a domestic environment. Think about whether you can make the emotional commitment to a rabbit. For more about the emotional aspect of owning a rabbit, see Chapter 14.

Of course, before you go out and get that rabbit, make sure that you did your homework and know *exactly* how to take care of this delightful creature. (See Part II in this book for more on housing, nutrition, and healthcare.) Find out about rabbit breeds to make sure that you know what kind of rabbit you want. Study up on rabbit behavior, so you'll understand your pet right from the get-go and be sure to make that all-important decision about whether your rabbit will live indoors or outdoors before you bring your pet home. Find a veterinarian experienced in the treatment of rabbits before you make your purchase rather than *after* an emergency arises.

All rabbit owners must do a number of tasks that take time, but you must also determine who can perform them. If you live alone, you'll obviously perform them. (No rabbit likes to clean his own hutch.) If you have a family and the rabbit will belong to everyone, then tasks must be delegated. Before your rabbit comes to live with you, sit down with your family and have a meeting. Discuss the tasks described in this chapter, as well as who will perform them, and when. A written schedule can do wonders to encourage slackers to keep up their end of the bargain. This is a great way to find out if your family isn't committed to owning a rabbit. If this is the case, then you can put off any plans for a new pet rabbit and thus spare your family and the rabbit from going through the hassle.

However, for the family that's willing to undertake a few extra chores for the sake of a furry new pet, taking care of a rabbit isn't too hard, especially if everyone in the family agrees to pitch in. Table 1-1 has some tips on who may best be able to perform the various tasks required of rabbit owners. (All these tasks are described in detail in Part II.)

Table 1-1:	Divvying Up the Tasks	
Task	*How Often*	*Who*
Feeding the rabbit	Daily	Kids of all ages can easily perform this task as long as an adult monitors them and makes certain the child is performing this important job. An adult should wash and cut up fresh foods for the child's safety and measure out pelleted feed beforehand.
Changing the water	Daily	Older children can make sure the rabbit has fresh water daily; adult supervision ensures the job gets done.
Spot cleaning	Weekly	Older children can remove soiled bedding and wipe down the dirty spots of the cage each day. Adults need to make certain that this is being done; a dirty cage can result in health problems for the rabbit.
Cage cleaning	Weekly	Depending on the type of cage (a hutch or smaller indoor cage), an adult or an older child should do this job.
Exercise	Daily	A child of any age can help a rabbit exercise by playing with the bunny or simply watching to see that the rabbit doesn't get into anything he isn't supposed to as the rabbit runs around on his own. It's important that adults be the one to lift and carry the rabbit if the children are young. Children should be monitored when they're playing with the rabbit to ensure that they don't chase or accidentally hurt the bunny in any way.

Chapter 2

Getting Under a Rabbit's Skin

The two most common pets in North America, if not the world, are cats and dogs. Rabbits, on the other hand, aren't as common. As a result, many folks don't know too much about them.

Rabbits are complicated creatures, both physically and psychologically. In addition to their uniquely designed social structure, their bodies have helped them to survive as a species for eons. As the caregiver to one of these special animals, it behooves you to understand the inner workings of the rabbit. If you do, you'll not only be able to take better care of your pet, but you'll also have a greater appreciation for this special member of the animal kingdom. (See Chapters 9 and 10 for more information about the health of your rabbit.)

Admiring from Afar

Rabbits are mammals, which means they are in the same general classification as dogs, cats, horses, sheep, tigers, elephants, humans and a lot of other animals. To be a *mammal* means you are *warm blooded* — that is, your body regulates its own temperature (as opposed to a reptile who needs an outside heat source to maintain its body temperature). Your species also gives birth to live young and nurses them with milk produced by mammary glands (hence the name *mammal*).

The rabbits body is uniquely designed in large part to escape predators. The rabbit is also put together in a way that helps him take in food, which in turn provides energy for escape and reproduction.

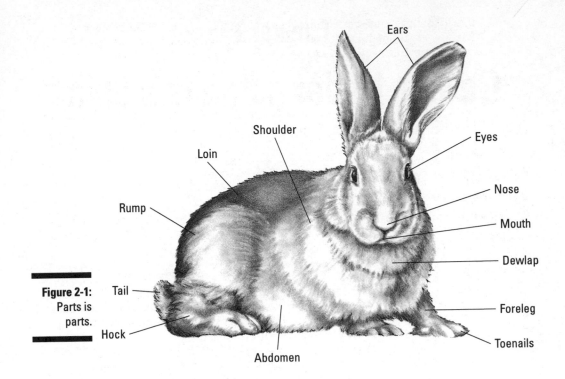

Figure 2-1:
Parts is
parts.

Labels: Ears, Shoulder, Loin, Eyes, Nose, Mouth, Dewlap, Rump, Tail, Hock, Abdomen, Foreleg, Toenails

Digesting This Information (and That Carrot)

One of the most interesting aspects of a rabbit's body is his digestive system. Unlike a cat or dog, rabbits can eat a wide variety of plant material. They can process and extract nutrients from many plants that are indigestible to less adaptable herbivores or omnivores. This helps make them highly successful in a variety of environments around the world. (Your mom referred to it as roughage, and your salad-hating friends refer to it as rabbit food.) Understanding how your rabbit's digestive system functions is important so you feed him in a way that's most efficient for his body.

Munching on fiber

Rabbits are *herbivores,* meaning that they dine only on plant material. A rabbit has an esophagus, stomach, and intestinal tract like other mammals. However, since they often dine on plants that are high in fiber, they have developed a strategy for dealing with this called *hind gut fermentation.* This is where the indigestible materials are broken down into manageable chemicals. (I talk more about this interesting process in a minute.) Many other herbivore friends, including horses, guinea pigs, and chinchillas, have this specialization of the digestive system.

Rabbits have a large stomach for their body size to enable them to eat large amounts of plant material quickly. They are *crepuscular,* meaning they eat primarily at dawn and at dusk. They don't need to eat small amounts all day long. They graze primarily in the a.m. and p.m. with little during the rest of the day, depending on what's available, the weather, and so on. Rabbits can do nicely eating a large meal twice a day.

The digestive process begins in the rabbit's mouth. The rabbit's *prehensile* lips grab the plant material first and then the front teeth called *incisors* — four upper and two lower — neatly slice off pieces of plant matter. The food is then passed to the molars (the back teeth), where it's chewed into small particles and finally swallowed.

All of the rabbit's teeth grow continuously throughout its life. If he is on a good diet, like that described in Chapter 7 and is given some additional materials to munch on throughout the day, he is less likely to pick something else such as your couch legs, your bed legs, or your legs. Chapter 17 lists some toys that make for fun and for shorter teeth.

Dining on delicacies

If you look at this rabbit habit scientifically and leave out the all-too-human judgment, it's actually a fascinating function. Rabbits have a particularly efficient way of dealing with the indigestible parts of their plant diet.

Rabbits have a very large blind sac called a *cecum* that is located where the small intestine and the large intestine join together. This would be in the same place as our appendix, but in the rabbit this organ is very large and contains a wonderfully diverse population of healthy bacteria, yeast, and other organisms working to help the rabbit digest his food.

When the food in the small intestine reaches the cecum and large intestine, the gastrointestinal tract knows which materials to divert into the cecum for further break down. The materials that were already digested in the small intestine and that don't need to make this little side trip to the cecum pass directly into the large intestine as waste. This leaves the body as the little round droppings you see in your rabbit's litter box.

What is happening in the cecum? The multitude of microorganisms are breaking down the indigestible fiber and turning it into digestible nutrients. In order for the rabbit to use these nutrients he must take this material and move it through the digestive tract one more time. So, at certain times of the day (which coincides with several hours after a rabbit eats a big meal) the material from the cecum is packaged up into small round moist pellets called *cecotropes*. The rabbit gets a signal in his brain about when these little delicacies are ready to be passed out of the body; he eats them the minute they emerge. Your rabbit will often look like he is grooming his hind end, but actually he is taking in these nutrient-rich cecotropes.

The various types of fiber in a rabbit's diet is not only there to be used for nutrition, but is they are vital to keeping the rabbit's gastrointestinal tract in excellent working order. The indigestible fiber is particularly important in making the intestines move along smoothly. You could think of it as sort of "tickling" the lining and keeping things moving smoothly. A diet that is low in appropriate types of fiber and too high in rich carbohydrates can lead to a sluggish intestine and cecum and subsequent serious disease. More about that in Chapter 9.

Normally you will not see any cecotropes in your rabbit's cage or at the most a rare one here or there. They are soft, green to brown, mucous coated, and have a stronger smell. If you see a number of them in your rabbit's cage, it may indicate a diet too rich in protein or another more serious condition. Please consult your vet.

Taking Advantage of Skin and Bones

Watch rabbits run and leap in play, and you get a sense of the complexity and flexibility of their skeletons and muscles. Nature equipped rabbits with this kind of flexibility to allow them to make lifesaving maneuvers when being chased down by predators. Basically, the rabbit's bones and muscles are what keep it ahead of the game.

The rabbit's skeleton has a skull, spine, rib cage, and leg bones. However, poor diet, poor housing, no exercise, and poor handling can be dangerous for a rabbit's skeleton. If a rabbit doesn't get any exercise, *osteoporosis* (bone disorder characterized by weak and brittle bones that break easily) can result, such as can happen in any animal (or human) who is sedentary and should have been active. If the normal stress of weight bearing through exercise on the bones is lacking, then the bones lose density. The rabbits that most frequently have spinal injuries, even with proper handling, are those that are confined to cages and never allowed to exercise or rarely exercise. A rabbit that's on a healthy diet and gets ample exercise rarely has a problem with a spinal injury due to a sudden leap in the air. (Wild rabbits are often seen to leap and twist in the air. It appears that their "dancing" is to practice changing direction suddenly for when they're being chased.)

Doing the doggie paddle

Rabbits are excellent swimmers, but taking them for a dip in the pool with you isn't a good idea. Although the rabbit's skeleton and muscles allow it to swim effectively, swimming is reserved for life-and-death escapes. Needless to say, this is not a pleasant situation for a rabbit to be in, and your bunny won't enjoy any excursions in the pool.

For this reason, it's important that

- Outdoor rabbits have housing that keeps them well protected from predators. Although wire may separate a predator from a rabbit inside a hutch, the rabbit may leap away in fear and literally break its back. See Chapter 6 for hutch information.

- You handle your rabbit properly (see Chapter 8). Incorrect handling or lifting can result in your rabbit twisting his spine or falling to the ground, and a consequentially serious if not fatal injury. (See Chapter 9 for more information about your rabbit's health.)

As for a rabbit's spine and muscles, they're incredibly flexible and allow the rabbit to move in ways that often defy description. The large groups of muscles in the hindquarters give the rabbit the power to sprint at breathtaking speeds, permitting twists and turns that seem almost impossible.

Taking a Whiff

Rabbit noses are always on the go. They wiggle almost incessantly. Although much of this wiggling is a result of the rabbit's rapid breathing, it also helps facilitate taking in certain odors when the rabbit needs to do so. For a highly social animal, such as a rabbit, being able to smell your fellow rabbits is vital: You determine who they are, what their sex is, and whether they're available to mate. Rabbits can tell much about a situation just by taking a good whiff.

Rabbits are much like cats and dogs in that their olfactory sense provides an entire unique world to them that we humans are not privy to. Rabbits can smell even the faintest odor and use their noses to do the following:

✔ Distinguishing one rabbit from another or one sex from another.

✔ In the case of males, finding out if a female rabbit is ready to breed.

✔ In the case of a mother rabbit, identifying her own babies.

✔ Determining if they want to eat a particular food.

✔ Detecting danger from predators and from weather conditions.

You can see your four-footed friend applying his nose to just about everything. Expect your bunny to smell first before dining and use this knowledge to head off your pet's efforts to chew on whatever he shouldn't (such as table legs, carpeting, and so on). See Chapter 5 for information on how to rabbit proof your home.

Also, given your rabbit's sensitivity in the olfactory department, refrain from using harsh chemicals, perfume, or anything particularly strong smelling in his presence or around his cage. His nose will thank you for it.

Putting Those Ears to Good Use

Rabbits haven't survived for eons just on their good looks. Their profound sense of hearing has served them well over time. (For a prey animal like the rabbit, being able to hear predators approaching and detect the warning thumps of other rabbits is crucial to the *colony,* a group of rabbits living together in a *warren,* a series of dens and tunnels.)

The shape of a rabbit's ears allows them to pick up barely detectable sounds in its environment. (Hey Bugs, it's those darned predators again!) The ears are sort of like radar dishes. The large exteriors intercept sounds and funnel them into the ear canal where the ear drum is located. Rabbit ears are also flexible. They can pivot around at the base to help detect the exact location where a sound is coming from.

What does all this mean to you, the rabbit owner? Be aware of the sensitivity of your rabbit's ears and treat him accordingly. Spare him loud music, screaming children, barking dogs, and any other nerve-frazzling racket. Your rabbit is less stressed if his environment is free of harsh, jarring noises.

Rabbits also use their ears to release excess body heat. That's why rabbits from hot environments, such as *jack rabbits,* have such large ears as compared to the *cottontail* from a temperate environment or an *artic hare* from a cold environment with small ears to prevent heat loss. Applying cool wet cloths to his ears (if he hasn't gone into shock already) can help to cool down an over-heated rabbit. Thus, cool blood circulates through his body and lowers his body temperature.

Rabbits and Humans: Friends and Foes

You may love your rabbit, and your rabbit may love you, but underneath your bunny's overt affections, a worried creature still exists. Think about it: For thousands of years, humans have hunted rabbits for food and fur. In fact, they still do!

The genetic make up of the wild rabbit enables him to recognize human beings as predators. Try walking up to a wild bunny and you'll see what I mean. In places where rabbits are regularly hunted, you won't see a rabbit anywhere in plain sight as you stroll. In areas where rabbits are protected, they let you see them but freeze if you get too close, hoping you won't see them. If you continue moving in their direction, they are gone within seconds.

Although your pet rabbit is tame and comes from a long line of domesticated rabbits, that innate fear of humans still prevails. You can win your bunny over to the point where he is incredibly comfortable with you, but be aware that he is easily frightened by quick movements, loud noises, and rough handling. In fact, some rabbit experts believe that even lifting a rabbit off the ground can be terrifying to the animal since this is a sensation that would normally come with being carried off by a predator.

For this reason, treat your rabbit gently at all times. You can get more details about how to ease your rabbit's inborn fears by reading Chapter 10.

Chapter 3

So Many Breeds, So Little Time

So now that you have read Chapter 1, which helps you decide if a rabbit is the right pet for you, you're certain that you want a rabbit for a pet and are ready to go out and get your bunny. Finding the rabbit who can ultimately be your companion may be one of the most exciting aspects of entering into rabbit ownership. Another exciting part is going to the pet supply store and loading up on goodies for your new bunny!

Actually choosing your rabbit can also be one of the most daunting parts of getting a rabbit, however. With all the types of rabbits out there, how do you know which one to get? Read on and find out.

Would You Like Some Heinz 57 with Your Rabbit?

Your first job in the rabbit selection process is to decide if you want a purebred rabbit or a mixed breed.

As you read this chapter, you'll find that you have many good reasons for choosing a purebred or a mixed-breed rabbit. If you're starting out with just one bunny at first, then you have to make a choice. Of course, if you want more than one, you can do one of each. The choice is yours.

When you decide that you definitely want to be a bunny's friend, you have plenty to consider. In addition to those listed later in this chapter, consider this:

Age

Regardless of whether you plan to get a purebred rabbit or a rabbit "mutt," you need to think about the age of the rabbit that you want. Baby bunnies are cute, and saying no when you see one is difficult. On the other hand, before a baby rabbit can become an adult, he must go through the dreaded adolescent stage — the rabbit equivalent to being a teenager. Many people prefer to skip this rather bratty period in rabbit development by buying or adopting an adult rabbit.

Boy oh girl

After you settle on a breed or type of rabbit and an age, your next decision is whether to get a male or a female. Depending on whom you talk to, both genders have their benefits, and the final decision is usually a matter of personal choice.

Bucks (males)

Having a reputation for being aggressive with people and other rabbits, males also tend to be distracted by their constant impulses to breed. This isn't true of every buck, of course, but enough male rabbits act that way to make it a valid generalization. Bucks also have the unpleasant habit of marking their territory, spraying urine around the house on vertical surfaces.

Does (females)

Often said to be territorial and aloof, females only care about reproducing to the point that they even conjure up false pregnancies if they aren't bred. Some female rabbits spray urine to mark their area, much like the buck.

Let's face it — neither one of these options sounds particularly appealing. In fact, if you read them again, you may start to wonder why anyone would ever want to keep *either* gender for a pet. It seems that raging hormones are the problem for both genders and are a large part of the reason that rabbits are so well known for reproductive tendencies. Luckily for those who love to share their lives with rabbits, a solution exists. Simply have your buck neutered or your doe spayed, and you're relieved of many of these behavioral problems. In fact, the sooner you spay or neuter your rabbit, the more likely your pet will never develop any of the unpleasant behaviors discussed here and in Chapter 12.

After taking all this into consideration, you may opt to just keep one rabbit for now. You can always add another bunny to your household later on. Or you may find that one rabbit is just right for your family and your situation. If you're pretty sure that you want to add more than one rabbit to your household, study up on the best way to do this for successful results. For details on how to help your bunny get along with another rabbit, as well as your other pets, see Chapter 13.

More than one

More than one bunny means all the more fun, right? Sure it does, but it also means more work and a bit of planning and thought, too.

- **Most rabbits love other rabbits.** Rabbits are social creatures and love the companionship of their own species. If the time that you have to spend with your rabbit is limited, providing a home to at least two bunnies can ward off loneliness for both pets.

- **Some rabbits don't like other rabbits.** Although rabbits enjoy the company of other rabbits, like people, each has its own personality as well as likes and dislikes. In other words, not all rabbits get along well together. Putting strange rabbits together, whether intact or not, is serious business and should be done with great care. Some rabbits *never* get along.

  Unless two rabbits grow up together, they're likely to fight or at least be disagreeable toward each other in the beginning. Introductions need to be made slowly and carefully to ensure that the rabbits don't get into a literal bunny free-for-all. Putting several rabbits together requires a large space. See Chapters 5 and 6 for more details on housing your rabbits.

  In fact, rabbit fights can be downright dangerous, and rabbits have been known to seriously injure and sometimes kill each other. Keeping siblings together is the best bet for rabbit harmony, as long as both pets are spayed or neutered.

- **Two rabbits mean double work.** When it comes time to clean up after your rabbits, two rabbits are twice as much work as one. You have much more to do when you have two rabbits sharing a hutch or two rabbits in their own cages. Also you need to feed two rabbits, provide water to two rabbits, and give exercise and vet care to two rabbits. All this is more time-consuming and more costly.

- **If you want a rabbit for a companion, stick with only one rabbit.** Rabbits who spend more time with other rabbits than humans tend to have a stronger bond with members of their own species rather than their human caretakers. If you want your rabbit to be more focused on you than a rabbit companion, have only one rabbit and spend a considerable amount of time with your pet.

- **Littermates do well together.** However, if they're male and female, as soon as they're of age (4 months), they do what rabbits do — incestuous or not.

If you plan to have more than one rabbit, introducing the bunnies carefully to avoid a fight is important. Rabbits are territorial, and it may take some convincing to get your resident bunny to accept a newcomer. Also, because rabbits have strong hierarchies in their social groups, your rabbits will probably scramble to see who is going to be the boss.

The first step toward a successful friendship between rabbits is spaying and neutering. Raging hormones can cause rabbits to fight when they might otherwise get along. Altering your rabbits means getting rid of those pesky hormones, resulting in a calmer and more docile bunny.

When deciding whether two rabbits can become friends, keep in mind that sex can be an important factor, too. Spayed females tend to get along best with neutered males.

When making the initial rabbit-to-rabbit introduction, follow these guidelines:

1. **Make the introduction on neutral territory.**

   Pick a spot where neither rabbit has had a chance to stake a claim. This can be a room in the house where neither has ever been. Placing the rabbits on unclaimed turf will temper their instinctive urge to defend territory.

2. **Keep the rabbits in individual cages at first and put the cages next to each other so they can see one another.**

   Leave them together like this as often as possible.

3. **After the rabbits seem comfortable with each other through their cages, place them together in the neutral territory while they're wearing leashes and harnesses.**

   Make sure there are plenty of hiding places to allow escape should it be necessary. Let them spend time together (as much as you can) but don't allow them to get too close to each other.

4. **When the rabbits seem comfortable together and you don't detect any aggression, allow them to get a little closer while still on their leashes.**

   If they do start to fight, you can separate them more easily because they're leashed.

5. **If you don't see any signs of hostility, you can let the rabbits loose together in the neutral space.**

   If they do squabble, break it up by squirting a water gun or spray bottle at them. Provided that you're dealing with neutered rabbits, the two can eventually work things out between them. If they do fight in the beginning, their personalities may be such that they never become best friends, but at least, they need to tolerate each other.

Bunny mutts

If you're simply looking for a companion rabbit and have no notions of breeding or showing (see Chapters 15 and 19 for more on these topics), a mixed-breed rabbit is very satisfactory. In fact, you're more likely to find a mixed breed in need of a home at animal shelters or rabbit rescue groups than a purebred.

A few good reasons to bring home a mixed-breed rabbit are as follows:

- ✔ If you go to a shelter or rescue group to adopt a rabbit, you may have to pay an adoption fee, but you'll be providing a home to a bunny who desperately needs one. This is a great feeling!
- ✔ Rabbits within a breed tend to all look alike to the untrained eye, but mixed-breed rabbits are truly unique. No two are exactly alike.

If you choose to adopt a rabbit from a rescue group or animal shelter (a terrific idea that's discussed in Chapter 4), you're likely to end up with a rabbit of unknown parentage. If you study photographs and descriptions of each rabbit breed in this chapter, you can probably see elements of these purebreds in your mixed-breed rabbit. Known in the rabbit world as *scrubs,* rabbits who are obviously not purebreds to a trained eye are assumed to be a mixture of breeds.

Of course, you don't need to know your mixed breed's ancestry to love her, but it could come in handy when dealing with issues such as coat care, ear care, and size. Mixed-breed rabbits come in a variety of shapes and sizes as a result of their varied bloodlines. If you would like to adopt a mixed-breed bunny, you should think about its coat type, ear type, head shape, and its size.

Rabbit coat types

Generally speaking, rabbits come in two different coat types: longhair and shorthair, both of which are shown in Figure 3-1.

Figure 3-1: Longhairs to the left, please. Shorthair? To the right.

- ✔ **Longhair rabbits** need frequent grooming. If your rabbit seems to have fur that looks similar to an Angora's coat (see further along in this chapter for more information on what that looks like), your bunny probably has some Angora breeding and should be treated like an Angora when it comes to grooming. Brush a longhair rabbit to keep the hair from matting, which can lead to skin disease. In the case of matting around the anal area, brush out the hair to avoid the accumulation of stool and urine that can burn the skin.

- ✔ **Shorthair rabbits,** on the other hand, do need grooming but not as often.

Head shape

The breeds that have shortened faces or small heads have a higher incidence of dental disease caused by *malocclusion* (the upper and lower teeth are not properly aligned). Rabbit teeth grow throughout their lifetime, and they must wear properly on each other in order to stay in alignment. Therefore, in rabbit breeds such as the lop-eared which has a flatter face, and the dwarf which has a smaller head, pay particular attention to the appearance of the teeth when looking for a pet. Some dental disease won't show up until the rabbit is four months old. It's therefore important to have your rabbit checked by an experienced veterinarian within its first year of life.

Size

Just like with purebred bunnies, you're likely to see a wide range of sizes in mixed-breed rabbits. Mixed breeds can range from 4 to 12 pounds. Most mixed-breed bunnies fall somewhere in between:

- Dwarf is 2-3 pounds.
- Small is 4-5 pounds.
- Medium is 6-7 pounds.
- Large is 8-9 pounds.
- Giants are over 9 pounds.

Myth of the hairballs

Contrary to popular myth, hair in a rabbit's stomach is not a big problem. Rabbits always have some hair there because they're constantly grooming themselves. What has traditionally been referred to as a "hairball" is really a dehydrated mass of food mixed with the normal hair that doesn't want to move. This compact mass is caused most commonly by a diet that is low in certain types of fiber and also low in moisture. The hair in itself is not the problem, but the diet is. For more on rabbit diet, see Chapter 7.

✔ **Larger:** Size is an important consideration because the larger the rabbit, the more space the pet needs.

✔ **Smaller:** The smaller the rabbit, the harder the rabbit is to handle because small rabbits tend to be flighty and nervous. Although the two-pound Dwarfs (see Figure 3-2) are a problem to handle, rabbits that are four to five pounds are a better choice for children.

Young kids shouldn't be permitted to lift and carry any rabbit because of possible injury to the bunny. (See Chapter 9 for more on lifting and carrying rabbits.) Smaller rabbits are particularly vulnerable — not necessarily just due to its size but because of its temperament. Conversely, older children who are gentle, responsible, and carefully monitored can lift and carry both medium-size and smaller bunnies without a problem.

Figure 3-2:
A dwarf is a dwarf, of course, of course . . . A giant breed is to the left, a dwarf breed to the right, and all this in comparison to an apple.

Bunny bluebloods

In the last hundred years or so, rabbit fanciers around the world have worked hard to create the various breeds of rabbits that exist today. But not all of them are easily available in North America and in many other parts of the world.

If you lean toward a purebred, you have many rabbits to select from. The American Rabbit Breeders Association (ARBA) recognizes 45 rabbit breeds (purebred rabbits other than the 45 ARBA breeds are out there, too), and if you want a purebred rabbit, you'll most likely be choosing from one of these fascinating types. However, you'll be happy to know that even though so many rabbit breeds exist, each one is distinctive enough in appearance to make your decision easier. Size, coat type, and color — even personality — can differ significantly between rabbit breeds. And you have all the various mixed-breed rabbits to pick from, each different from the other.

You pure about that?

You may be wondering what exactly makes a rabbit purebred. A *purebred* rabbit or animal of any kind is a member of *breed* — a group of individuals within a domesticated species that has common ancestors and characteristics that are different from other groups of individuals within the same species. Rabbit breeds are similar to dog breeds, such as *Cocker Spaniel* and *Collie,* in that respect. Both dog breeds and rabbits breeds have distinct body types, head shapes, colorations, and other traits that all combined, result in a unique kind of dog or rabbit.

Purebred reasoning

Before you decide on a mixed breed or purebred rabbit, give the following issues some consideration:

- **Appearance:** If you prefer a rabbit with a particular type of fur or general appearance, you can get exactly what you want if you go for a purebred. Also, keep the coat type in mind. Different rabbit breeds have different coat types. *English Angoras* and *Jersey Woolies,* for example, are known for their profuse coats. These coats are beautiful to look at but require considerable time and care to keep groomed. Shorthair breeds, such as the *Rex* and *Dutch,* on the other hand, need little grooming. Think long and hard about whether you have enough time and interest for a longhair rabbit.

- **Breeding:** If you want to get involved with rabbit breeding (see Chapter 15), you should get a purebred. The world has many bunnies out there in need of homes, so indiscriminately breeding rabbits without the purpose of improving the breed is irresponsible. Responsible rabbit breeders are involved in the business of purebred rabbits, understand the ins and outs of rabbit husbandry, and have good homes lined up for the rabbits before they breed.

- **Disposition:** Many breeds of rabbits have distinct dispositions that are unique to them. If you want a quieter rabbit, opt for a breed known for its gentle temperament. If you prefer a challenge, go for a feistier breed. (Of course, all rabbits are individuals, and temperament can vary even within a particular breed.)

- **Showing:** If you plan to show your rabbit in the American Rabbit Breeders Association, Inc. (ARBA) shows, you must have a purebred. (For more on the ARBA, go to the resources chapter.) If your child wants to show rabbits in 4-H, a purebred offers more opportunities for showing than a mixed breed. See Chapter 17 for more showing details.

✔ **Size:** With a purebred rabbit, you know exactly what size the bunny will be when he's grown. For example, if you buy a purebred baby *New Zealand* rabbit, you know that it will grow up to weigh about ten pounds, max, because that's typical of the *New Zealand* breed. Purebred rabbits come in an assortment of sizes, from the tiny 2-pound *Netherland Dwarf* to the huge 14-pound *Flemish Giant* and a number of sizes in between. The smaller breeds are easier to house and handle than the larger breeds. The large breeds require bigger cages and bigger biceps to lift. The majority of breed sizes is in between, which is the typical size that most people think of when they imagine a pet rabbit.

Showing off beautiful fur

Rabbits come in a vast array of colors and patterns according to ARBA. ARBA declares that a few coat variations exist within the breeds, too. "What's the difference?" you ask. Well, I'll tell you:

✔ **Coat.** The kind of fur a rabbit has. Rabbits come in one of four different kinds of fur, the first three of which are considered shorthair:

  • **Normal** rabbit fur is the kind of coat that you see on most rabbits. It comes in two layers: an overcoat and undercoat. Both layers are about an inch in length. The undercoat is soft and serves as insulation to keep the rabbit warm.

  • **Rex** fur looks and feels like velvet and is shorter than normal fur. Cottony and airy to the touch, Rex fur, shown in the insert, is stands upright instead of laying flat against the rabbit's body.

  • **Angora** coat is long and fluffy and is often used for spinning because of its warmth. Because it's used to make clothing, the angora coat is often referred to as *wool*. The fur stands away from the rabbit's body, giving it a fuzzy, puffy appearance.

  • **Satin** fur has a silky, shiny appearance, the result of its fine, somewhat translucent hair shafts. Satin coats are about the same length as normal fur coats but can be distinguished by their distinctive luster.

✔ **Color.** Rabbit colors are arranged in Pattern Groups. Individual colors exist within each Pattern Group. (Some have the same name as the Pattern Group, but are considered distinct colorations and not just Pattern Groups.) Each breed has its own breed standard and allowed color varieties, but a host of common colors can be found in many different breeds.

✔ Patterns are made of the following:

  • **Agouti:** Agouti-colored rabbits has three or more bands of color on each guard hair shaft, usually with a dark gray base. (*Guard hair* is the coarse, outer hair on most mammals.) Two or more alternating light or dark rings are also present. The head, feet, and ears of a rabbit of this color are usually *ticked* (darker), while the circles around the eyes, the fur on the belly and under the jaws tend to be lighter. Agouti-colored rabbits come in chestnut, chocolate, sable, lilac, and smoke pearl.

- **Brindle:** Brindle, a color also seen commonly in certain dog breeds, such as the Greyhound and American Pit Bull Terrier, is an intermingling of two solid guard hair colors, a dark and a light. Black and orange as well as black and white are the prevalent color combinations. The brindle pattern appears consistently throughout the body.

- **Broken:** Two different subdivisions can be found within the broken pattern: bi-color and tri-color. A bi-colored broken pattern consists of any normal rabbit color appearing with white. For example, a bi-colored rabbit may be white with black spots. A tri-colored rabbit, on the other hand, has white along with two other colors.

- **Marked:** Rabbits of marked patterns are usually white with patterns consisting of another color throughout their bodies.

- **Pointed white:** Much like a Siamese cat, this type of rabbit is all white with a darker color on its nose, ears, feet, and tail.

- **Self:** Used to describe solid-color rabbits, this term applies to those bunnies who have a uniform color throughout their entire body.

- **Shaded:** Shaded rabbits show a gradual shift in color, beginning with a darker color on their backs, heads, necks, ears, legs, and tails. This color eventually turns into a lighter version of the same color when it reaches the rabbit's sides.

- **Solid:** Similar to the self-pattern, this pattern may also include agouti and other mixed-color fur, as long as they don't create a pattern or marking.

- **Ticked:** Contrasting the rabbit's main color, solid or tipped guard hairs throughout the coat distinguish this pattern.

- **Wide band:** Rabbits of this coloration have the same color on their bodies, heads, ears, tails, and feet. Their eye circles, underside of tail, jaws, and belly have a lighter coloration.

✔ **Common colors.** In addition to black and white, the colors listed here are those you'll see most often:

- **Beige:** Rabbits of this color have a beige pigment throughout their bodies except for the napes of their necks, which is lighter. They have a bluish-white color on their bellies, along with *eye circles* (coloration around the outside of the eye) of the same color. Their eyes are brown with a ruby glow.

- **Blue:** The Blue coloration in rabbits is best described as a medium shade of gray with a blue or lavender cast. The eyes of a blue-colored rabbit are blue-gray.

- **Castor:** A rich dark chestnut color, castor has also been described as mahogany brown. Castor fur is lightly tipped with black evenly distributed over the body, head, and legs. The belly of a castor rabbit is white or tan, and the eyes are brown.

- **Chinchilla:** Chinchilla-colored rabbits possess a blend of black and pearl hairs with a dark gray base. Named after the coloring seen on actual chinchillas, a rodent known for its lush fur, chinchilla rabbits also come in a chocolate version.

- **Chocolate:** A deep dark brown, the chocolate coloration features a light gray undercoat. The eyes are brown with a red cast in subdued light.

- **Fawn:** Fawn-colored rabbits are a deep golden color over their backs onto their flanks and chests. Their eye circles, insides of ears, under jaws, tails, and bellies are white. Fawn-colored rabbits have gray or brown eyes.

- **Lilac:** This coloration features a medium-gray hue with a pinkish tint over the rabbit's entire body. The eyes are the same color as the fur and have a ruby glow in subdued light.

- **Lynx:** The body and the top of the lynx-colored rabbit's tail are tinged with lilac and light orange with a sharper orange color showing through. Areas underneath the tail, belly, and jaw are white. The eye circles and insides of the ears are also white. The eyes of a lynx-colored rabbit are blue-gray.

- **Opal:** Opal-colored rabbits feature a pale bluish color on the top of the hair shaft with a fawn band below it and a dark gray undercoat. The ears of the opal are laced with blue. The eye circles and underside of the rabbit are white with a dark gray undercoat. The eyes are gray.

- **Siamese:** Not surprisingly, Siamese-colored rabbits look much like seal-point Siamese cats. They have dark brown color on their ears, head, feet, belly, and tail with a lighter body color so that the dark points can be seen. The eyes are brown.

- **Squirrel:** A strange color name for a rabbit but often used nonetheless. The hair shaft of rabbits with the squirrel coloration consists of a blend of gray and white bands. This color extends from the rabbit's back down to its sides, where it's met by white on the belly and top of the hind feet. The nape of the neck, chest, and eye circles are a lighter version of the original color. The upper part of the ears has a dark blue edge. The eyes are gray.

- **Steel:** This interesting color pattern comes in black, blue, chocolate, lilac, sable, and smoke pearl. The entire body of the rabbit features one of these colors, the hairs of which are diffused with a small amount of gold or silver tipping, depending on whether the rabbit is a gold steel or a silver steel. The eyes are brown or gray.

- **Tan Pattern:** Different from beige, the tan coloration features a solid color on the head, back, sides, outside of ears, back legs, front of forelegs, and top of the tail. A lighter color appears on the eye circles, nostrils, jaw, chest, and underside of the rabbit's body.

- **Tortoiseshell:** Rabbits with this coloration don't have a shell that they can duck into, but they sport a lively orange on their bodies, which mingles into a grayish blue shadowing over the rump and haunches. The top of the tail matches the orange color, but underneath is the color of the shadowing. Tortoiseshell-colored rabbits have brown eyes.

Even though it may seem hard to visualize the patterns and colors listed in descriptions of these breeds, they can be broken down into more simple terms. Start with the various types of coats that rabbits have and then move on to the different colorations and patterns.

Breeding All About It

A *breed club,* a group of people who specialize in each of the breeds, represents each ARBA rabbit breed. All the ARBA rabbit breeds have a unique history and a set of fans that believe *their* breed of rabbit is the absolute best. Take a look at these 45 breeds and judge for yourself. See the Appendix of this book for ARBA contact information and the 45 recognized breed clubs.

American

Compact in appearance, the American is a medium-size rabbit, weighing around ten pounds. Its mandolin-shaped body provides a slight arch over the loins and hindquarters and a taper from the hindquarters to the shoulders. In existence nearly 100 years, the American breed comes in two color varieties: blue or white. The blue variety has blue-gray eyes, and the white version has pink eyes.

American Fuzzy Lop

The Fuzzy Lop, which is related to the Holland Lop and the Angora, is available in many colors. This along with its furry coat and long, floppy ears make it a popular breed with rabbit lovers. The American Fuzzy Lop is shown in six different groups based on its color pattern: broken, pointed white, wide band, agouti, shaded, and self. Within those groups, the agouti colors of chestnut, chinchilla, opal, and lynx can be seen. The broken colors of any recognized rabbit breed are allowed, as are the solid colors of black, white, lilac, blue, and chocolate. A number of other color patterns are also available in this small rabbit, whose body is short and stocky. This cobby (stocky) little rabbit's coat is long and woolly, requiring frequent grooming.

American Sable

The ears, face, legs, and tail of the American Sable are darker than the main part of its body. This rabbit is well named because its coat is a beautiful dark brown — the result of crosses with the Chinchilla. A medium-size rabbit sporting a slightly arched back, the American Sable is an attractive pet, weighing around nine pounds.

Angora

Angora rabbits come in one of four types:

- **English Angora:** Originating in Turkey, the English Angora breed is at least 200 years old, if not older. This rabbit comes in six color groups: the pointed white, self, agouti, shaded, wide band, and ticked. Within these groups, the colors available are white with black; blue lilac or chocolate points; solid blue, black, chestnut, agouti, chinchilla, chocolate agouti, chocolate chinchilla, copper, lilac, lilac chinchilla, lynx, squirrel, opal and wild gray; shaded blue cream, chocolate tortoiseshell, dark sable, frosted pearl, lilac cream, smoke pearl, sable and tortoiseshell; solid cream, red and fawn; and ticked chocolate steel, lilac steel, steel and blue steel. Compact in size and stature, the English Angora weighs in at around six pounds.

- **French Angora:** The French Angora was developed before the English Angora, specifically for its wool. The French people used to hand pluck its wool and spin it for clothing. This breed comes in the same four-color varieties as the English Angora and in the identical colors. While the two breeds are similar, the French Angora is somewhat bigger than the English, weighing in at around nine pounds. The French Angora also has less hair on its head, ears, and legs.

- **Giant Angora:** Bathed in fur, the Giant Angora, with its dramatic appearance, tends to stand out among the rest of the Angora breeds. Unlike the other Angoras, the Giant is only available in white, with blue eyes or ruby eyes. It's larger than the English or the Satin, weighing in at around nine pounds. Its coat is similar to the English Angora in that it has longer *furnishings* (hair on its ears, face, and legs).

✔ **Satin Angora:** Slightly smaller than the English Angora, Satin Angoras usually weigh around seven pounds. The Satin Angora comes in the same color varieties as the English and French Angoras. The main difference between the Satin and the other Angoras is its coat. The Satin, as its name would imply, has shinier, silkier hair than its counterparts.

Each one of these Angoras is a separate breed and has the characteristic long, woolly hair typical of this rabbit family. Angoras come in a vast array of beautiful colors and come in two color classifications: white and colored.

Because of the Angora's dense coat, which measures about three inches in length, this breed needs plenty of grooming. You should only consider owning an Angora if you have the time and patience to spend brushing its luxurious coat. Chapter 8 offers grooming information.

Belgian Hare

Europeans developed the Belgian Hare in the late 1800s specifically for the lean, racehorselike appearance. Despite its name, the Belgian Hare isn't really a hare but is actually a domestic rabbit. However, its long legs and ears give it the appearance of a hare, hence its name. Only available in red chestnut, the Belgian Hare is a large-size rabbit of about nine pounds.

Beveren

A large rabbit of about ten pounds, the Beveren has a thick, silky coat. It's of medium length and has a slightly arched back. Not as frequently seen in the United States as some other breeds, the Beveren was developed in Europe, and comes in the color varieties of white, blue, and black.

Britannia Petite

Known for being curious and alert, the tiny, fine-boned Britannia Petite can make a good pet for older children who can treat this light-stature breed gently. This rabbit is all white or black otter-colored and weighs only about two pounds.

Californian

Originally bred in the Golden State in the 1920s, the Californian is related to the Himalayan, which is similar in appearance. This popular rabbit looks much like a Siamese cat, with its white coat and black-tipped ears, nose, feet, and tail. Somewhat large in size, the typical Californian weighs about nine pounds. Its body is plump and firm to the touch.

Champagne d' Argent

The Argent, an old breed, was originally bred in the Champagne province of France for its fur and meat. Weighing about ten pounds, the medium-size Argent is a popular pet in the United States. The Argent coat contains a marvelous mix of colored hairs that has a silvery effect.

Checkered Giant

The Checkered Giant was first brought to America from Europe in 1910 and sports a long, well-arched body. Another popular breed, the Checkered Giant comes in black and blue color varieties. The breed is typically white with dark markings, including a "butterfly" on the nose, dark ears, dark circles around the eyes, spots on the cheeks and various other dark patches on the body. Weighing a solid 11 pounds or more, the Checkered Giant is related to the Flemish Giant.

Chinchilla

The Chinchilla comes in three breeds: the Standard, the American, and the Giant. All three types have the coloring of an actual chinchilla and are popular pets because of their attractive coats.

- **Standard Chinchilla** is the foundation of the Chinchilla breed, weighing around six pounds. Reportedly developed in France by crossing a wild gray rabbit with some domestic strains, the breed was first shown in 1913. It has a medium body with a slight arch to the back.

- **American Chinchilla** is the middleweight of the three Chinchilla breeds, coming in at around ten pounds. It was bred down from the Standard variety for its size.

- **Giant Chinchilla** is the largest in this family and the result of a cross between the Flemish Giant and a smaller Chinchilla by an American breeder sometime after World War I. It was developed as a meat rabbit, but makes a nice, albeit large, pet at about 14 pounds.

Cinnamon

This breed comes only in a reddish color synonymous with its name. The ears, face, and feet bear a darker shade of this same color. Occasional shades of gray on various parts of its body contribute to this breed's unusual appearance. Cinnamons, which are related to the New Zealand White, the Checkered Giant, the Californian and the Chinchilla, weigh approximately ten pounds.

Crème d' Argent

The Crème d'Argent, which originated in France, is a handsome rabbit with an exquisitely colored coat of pale orange. Lighter guard hairs give this rabbit a smooth and silky appearance. Typically, the Crème d'Argent weighs about nine pounds.

Dutch

Originally from Holland, the Dutch is one of the oldest established rabbit breeds. Small and compact, these rabbits weigh around four pounds. The Dutch is an extremely popular rabbit and easily recognizable because of its markings; they have a band of white around the chest. Available in six color varieties, the Dutch has a dark head with a white nose, a white *blaze,* (a white stripe starting at the nose and going upward toward the face) and dark *britches* (the back half of the rabbit). Its dark eyes blend into the color on its face, which can be black, blue, chocolate, tortoiseshell, steel, or gray.

Dwarf Hotot

Only seen in white with dark eyes, the Dwarf Hotot weighs about three pounds and was bred down from the Hotot in the 1970s. At first sight, the tiny Dwarf Hotot appears to be wearing eyeliner. The breed's characteristic black eye bands give it this look.

English Spot

An old breed whose popularity began in England in the late 1800s, the English Spot is still a favorite breed and makes a good pet. The English, for short, is reminiscent of a Dalmatian with its white coat and dark spots. The breed comes in seven different color varieties of which the breed's markings are made: black, blue, chocolate, gold, gray, lilac, and tortoiseshell. A capped nose, dark ears, eye rings, and a stripe along the back are all characteristic of this breed, which weighs about eight pounds.

Flemish Giant

Seen quite often at rabbit shows, the Flemish Giant originated in Belgium as its name suggests. Massive in size, the Flemish Giant is the largest breed of rabbit and weighs over 14 pounds. Available in steel gray, light gray, black, blue, white, sandy, and fawn, this breed is popular as a pet because of its large size. In general, the larger the rabbit, the greater the tendency to be more laid-back and relaxed than the dwarf breeds.

Florida White

This breed, a cross between the Dutch, Polish, and New Zealand White, the Florida White is relatively new; the American Rabbit Breeders Association, Inc. accepted this breed in the early 1960s. The Florida White is the one most commonly used for laboratory research. This breed comes in white only, as its name implies, with pink eyes. It weighs about five pounds.

Harlequin

The Harlequin, developed in France in the 1800s, is an interesting, medium-size rabbit of about eight pounds with unusual markings. Available in two color groups and four actual colors, the Harlequin is best described as having an "ice-cream sundae" look to its coat. Different colors swirl and blend in unique configurations. The heads of Harlequin rabbits are split in half by color, making them look like a different rabbit from one side to the next! Harlequin base colors are black, blue, lilac, and chocolate. Two types exist:

- **Japanese Harlequin** sports a coat that has a base coloring that interchanges with strips of orange or a lighter version of the base color.
- **Magpie Harlequin** base coloring alternates with strips of white.

Havana

The small, shiny Havana was created from a single rabbit born to an unpedigreed doe in Holland in 1898. First appearing in chocolate, the Havana is now available in blue and black varieties as well. Prized for its coat, the Havana is short and stocky *(close coupled)*. Its weight of six pounds and its compact build can make it a nice pet for an older child.

Himalayan

More widely distributed around the world than any other breed of rabbit, the Himalayan is popular in China and Russia, as well as in the United States. The breed has been around for many years, reportedly originating near the Himalayan Mountains. Distinctive because of its white coat and blue or black markings, this small-size rabbit weighs only about four pounds.

Hotot

The breed was first imported into the United States in the late 1970s. In France, this breed is known as the Blanc de Hotot, translated *the white of Hotot*. Hotot is the area where the breed was developed. Available only in a frosty white color with thin black eye circles, the medium-size Hotot weighs around nine pounds.

Jersey Wooly

A recently developed breed of rabbit created in the 1970s through crossbreeding, the Jersey Wooly was created specifically for its luxurious coat. The fur of the Jersey Wooly is available in agouti (chestnut, chinchilla, opal, and squirrel), pointed white (black or blue markings), self (black, blue, chocolate, lilac, blue-eyed white, and ruby-eyed white), shaded (sable point, seal, Siamese sable, smoke pearl, tortoiseshell, and blue tortoiseshell) and tan pattern (black otter, blue otter, silver marten, sable marten, and smoke pearl marten) color groups. A small rabbit, the Jersey Wooly weighs about three pounds.

This breed, shown in the insert, is known for its gentle temperament and for being an exceptional pet. However, because of its long coat, the Jersey Wooly does require regular grooming.

Lilac

The Lilac comes in one color: a light pinkish gray. Originally considered a deviation from the norm, the Lilac began as a result of an unusual coloration within the Havana breed. Weighing about seven pounds, the body of the Lilac is substantial and compact. This breed makes a good and attractive companion rabbit.

Lops

The Lop rabbits are probably the most distinctive and easily recognizable of all the breeds. The Lop has huge ears that flop down beside its head like a hound dog's ears, giving it a special look unique to the breed. Along with those big ears comes a wonderful personality. Because Lops are bred specifically for show and pet purposes, they tend to be people oriented. Owners of Lops report that they're amusing rabbits to live with and can also grow to be affectionate and sensitive to their owners' feelings.

Lops come in four different breeds, each unique in both its appearance and history:

- **English Lop:** Developed at least as early as the 1800s, the English Lop is one of the oldest breeds of domestic rabbit still in existence and the first of the lop-eared breeds. The ears of an adult English Lop measure 25 inches or more in length. Weighing approximately ten pounds, the English Lop comes in broken and solid color patterns. Within those patterns, many of the typical rabbit colors are found. When being judged at rabbit shows, the ears are the most important aspect of this well-balanced breed.

- **French Lop:** Developed in France in the 1800s from the English Lop and the Flemish Giant, the French Lop differs from the English in that it sports a heavier stature and shorter ears. The French Lop weighs in at around ten pounds and comes in two color varieties: solid and broken. It can be found in many different rabbit colors. The French Lop is a close relative of the English Lop, which was used in its creation.

- **Holland Lop:** Also known as the Netherland Dwarf Lop, the tiny, compact Holland Lop weighs only about four pounds. The Holland Lop is a dwarf breed of Lop, created in Holland in the 1960s. It falls into the same color varieties as the French and English: agouti, broken, pointed white, self, solid, shaded, and ticked.

  Holland Lops are available in any recognized rabbit color, one of which is shown in this book's insert.

- **Mini Lop:** Developed in the 1970s in Germany, the Mini Lop was originally called the Klein Widder until its named was changed in the 1980s, when the American Rabbit Breeders Association, Inc. recognized it.

  The Mini Lop, shown in Figure 3-3, is similar to the French Lop, although it's much smaller at around five pounds. The breed comes in the usual Lop color varieties of agouti, broken, pointed white, shelf, shaded, solid, and ticked. All recognized rabbit colors are seen in the Mini Lop.

Figure 3-3:
The Mini Lop is a relatively new breed of Lop.

Mini Rex

The Mini Rex breed, shown in Figure 3-4, is growing in popularity as a pet and show rabbit because of its luxurious fur, which is short yet plush, and its small size. Cottony and airy to the touch, Rex fur looks and feels like velvet (you can see a detail in Figure 3-5) and is shorter than normal fur. Their guard hairs are erect and short and the undercoat is erect, which gives it that cut fur look. *Guard hair* is the coarse, outer hair on most mammals.

This breed was developed using the standard-size Rex. Weighing about four pounds, the Mini Rex is available in the same color varieties and colors as its larger cousin, the Rex.

Foot disease is more common in rabbits with Rex fur because of the lack of heavy protective fur on the foot pad. Rex rabbits owners need to take care to keep their pets from becoming overweight and house the pets on a surface that provides some softness.

Figure 3-4:
Mini Rexes
are
becoming
a more
popular
breed.

Netherland Dwarf

Part of the Netherland Dwarf's appeal is no doubt the result of its babylike features; fully grown adult Netherland Dwarfs still resemble what's commonly known as *kits* (baby rabbits) among rabbit lovers. This popular breed, shown in the insert, is the smallest of domestic rabbits, not weighing more than two pounds. Its tiny stature, wide availability of colors, small ears, and large eyes make it a popular pet. The Netherland Dwarf comes in the following color varieties and colors: self (white with ruby eyes, white with blue eyes, black, blue, chocolate, and lilac); shaded (Siamese sable, Siamese smoke pearl, and sable point); agouti (chinchilla, lynx, opal, squirrel, and chestnut); tan pattern (sable marten, silver marten, smoke pearl marten, otter, and tan); and any other variety (fawn, Himalayan, orange, steel, and tortoiseshell).

This breed is definitely more prone to dental disease due to the small size of their heads and shortened jaws.

New Zealand

Despite its name, the New Zealand was developed in the United States, where it was created for meat, fur, and research purposes. In spite of its original function, however, the New Zealand has become a popular pet and show rabbit. This breed comes in three distinct color varieties: white, black, and red. The red was the first color to appear after what experts believe was a cross between a Belgium Hare and a white rabbit. Typical New Zealands weigh about ten pounds.

Palomino

The Palomino's golden color is similar to the coat colors seen in the Palomino horse. (Surprise!) A newer breed, the Palomino was developed in the United States and comes in two color varieties: golden and lynx. Weighing about nine pounds, the Palomino has a slightly arched back and makes a good pet because of its easygoing personality.

Polish

Some experts believe that the name of this breed doesn't refer to the country of Poland but rather to this rabbit's shiny coat. A tiny bunny weighing only about three pounds, the Polish is believed to have developed in England in the 1800s. Commonly seen at rabbit shows, this breed comes in five color varieties: blue, black, chocolate, blue-eyed white, and ruby-eyed white.

Rex

The Rex, which comes in a wide variety of colors, is popular as a pet and show rabbit. Rex rabbit fur looks and feels like plush velvet, as shown in Figure 3-5. Created in 1919 from a mutation, the Rex's unusual coat can be attributed to erect, short guard hairs and erect, short undercoat. Weighing approximately nine pounds, the Rex comes in black, black otter, blue, Californian, castor, chinchilla, chocolate, lilac, lynx, opal, red, sable, seal, white, and broken group varieties. All known rabbit colors are seen in the Rex.

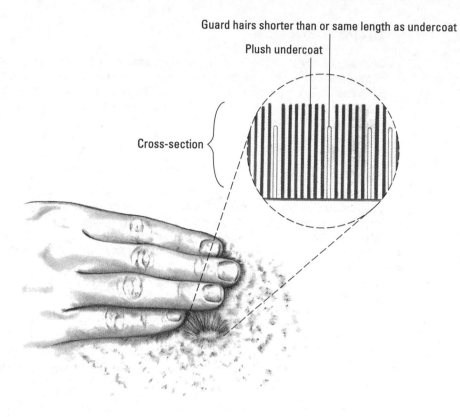

Guard hairs shorter than or same length as undercoat

Plush undercoat

Cross-section

Figure 3-5:
A Rex's
hair is
short but
plush.

Rhinelander

Developed in Europe, the Rhinelander is a medium- to large-size rabbit weighing anywhere from seven to ten pounds. The Rhinelander has an unusual coloration that can best be described as patches of calico, much like the coloring on the calico cat. The breed's base color is white, with markings of black and orange on its nose, ears, cheeks, eyes, back, and sides.

Satin

Created in the United States from a mutation within the Havana breed, the Satin comes in ten different color groups: black, blue, Californian, chinchilla, chocolate, copper, red, Siamese, white, and broken. The Satin is so named because of its soft, shiny coat. This is a medium-size rabbit with a weight of about nine pounds.

Silver

Believed to have originated in India centuries ago, the Silver breed was refined in England during the height of rabbit show popularity. The Silver got its name from the silvery sheen on its coat, created by a mixture of white hairs against a dark background. Available in black, brown, and fawn, Silvers weigh anywhere from four to seven pounds.

Silver Fox

Formerly called the American Heavyweight Silver, the Silver Fox is large, weighing about ten pounds. Originally bred in Europe for its fur, the Silver Fox has an unusual coat. Measuring an inch or more in length with a thick undercoat, the fur of the Silver Fox comes in black or blue varieties.

Silver Marten

Created using the Chinchilla rabbit, the Silver Marten has guard hairs that are gray-tipped on a dark background of black, blue, chocolate, or sable. The area around the eye and nose are also gray. Silver Martens typically weigh about eight pounds.

Tan

Supposedly the result of an accidental mating between a wild buck and a Dutch doe in England during the 1800s, the Tan has been popular for decades. The color and markings of this breed are reminiscent of a Doberman Pincher, particularly the black and chocolate varieties. The top part of the body is dark, but the underside is tan. The tan coloring also appears around the eyes and nose, under the neck, and inside the brims of the ears. The Tan is a small- to medium-size rabbit, weighing approximately five pounds.

Chapter 4

Hiding in Holes, Shelters, and Shops

*O*kay, so you can't wait to get a rabbit. You can't wait to make that furry face and long set of ears a part of your family. But since rabbits don't grow under rocks, you need to go out and find a good source for your new pet.

As a potential rabbit owner, you have several options when it comes to "shopping" for the bunny you've decided upon (which is discussed in detail in Chapter 3). The source you ultimately choose depends on exactly what you are looking for. Before you go, think about what you want to do with your rabbit — show him or keep him just as a pet — and put that scenario together with what you are about to read.

Donning Your Cape: Rescuing a Rabbit

The true guardian angels of the rabbit world are those who take care of unwanted rabbits and struggle to find them good homes. These people are found working in animal shelters and within private rabbit rescue groups.

Shelters are the very same that take in unwanted dogs and cats and from where most municipal animal control agencies work. *Rescue groups* are private, non-profit organizations mostly run by volunteers. You can look for a rescue group in your area in the Appendix, by contacting the House Rabbit Society, or by looking on the Internet for a group in your area.

If you are looking for a rabbit, and don't mind one that is full grown (few babies are put up for adoption), consider adopting a bunny. Unwanted rabbits are euthanized every year in animal shelters because they have nowhere to go. Adopting a bunny essentially means saving his life.

Presenting the problem

You may be wondering why rabbits would need rescuing. Do that many unwanted rabbits exist? If you're familiar with the pet overpopulation that plagues cats and dogs, then you'll easily understand the situation with rabbits. It's virtually the same dilemma. A lot of domesticated rabbits are alive in this country, and not enough of them have homes.

Most of the rabbits that are homeless are in this situation through no fault of their own. Common reasons given for abandoning rabbits to shelters and rescue groups include:

- ✔ The kids (or sadly, the adults) got tired of taking care of the rabbit.

- ✔ I didn't know that rabbits like to chew on everything. (See Chapter 11 for training help.)

- ✔ We got a baby rabbit for Easter and then it grew up.

- ✔ The adolescent rabbit's behavior is difficult to handle. I don't want to deal with it.

- ✔ My rabbit is urinating or defecating outside his litterbox. (Again, see Chapter 11 for training help.)

- ✔ My rabbit has chronic health problems that I can no longer financially or time-wise handle.

Seeking the solution

When unwanted rabbits come to animal shelters or rescue groups, they are put up for adoption.

In order to ensure that you will provide a good, permanent home for the rabbit you are adopting, be prepared to answer some questions. Some shelters and nearly all rescue groups

- ✔ Screen to make sure that you have the facilities and willingness to provide a lasting home for a rabbit. Don't be offended by their questions. Remember that these people have the best interests of the rabbit in mind.

- ✔ Require that you pay an adoption fee. This is to help offset the cost of caring for the rabbit you have adopted. These fees help the groups continue to operate so they can continue to provide help to rabbits in need.

> ✔ Have only a few rabbits available at any given time in your area, so you
> will probably only have to choose from a handful of bunnies.

Each one of these groups works a bit differently. Read on to find out which
adoption route you prefer to take.

Shelters

Rabbits held in shelters — particularly ones run by local government
agencies — are usually placed up for adoption shortly after arrival. At shelters
where unadopted pets are euthanized, rabbits are destroyed if they are not
adopted within a specified period of time. *No-kill shelters* keep rabbits until
they are adopted.

If you go to an animal shelter to rescue a bunny, follow these steps:

1. **Call to make sure your local shelter has rabbits on the day you decide
   to go.**

2. **Peruse the rabbits, deciding which one most catches your interest.**

3. **Ask the staff for some information about the rabbit's personality.**

   You will probably get a good sense of who the rabbit is from talking to
   the people who have been caring for the bunny for a period of time.

4. **Interact with the bunny yourself.**

   Keep in mind that an animal shelter full of barking dogs and strange
   smells can be overwhelming to a rabbit, so your interactions with the
   bunny might be rather one-sided.

   If possible, ask the staff if you can take the rabbit to a quiet area away
   from other animals. Sit on the floor and watch his behavior. Unless the
   rabbit is obviously aggressive or is completely terrified, even in a quiet
   environment the bunny will probably make a good pet. Chapter 10 tells
   you more about how to read a rabbit's body language.

5. **Check the rabbit over for signs of ill health (discussed in this chapter's
   "Choosing the rabbit") to make sure the bunny is in good shape.**

   If the rabbit seems sick and you are interested in adopting him anyway,
   talk to the staff about having the shelter veterinarian treat the rabbit at a
   reduced cost or for no fee if you adopt the animal.

Rescue groups

These private non-profit organizations usually consist of a network of foster
homes that provide refuge to unwanted rabbits until permanent homes can
be found. Individuals within these groups are almost always volunteers who
provide this service because they love rabbits and want to help them.

1. **Contact a rescue group.**

   You can find rescue groups in this book's Appendix, online, and through a local veterinarian. You're likely going to be screened over the phone (to make certain you can provide a good home) before you're invited to see the rabbits.

2. **Once the group decides you are qualified to adopt a bunny, you're directed to rabbits in the area in need of homes.**

   More than likely, the bunnies needing adoption stay in foster homes within the area. The rescue coordinator sets up one or more appointments for you to meet rabbits.

3. **When meeting the foster parents, ask about the rabbit's personality.**

   The foster parent can give you his impressions of whether you (and your family) are a good match with this particular rabbit.

4. **Watch him in his element: running around the house, hanging out in his hutch, and so on.**

   This provides a great way to see the animal's personality. By visiting a rabbit in a foster home, where she is comfortable, you get a good sense of who the rabbit really is. Ultimately the decision is yours, but the advice of someone who is knowledgeable about rabbits and knows an individual rabbit can be invaluable.

5. **Look the rabbit over for signs of good health, discussed in this chapter's "Choosing the rabbit."**

   Reputable rescue groups only place healthy rabbits for adoption, so illness should not be a problem. Still, it doesn't hurt to be on the safe side.

An oldie but a goodie

Baby bunnies are unbearably adorable, there's no doubt about that. But as cute as they are, these youngsters come with issues that older rabbits just don't have. Baby bunnies

- Need to be trained. They have to be shown how to go in a litterbox (a must if you plan to have your rabbit hop around the house).

- Eventually become "teenager" bunnies. That means they go through a phase of general orneriness.

Another great thing about adult rabbits is that they know who they are — and that means you know exactly what you are getting. Adult rabbits have already reached their full size, so you won't get any surprises in that department. They have also developed their personalities. Keep in mind, however, that the behavior of the adult rabbit you're considering adopting may never change, particularly if you don't have the time or experience for training. Younger rabbits may be more able to train and socialize.

TIP

Save a stray

It may sound strange, but stray domestic rabbits are more often turning up in urban areas. These rabbits are usually family pets that have been dumped by uncaring owners.

1. Buy a humane trap. You more than likely have to use a humane trap. The rabbit probably won't let you approach him. *Humane traps,* which baits the rabbit and holds him until you're ready to retrieve it, are available from

   - mail order catalogs
   - humane societies
   - animal control agencies
   - fish and wildlife agencies
   - wildlife rehabilitation centers
   - local pet supply stores (to order)

   Buy a trap made of a lightweight material or that allows the tension to be set lightly on the trap door. A door that slams down hard on a rabbit's back can permanently injure the animal's spine.

2. Take the trap to where you've seen the rabbit, set it, and use pieces of carrot, strawberry, peach, or banana as bait.

   Try to do this early in the morning or evening, since this is the time most rabbits feed. Avoid setting the trap at night when you won't be able to monitor it. If the rabbit is trapped and a predator approaches it in the dark of night, the rabbit may literally be frightened to death.

3. Cover the trap with a dark towel or blanket, leaving the open door accessible. This gives the rabbit a sense of security once it is caught inside.

4. Check the trap every few hours to see if the rabbit has entered it.

5. Take the bunny right away to a veterinarian experienced in rabbits. Ask the vet to examine the rabbit for any health problems and parasites. If the rabbit is in good health, you can take it home and provide it a good environment and diet. If the rabbit is suffering from a health problem, the vet can advise you on what is needed for treatment. (Parasites like fleas and ticks are almost certain to be present on the rabbit, especially in the spring, summer, and fall months.)

Rabbits are wonderful escape artists (they can dig their way out of just about any yard if left unsupervised), and the stray rabbit you found might actually be someone's lost pet. If no one claims the rabbit after a month, you can feel pretty confident that you have rescued an abandoned pet. Once you capture the rabbit and bring it home, try

- Posting signs in the neighborhood where you found it.

- Noting your find in your local newspaper's lost and found section (which are usually free).

- Contact local veterinary clinics that deal with rabbits, animal shelters, and animal control agencies where a person may have reported a lost animal.

If you prefer not to capture the stray yourself, call your local humane society and ask them to pick up the rabbit. Animal control may not have the manpower to trap the stray rabbit right away. Once the humane society retrieves the rabbit you can begin adoption procedures. Most shelters hold new animals for a few days to see if the pet was lost and will be claimed. Monitor this on a daily basis so you know exactly when the rabbit is available for adoption.

Calling the Classifieds

Another way to get a rabbit is through a classified ad in a local newspaper. You may see ads for baby rabbits for sale, both purebred and mixed. Of course, you'll find pros and cons to buying a rabbit through the method; Table 4-1 presents these pros and cons.

Table 4-1	Pros and cons of classified ads
Pros	**Cons**
You experience little or no waiting. If you want a baby bunny now, you can probably get one by the end of the day.	This is not a popular place to advertise rabbits, so you won't have many ads to choose from.
You may be able to find someone very close and won't have to take a long drive out to the middle of nowhere.	Responsible breeders tend to use other methods to advertise their rabbits for sale (most often word of mouth).
Rabbits sold through classified ads are generally cheaper than those purchased from a breeder or pet shop.	People who sell rabbits through classified ads are often not very knowledgeable about rabbits and their care, and you may not find a healthy rabbit when you arrive at the seller's home.

When pursuing these kinds of ads, be on the lookout for rabbits that might not be well cared for. Unlike rabbits placed up for adoption through reliable rescue groups, rabbits put up for adoption by individuals using classified ads have not been screened for good health. To get a sense of the rabbit's general health, ask to see where the rabbit is currently living, and make sure those quarters are clean. For more detailed health signs, see this chapter's "Choosing the rabbit."

If the rabbit seems healthy, ask the owner if you can take the bunny on a trial period. If the owner agrees, immediately take him to a veterinarian for a full examination. If the rabbit is suffering from a health problem, the veterinarian will let you know what treatment is needed. You then have to decide if you want to assume responsibility for a sick rabbit or if you want to return the rabbit to its original owner.

Reading about Breeders

Hopefully you have read Chapter 3 and are familiar with the various types of rabbits out there. If you haven't read it yet, go do it right now. I'll wait.

Probably the best place to get a purebred rabbit is a rabbit breeder. Here are some good reasons to go in this direction:

- ✔ Responsible rabbit breeders take very good care of their animals, and make an excellent source for a rabbit if you are looking for a healthy, well-socialized purebred bunny.

- ✔ Breeders usually have baby bunnies available, a real plus if you have your heart set on getting a very young rabbit.

- ✔ Your rabbit's breeder will be a contact for life, and can help you with bunny related questions and problems that may come up. He or she may even be willing to help you get started in showing and breeding rabbits, if this is your ultimate goal. A responsible breeder will also take the rabbit back if you can't keep it for any reason during the animal's life.

- ✔ You may be able to meet your future rabbit's *sire* and *dam* (father and mother) at the breeder's rabbitry, which will give you a good idea of what your rabbit's personality will be like.

- ✔ A good breeder will help you make good decisions about how and where to keep your new rabbit, and even whether you'e ready to take on a rabbit right now.

Here are some downsides:

- ✔ Lots of shelter rabbits out there need good homes.

- ✔ Buying from a breeder is expensive.

Unless you're set on showing or breeding, consider getting a purebred or mixed breed from a shelter. More than a fair share of purebreds make their way to shelters.

Getting a connection

You have these sources for finding rabbit breeders in your area:

- ✔ **American Rabbit Breeders Association (ARBA).** ARBA is a national organization, but works with national clubs for each of the breeds its recognizes. These breed clubs keep records of all the breeders in the United States, and can be contacted for the names and numbers of breeders in your area. For a list of national rabbit breed clubs, see the appendix.

✔ **Local 4-H club.** Most 4-H clubs have rabbit projects, usually run by breeders who do this in their spare time. You can find out who the rabbit contact is in your local 4-H club by contacting your County Extension office. You can find your County Extension office by calling directory assistance within your area code.

✔ **Rabbit shows.** ARBA shows are the best events to attend since breeders of nearly every type of rabbit can be found at these shows. Spend some time at the show, and make conversation with breeders to see if they have rabbits available for sale. Be sure to wait until *after* the breeder has finished showing in his or her class, however, since breeders are usually busy readying rabbits just before they take the rabbit to the show ring. You can read more about shows in Chapter 17.

✔ **Veterinarian with rabbit experience.** These people know the responsible breeders in the area; they see these animals in their practice after they're sold as pets. Vets also receive personal recommendations of breeders from clients.

Checking over your breeder

Once you have come up with the name of a breeder or two, your next step is to scope out his or her rabbitry (the place where the rabbits are kept) and find out if this is really the person from whom you wish to buy your rabbit.

Take the following steps to help make this decision:

✔ Call the breeder and ask her about the breeding operation. Your job is to get a sense of who the breeder is. Find out:

• How many rabbit breeds this person is involved with (many breeders dabble in more than one breed).

• How many rabbits this person currently keeps. If the breeder has more than a dozen or so rabbits, ask if the breeder has help. It's a lot of work to properly care for a large group of rabbits!

✔ While you are on the phone with the breeder, find out if she shows rabbits. This is important for two reasons.

• A breeder involved with showing is an expert on the breed (or breeds) in her rabbitry.

• You can't expect to buy a show-quality rabbit from a breeder who doesn't show. If you're looking to buy a rabbit you can show, the answer to this question is doubly important.

On the topic of buying a show rabbit, make sure you tell the breeder up front that you want a rabbit you can show. Expect to pay a higher price for a show-quality rabbit.

✔ Visit the breeder's facilities. Ask him or her if you can come and check out the rabbitry. If the breeder says no, even with an appointment, shop for your rabbit elsewhere. A breeder who won't allow buyers to see the general environment where his or her rabbits are kept is most likely hiding something. (Some areas of the rabbitry may be off limits to visitors to protect from transmission of disease.)

When you do visit the rabbitry, look for healthy rabbits in a clean environment. That means the cages should be clean and the smell should not be overwhelming. The rabbits themselves should be bright eyed, have well groomed coats and be free of diarrhea or any respiratory ailments.

Choosing the rabbit

Once you've picked your breeder, it's time to pick your rabbit. The breeder should be able to help you with this decision.

✔ Make sure the rabbit you buy appears healthy. Stay away from a rabbit with

- Runny, not clear, eyes

- Matted, not clean, coat

- Fur matted with stool or urine

- Sores on the bottoms of the feet

- Crusty ears

- Any kind of nasal discharge or apparent respiratory difficulty

✔ Look for a personable rabbit. Even if you plan to show your rabbit, you'll likely also want to enjoy your bunny as a pet. Rabbits who kick repeatedly and bite when you or the breeder handles them are probably not well socialized and may not make good pets.

If you are looking for a show prospect,

✔ Study the standard for your breed before you purchase the rabbit.

✔ Ask the breeder to select the best show animal available in the breed you're seeking. The breeder should show you the rabbit's coat and *conformation* (the way he's put together), explaining how the rabbit holds up to the breed's standard. The *breed standard* is the blueprint of the ideal rabbit.

- ✔ Ask the breeder to point out the rabbit's good points and faults before you purchase.

- ✔ Try to get the best rabbit you can afford: the one with the least amount of faults.

Be aware that if you are purchasing a very young rabbit, both you and the breeder won't know for sure if your rabbit will grow up to be a winner in the show ring. Only time will tell. (See Chapter 17 for more information about the show ring.)

A Rabbit in Store for You: Pet Shops

If you have a pet shop in your area that sells animals, an adorable baby bunny has probably lured you to a cage window. Rabbits for sale can be found in many pet shops, especially around Easter.

A pet shop can be an okay place to purchase a rabbit as long as you take the following points into consideration:

- ✔ **Rabbits sold in pet shops are not always purebred.** Many are mixed breeds of unknown ancestry. The few purebreds that can be found in pet shops are almost always "pet quality," which means you can't successfully exhibit them in ARBA rabbit shows.

- ✔ **The breeding, socialization, and early health care is unknown.** You will not be able to examine the rabbitry where the bunny was born or meet its parents. This means you don't know much about the rabbit you are buying, or its background.

- ✔ **The rabbit care information you receive from pet shop employees may be unreliable.** Expertise on rabbits varies from pet store to pet store, and you have no way of knowing if you are getting the right answers to your questions.

- ✔ **A lot of unwanted rabbits currently residing in shelters need homes.** The people who run these groups believe that with so many mixed breed rabbits available for adoption, rabbit lovers have a moral obligation to avoid purchasing rabbits from pet shops.

If you would like to buy a rabbit from a pet shop in spite of these realities, make sure you follow these guidelines:

- ✔ Take a close look at the conditions. The cage should be clean and fresh water and hay available. Groups of rabbits should not be crowded into small cages; this causes stress and increases the likelihood of disease.

✔ Examine the rabbit for good health. Stay away from a rabbit with

- Runny eyes

- Matted coat (especially with urine and stool)

- Crusty ears

- Sores on bottoms of his feet

- Nasal discharge or difficulty breathing

✔ Make certain the pet store provides a health guarantee for the rabbit. In the event that the rabbit becomes ill shortly after purchase (usually within 48 hours), the store should be willing to pay your vet bills. If the rabbit dies not long after you buy it, find out why it died. If the cause was related to the way the rabbit was cared for before you purchased it, you should be entitled to a refund. (A replacement rabbit is not an acceptable substitute for a refund since a dead rabbit indicates a serious illness among the bunnies available at the store.)

Part II

Keeping Your Rabbit Well Fed and Funk Free

The 5th Wave   By Rich Tennant

The way I see it, a visual inspection of my rabbit's feed, just isn't enough

In this part . . .

Properly caring for your rabbit is crucial and has many aspects. I show how to house your rabbit and help you decide whether your pet should be kept indoors or out. You read about the best cages for a rabbit, how to groom your pet, and most importantly how to properly feed your bunny for optimum health.

Chapter 5

Shacking Up with an Indoor Rabbit

....

....

In the old days, rabbits were considered strictly outdoor animals. Even rabbits kept as pets were relegated to hutches out in the backyard — never to put their fuzzy little bunny paws inside a human dwelling. But luckily for both rabbits and pet owners, attitudes have changed on this topic.

These days, rabbits are allowed to live indoors — in close quarters with their human companions. In fact, not only are they allowed, but also they're welcome! You must be wondering how in the world this works. Rabbits inside the house? Isn't that the same as having a sheep or goat hanging around the living room? Well, not quite. Read on to find out the benefits of living with a house rabbit.

Opening Your Eyes about Keeping Him Inside

Before we go any further, stop and take a look at all the really great reasons for you to keep your rabbit inside the house instead of outdoors in a hutch.

Safety

When Nature was doling out the cards to determine who would be prey and who would be predator, the rabbit got the ace of spades. Just about every predator on the planet regards rabbits as fair game.

Rabbits that live outdoors — whether in the wild or in the confines of a backyard — are constantly at risk for becoming dinner. Even in suburban areas, nocturnal predators lurk, yearning for rabbit stew.

Even if your bunny is tucked away in a hutch, he isn't completely safe. Critters, such as raccoons, are notorious for reaching their long arms between the wire of a rabbit hutch and grabbing for the terrified bunny. Other creatures — coyotes, snakes, and even cats — are attracted to a caged rabbit. Although most of these predators may not be able to gain access to the inside of the hutch, their mere presence can be enough to terrify your rabbit to death.

Rabbits kept indoors are completely safe from predators that lurk in the night (provided your other pets are rabbit friendly; see Chapter 3 for more information on this). For that reason and others, the average life span of the indoor rabbit is significantly higher than his outdoor counterpart.

Health

Pet rabbits that live outdoors in your yard are more susceptible to illness but not for the reasons that you may think. It's not because thousands of airborne rabbit-nabbing germs are floating around your yard or because wild rabbits may drop by and spread illness. (Although in some areas, wild rabbits actually do spread illness to pet rabbits.)

The main reason that the outdoor life for a pet rabbit means a greater possibility of illness is because outdoor bunnies spend less time with their owners. For a rabbit, less time with your owner means less likelihood of someone noticing that you're sick.

When rabbits don't feel well, they let us know in a variety of subtle ways, such as a change in appetite or acting depressed and lethargic. Others are sneezing, scratching, limping, and changes in their stool or urine output. (See Chapter 9 for more information on rabbit health issues.) Rabbits are prey animals, and they naturally hide signs of disease, so they won't become a snack for a predator the minute they're feeling a bit under the weather. If you don't spend much time with your rabbit, you're less likely to actually see your pet limping, sneezing, or being lethargic. You're also less likely to recognize any subtle yet important difference in your pet's behavior.

The House Rabbit Society

In 1988, a group of seven rabbit lovers got together to form an organization called the House Rabbit Society designed to help rabbits. They firmly believed, among other things, that rabbits should live indoors with their human companions.

Before the House Rabbit Society was organized, some people kept rabbits inside, but they kept quiet about it. Rabbits were traditionally considered livestock and were supposed to live outside. Or so most people thought. Today, with

the help of the House Rabbit Society, which promotes keeping rabbits indoors, bunny lovers around the world are finding out firsthand that rabbits make great indoor pets. The organization provides information to rabbit owners on how to best care for and live with their house rabbits.

For more information on the House Rabbit Society or to find a chapter in your area, contact them at House Rabbit Society, 148 Broadway, Richmond, California 94804 or go to their Web site at www.rabbit.org.

Another problem for outdoor rabbits is weather. Although rabbits tolerate the cold weather, heat is a killer for bunnies. A particularly hot day can spell doom for an outdoor rabbit, and controlling the temperature in an outdoor rabbit hutch is difficult if not impossible.

Bonding

For people who live with house rabbits, one of the most important reasons to keep a bunny inside is for the incredible bonding experience it offers. Sure, you can still bond with your rabbit if he lives outside in a hutch, but spending much time with your pet can only be had if your pet lives under the same roof and within the same walls as you.

If you live with an indoor rabbit, you and your bunny can share the following activities:

- **Watching TV:** What could be more relaxing than to come home at night and cuddle up on the couch with your favorite plant-eating mammal?

- **Reading:** Your rabbit will love it if you sit in your most comfortable chair to supervise his playtime as he romps around the room while you read a book.

- **Eating meals:** If you're a healthy eater who enjoys plenty of fresh fruits and vegetables, you can share some of your food with your rabbit. Watch your rabbit beg. Dogs that beg can be annoying, but a bunny that begs is downright adorable.

- **Playing together:** You can play indoor games with your rabbit or simply sit by and watch him play on his own with his toys.

- **Cleaning house:** Watch your rabbit help you as you straighten up around the house. If he's a real people-rabbit, he'll follow you around and do his best to assist.

Fun

Having any kind of rabbit is a hoot, but having an indoor rabbit is twice the fun. People who live with house rabbits can talk for hours about all the funny and adorable antics that their rabbits do, such as how they hop into your lap while you're napping, stare up at you from the ground while you're making dinner, or curl up under the covers with you when you're home sick from work.

Rabbits can be really hilarious to watch, too, as evidenced in Chapter 17. Playing with their toys, chasing each other (if you have more than one), or kicking up their heels in sheer joy — all antics enjoyed by indoor rabbits and easily viewed by indoor rabbit owners.

REMEMBER

Enjoying your house rabbit

One of the best reasons for keeping your rabbit indoors is all the neat stuff that you'll witness. Chapter 10 gives details about reading your rabbit's body language. For example:

- **Sounds:** You get to hear all the sounds that rabbits make. They make a honking noise when they want attention from you or are begging for something to eat. A kind of purring sound resonates from a rabbit who is happily being scratched behind the ear while you're watching TV, and they "cluck" when you give them a snack that they really enjoy.

- **Body language:** A relaxed house rabbit expresses himself physically as well as

vocally. A completely stretched out rabbit is happy, secure, and content. A rabbit who has flopped over on his side or back is in a deep sleep and probably dreaming. A shuddering bunny has just smelled something that he doesn't like. (See Chapter 10 for more information on bunny body language.)

- **Many moods:** Just like people, rabbits have shifting moods. Your pet may feel playful on any given day but act relaxed and sleepy the next day. One evening, he may beg for affection, but tomorrow, he's content to just huddle on a cushion nearby.

Making Sure Everyone's Comfy

If you think that you may want to try keeping your rabbit indoors, you need to know how to provide the right environment. Having an indoor rabbit doesn't mean that you let your little hopper have the run of the place. Far from it. You need to provide a well thought out and careful environment for your rabbit, for both his sake and yours.

Picking up some essentials

It's easy to find items for your rabbit if you know where to look. Pet store chains and independent pet stores are good sources, as are mail order catalogs for pet products. A number of general online pet supply resources carry rabbit products, and some web sites carry goodies exclusively for rabbits. See the Appendix for contact information on a number of these sources.

Shopping for miscellany

Your indoor rabbit's cage is just one of several items that you need to pick up at a pet supply store before you bring home your bunny. Scope out the following house rabbit necessities:

✔ **Litter box:** All good house rabbits know how to use a litter box, and yours should be no exception. Get a box that's small enough to fit into your rabbit's cage yet big enough for your bunny to sit in comfortably. A small cat litter box can do, or you can find a rabbit-size box in a bunny catalog or on an Internet shopping site. Figure 5-1 is an example of a box that fits into the cage's corner. (See Chapter 11 for advice on litter box training your rabbit.)

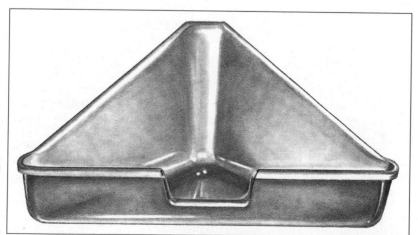

Figure 5-1:
Please
don't litter!

- **Litter:** You need to put something inside that litter box besides your rabbit. Avoid the temptation to use your cat's clay-based litter. Although this type of litter is fine for cats, the dust is irritating to the rabbit's respiratory tract and some rabbits have eaten the clay litter, resulting in a fatal intestinal impaction. Pelleted bedding is more absorbent than clay and if eaten, not harmful to the rabbit. In addition, pelleted bedding tends to draw moisture away from the surface so that it remains drier where the rabbit is sitting. Suitable bedding material includes those made of aspen, paper, and cellulose. Corn cob bedding isn't very absorbent and tends to mold easily which can present a health problem. Avoiding cedar and pine litters is best. Although they smell nice to the human nose, some experts believe the fumes may be too strong for rabbits.

- **Food bowl or feeder:** You see all kinds of food bowls in the store, but the crock-style bowls are the best kind (seen in Figure 5-2). These ceramic containers work great because they're hard to tip over, and rabbits are notorious tippers. Make sure the bowl that you buy isn't too deep for your rabbit to reach into. This is primarily a concern with baby bunnies and small dwarf breeds. Keep in mind that bowls are easy to clean: Just throw them in the dishwasher.

Figure 5-2:
Subvert the notorious tendency for rabbits to tip with these ceramic food bowls.

- **Water bottle:** Instead of providing a bowl of water like you would for a cat or dog, give your rabbit a gravity water bottle. This bottle, shown in Figure 5-3, has a metal tube at the end with a metal ball in the tip. These bottles keep the water accessible without letting it drip. When your rabbit is thirsty, he can sip from the metal tip of the water bottle. This sure beats giving him a bowl of water that he can tip over several times a day.

Figure 5-3:
Honey may
be the
nectar of
the gods,
but water is
pretty darn
important
to rabbits.

✔ **Nest box:** Rabbits take great comfort in having a small, dark space
where they can huddle when they need time to themselves. Check out
the huddling rabbit in Figure 5-4. A nest box, tucked into a corner of
your rabbit's cage, can provide that comfort. You can purchase a nest
box from a rabbit supply catalog or Internet site. Get one that's made of
metal with a wood floor or wood covered with metal mesh. If you opt for
a wood-only box, your rabbit will soon gnaw the box to pieces.

Figure 5-4:
Who doesn't
like to hang
out in a
small
nesting
box?

- **Bedding:** Put something in your rabbit's nest box to make it cozy for sleeping. Use the same pelleted bedding you put in the litter box. You can add a layer of hay or straw on top to make it more nest-like. Avoid cedar or pine bedding because of the strong odor it emits.

- **Hayrack:** Roughage is important in a rabbit's diet (as discussed in Chapter 7), and your bunny should always have a supply of fresh grass hay available for noshing. To keep the hay from being strewn all over your rabbit's house — and yours — you need a hayrack that hangs from the side of the cage. The rack, shown in Figure 5-5, keeps the hay in place as your rabbit munches on it throughout the day. Metal hayracks are available from rabbit supply retailers.

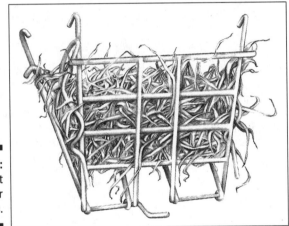

Figure 5-5: Hay's not just for horses.

- **Chew blocks:** Rabbit teeth are continually growing, and rabbits have a strong urge to gnaw as a result. Buy your bunny some chew blocks made for small animals, so he can work those teeth on the blocks (rather than your furniture). Chapter 14 has information on how to deal with rabbits who chew on your prized antique chaise lounge legs. The "Chewing" section, later in this chapter, offers tips on preventing this from happening.

- **Toys:** Rabbits love to play. Pick up a few toys for your pet while you're out shopping for supplies. Rabbits enjoy most cat toys, especially balls with bells in them. You can also give your pet homemade toys, such as empty toilet paper rolls and cardboard boxes. Use toys that are safe for your pet to chew, because he most likely will! Chapter 17 talks about toys in depth.

Craving his cage

Yes, even though your rabbit is living inside the house, he still needs a cage. Rather than thinking of it as a jail of sorts, think of your rabbit's enclosure as a den. That is, a place that he can call his own.

The purpose of your indoor rabbit's cage is to provide a confined spot for your rabbit when you can't supervise him. Because pet rabbits have a strong desire to hide in enclosed spaces left over from their wild days, your rabbit can appreciate having such a place where he can go to rest and escape from the world. You can appreciate having a place like this for him to go because your rabbit shouldn't be out and about in your house unless you can keep a close eye on him.

You can buy an indoor rabbit cage at a pet supply store, through a catalog, or over the Internet. (See the Appendix for shopping sites and catalogs.) A good example of an indoor cage is shown in Figure 5-6.

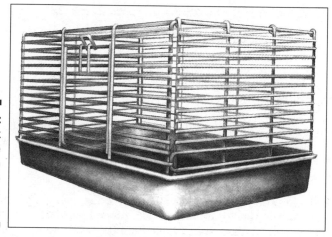

Figure 5-6:
It may look like a little rabbit prison to you but to him it's homey.

Your rabbit's indoor cage should:

✔ Be large enough for the rabbit to turn around comfortably and stand up on his hind legs without his ears touching the top. If your rabbit is a baby now, be sure to buy a cage that can fit him when he's grown. Chapter 6 tells you how you can figure out how large a cage your rabbit needs, based on his size.

✔ Have enough room to accommodate a small litter box, a nesting box (big enough for the rabbit to fit into), a food bowl, a water bottle, and a hayrack with openings no larger than 1 by 2 inches. Anything bigger and the rabbit may catch his leg or head in it. The floor of the cage may be made of wire, with square openings of about ½ inch. A slide-out tray below the wire catches waste material. Line the tray with newspaper or one of the pelleted beddings mentioned earlier. You can use a solid-floored cage instead, particularly if you're planning to litter box train your rabbit. The whole floor to the cage will slide out and you can again use newspaper or pelleted bedding to line it.

> # Moving on up
>
> You may see some pretty fancy many-tiered cages on the market designed for rabbits, but buyer beware. If the ramps are too steep, injuries may result. Rabbits are land animals and don't feel safe when high above the ground. In addition, the vertical nature of the cage gives the false impression that the rabbit has enough space, when in fact, it's the horizontal space that's important for exercise and movement. For these reasons, I don't recommend many-tiered cages (four-plus tiers) for rabbits, ferrets, or guinea pigs. They simply don't fit with the animals' natural physiology and psyche.

✔ Having a side door for your rabbit to enter through the cage is a must. For your convenience, try to get a cage that also opens from the top. Being able to open the cage roof makes reaching in to provide your pet with food or taking your rabbit out (if you need to) much easier.

Where you put your rabbit's cage is even more important than what it looks like. Rabbits are sensitive to climate and air quality and can quickly become ill if they're exposed to the wrong things. Keep the following in mind when you think about where you place your indoor rabbit's cage:

✔ **Avoid placing the cage in an area of your house where dramatic and extreme temperature fluctuations take place frequently.** High heat and humidity are particularly dangerous. Rabbits, other pets, or humans for that matter do *not* need a constant temperature range all the time. Some fluctuation is healthy; just try to avoid the extremes.

✔ **Never expose the cage to direct sunlight.** The sun's rays when magnified through glass can become hot and can cause heat stroke in a rabbit. Even direct sunlight through a window screen can be dangerous for a rabbit.

✔ **Don't put the cage near a heating or air-conditioning vent because sudden temperature changes take place there.** In addition, when the fan on the furnace or air conditioner starts up, it blows out all the settled dust, which can create irritation in your pet's respiratory tract.

✔ **An attic or basement is no place for a rabbit cage.** The dampness and lack of ventilation in these areas can prove hazardous to your pet's health.

✔ **The cage should be in a well-lit area where people come and go but shouldn't be in a spot where your rabbit never has any peace and quiet.**

✔ **Place the cage where the bunny can experience at least eight hours of darkness.** Constant bright lighting with no relief or inconsistent lighting (one night up late, next night not) can wreak havoc on a rabbit's endocrine system, which has some dependency on photoperiods for its function. At the least, cover the cage with a heavy cloth or towel that blocks light for at least eight hours out of each 24-hour period.

✔ **Don't put the cage near stereo speakers or a TV; the noise may drive your rabbit out of his mind.**

Rebellious rabbits

A big reason for keeping your rabbit inside instead of out is so that you can share house time with your pet. But before you let your rabbit go running through the halls, you need to take some precautions. These aren't only for the safety of your rabbit — who can get into more trouble than you can possibly imagine — but also for the well being of your home.

In order to adequately protect your house and your rabbit, get an idea of exactly what kinds of problems rabbits can get into when left to their own devices inside your home. Take a look at Figure 5-7.

Holding down the fort

One easy and economical way to confine your rabbit to an area of the home or outdoors is also moveable. A dog exercise pen, found in pet stores or dog supply catalogs, is comprised of 3 to 4 foot high by 2 to 4 foot long metal wire panels that quickly hook together with a long pin to make an enclosure. You can easily step over the fencing to gain entrance, or you can remove one pin and open the fencing. The panels can be formed to a variety of shapes and used indoors or out. When the panels aren't in use, the entire apparatus can be folded completely flat and stored against a wall or in a closet in a matter of minutes. The size that you get depends on the rabbits, but of course, the larger, the better. For large breed rabbits, I recommend the 4-foot fencing; other breeds do fine with three.

In addition, if you have carpeting or want to protect a floor, you can buy a sheet of no-wax flooring at any hardware store and place it under the fenced-in area; it doesn't have to be really high quality. The flooring can easily be rolled up and moved should you need to do so. Voila! You have no problems with soiled carpet or digging into carpet. The rabbit can be confined to the pen and still be in the room with you without danger of getting into mischief. They're invaluable, and some local House Rabbit Society chapters use them in foster homes.

You can also leave the fencing up all the time around the cage as a permanent exercise area. This works *great* outside as well and can be moved around the yard. Of course, don't leave your rabbit in his pen outside without supervision.

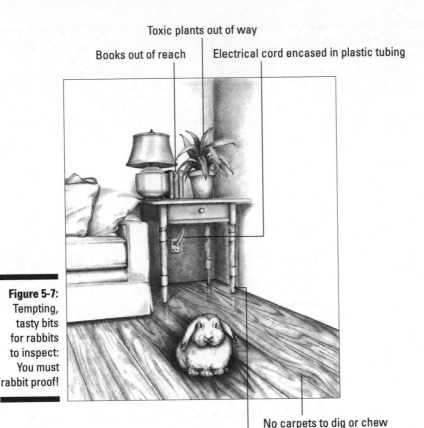

Toxic plants out of way

Books out of reach

Electrical cord encased in plastic tubing

Figure 5-7:
Tempting,
tasty bits
for rabbits
to inspect:
You must
rabbit proof!

No carpets to dig or chew

Wrapped in heavy plastic

Trouble Spots

Rabbits love to tuck themselves away into little corners. They're also curious and love to investigate new places. Put this combination together and you have potential for trouble in the house with your rabbit.

Before you give your bunny access to a room,

- ✔ Get down on all fours and look around carefully.

- ✔ Find any small spaces that your rabbit may be able to get into. Your bunny is apt to crawl into one of these spots and possibly get trapped.

- ✔ Block nooks and crannies with heavy objects, so your rabbit won't be able to get into them and then get stuck.

- ✔ Make sure no toxic chemicals or plants are placed within reach of your rabbit. (See Chapter 6 for more information on toxic plants.)

- ✔ Be certain that trash bags and buckets are well out of bunny's reach.

Chewing

Rabbits have a tremendous urge to gnaw. Although chewing doesn't give bunnies zits or cause them to have to let out their trousers, it can result in plenty of grief for both them and the owners they live with if they chew on the wrong things.

When inside a home, rabbits tend to make a beeline for the following objects, with teeth bared:

- ✔ Carpet edges
- ✔ Electrical cords
- ✔ Telephone cords
- ✔ Wooden furniture legs

As you can well imagine, rabbit teeth can do plenty of damage to these items. In a short time, wooden furniture legs can be permanently disfigured, telephone cords can be rendered useless, and carpet edges can be chomped and swallowed. Electrical cords that have been chewed through can be fatal for a rabbit and may even start a fire in your home.

However, you can enjoy your indoor rabbit without having to worry about those destructive teeth:

- ✔ **Limit your rabbit's activities to one or two rooms of the house.**

- ✔ **Don't let your rabbit run loose in the house without your constant supervision.**

- ✔ **Cover wooden furniture legs in accessible rooms with bubble wrap or thick plastic. Figure 5-8 shows you how to do this.**

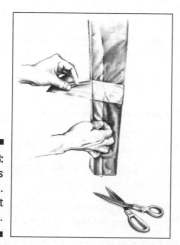

Figure 5-8:
Plastic is
pretty . . .
pretty rabbit
safe, that is.

- ✔ **Put telephone cords well out of reach.** This includes beyond the grasp of rabbits who like to hop up onto chairs.

- ✔ **Cover electrical cords with plastic aquarium tubing.** Cut the tube lengthwise and slip it over the cord, as is shown in Figure 5-9.

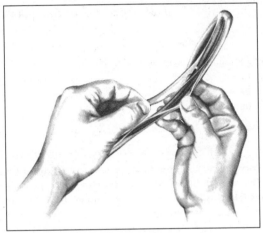

Figure 5-9:
Wrap up
that
electrical
wiring.

- ✔ **Leave chew toys around the room.** Your rabbit can chew on these instead of what he shouldn't.

Digging

Another bad bunny habit is digging. Rabbits love to dig. In the wild, they create their dens by excavating. A problem arises, however, when rabbits running loose in the house decide that they want to dig a tunnel through your carpeting. They usually choose a loose corner of the carpet to start their excavation. They also choose doorways if the door is closed, so you often need to protect the lower part of the door with Plexiglas or the like to keep them from damaging the wood. If this digging goes unnoticed, they can quickly tear up a good portion of the rug. In addition, if they eat the carpet, the fibers are indigestible, and the ingestion of enough of these can lead to an intestinal impaction.

TIP

To keep your four-legged shovel from messing up your carpeting

- ✔ **Check all the corners of the room where your rabbit will be roaming.**

- ✔ **Place heavy objects in the corners, so your rabbit can't get a toehold on a loose area of the rug.**

Putting off the perfume

I don't recommend spraying perfume on furniture legs to put off your chewy pet. Several animals have been known to develop respiratory disease from perfumes, and in the case of birds, some fatalities have occurred. Highly aromatic perfumes and perfumes that contain plenty of alcohol, which helps the scent spread, have been implicated most often. Don't use these products. In addition, more and more humans are allergic to these same perfumes and will break out in a rash or have an asthma attack after being exposed to the substance. It has also been my experience that most products that are designed to keep dogs and cats off of furniture do *not* work on rabbits.

✔ **Make sure carpet edges are securely tacked down.** You can cover them with a heavy plastic rug protector, as sold to protect rugs under office furniture. These rug protectors are often found in office supply stores and are made of clear heavy plastic with spikes on the back to hold them in place on the carpet. They can be cut to different sizes and help protect carpet corners from your rabbit's digging and soiling. You can also use a clear plastic carpet runner protector found in many hardware or carpeting stores. They're all smooth enough that when the rabbit digs at them, they get nowhere. Alternatively, you could use sheets of Plexiglas in the digging areas, but they're harder to secure.

✔ **Encourage your rabbit to dig somewhere else.** Provide him with a box full of sand or soil that he can rummage through. Make sure the box is deep enough to keep the dirt inside when your rabbit starts to excavate but not so deep that your rabbit can't jump in or out.

Also, rabbits like to dig at furniture. Your favorite couch, chair, or bed may be shredded. Protect these areas with a heavy cloth covering or prevent the rabbit from having access to them.

Putting Her on the Nautilus

Whether a rabbit is living indoors or out, the bunny needs exercise and plenty of it. Caged rabbits need at least two hours a day, every day, of free time outside the cage for exercise. For indoor rabbits, this need can be handled indoors or out.

Indoors

After you designate which areas of your home will be accessible to your bunny and have securely rabbit proofed these rooms or set up a rabbit pen with moveable panels, you can give your rabbit permission to roam, under your supervision. When you first turn your bunny loose in "her" room, she'll hop about and investigate. This will go on for several days. She'll scour the place and leave her scent on objects by rubbing her chin on them. (Don't worry; the scent is not discernible to the human nose.) Eventually, though, the novelty of the new room wears off, and bunny gets bored. To encourage her to do more than just sit in a corner and stare at you, you'll need to get active.

Some tips on getting your bunny to exercise:

- ✔ **Play with him:** If you've bonded with your rabbit, you'll be amazed at how easily he can learn to play with you. When playing with your rabbit, let the rabbit initiate the play. (See Chapter 17 for more details on playing with your rabbit.)

- ✔ **Teach him tricks:** A rabbit isn't going to fetch your slippers or rescue lost children, but you can show him some basic tricks and behaviors that result in food rewards. See Chapter 13 for details on how to do this.

- ✔ **Give him toys:** Now is the time to pull out those toys that you bought for your rabbit at the pet supply store. Toss him one toy at a time until you find the one that strikes his fancy. Don't forget the homemade stuff, too. A cardboard box, a toilet paper roll, and even an empty plastic soda bottle can prove terribly exciting to your rabbit. See Chapter 17 for information on toys for your rabbit.

- ✔ **Provide company:** If you have more than one rabbit, and they all get along, put them together for exercise playtime. Not only can they get plenty of exercise, but watching them, you'll also laugh your head off. But make sure that you provide them with several "hide" areas. These can be as simple as overturned cardboard boxes with a hole cut in the side — at least as many as the number of rabbits — in case a spat breaks out. If the rabbit has nowhere to hide or escape and another one is being aggressive, a serious injury may result.

Keep in mind that you should place your litter box somewhere in the room, so your rabbit can use it during playtime. If you have more than one rabbit, put at least as many litter boxes out as the number of rabbits. If you're in the process of teaching your rabbit to use the box, you may want to have two or more placed strategically around the room to encourage their use. Put newspaper or a sheet of heavy plastic under and around the boxes as rabbits may urinate over the side if the box isn't deep.

Outdoors

Just because you have an indoor rabbit doesn't mean that you can't take him outside for exercise. Just as with your indoor rabbit areas, your outdoor areas must be rabbit-proofed too, as shown in Figure 5-10.

No means of escape   No toxic plants present

Figure 5-10:
Indoors to outdoors: Just make sure you rabbit proof your yard.

Never leave rabbit unattended

Select an area where you plan to exercise your rabbit outdoors, and check it out for safety. For details on what this involves, see Chapter 6. You won't need to do as much work to encourage your rabbit to exercise outdoors. The sights, sounds, and smells of the great outdoors can keep your rabbit busy.

However, don't leave your bunny out there to do his thing. Watching with a close eye to make certain he stays safe from predators, you must stay outside with your bunny. Remember that just about every land-based predator on the planet considers the rabbit a potential meal.

One solution to this is to build your rabbit a secure, outdoor area where he can exercise without worrying about predators. You still need to keep a close eye on him, but you probably won't have to do more than just check on him every so often. You can also use the exercise pen for a temporary outside play area. See Chapter 13 for details on constructing a safe outdoor play area.

Keeping a Squeaky Clean Home

One of the most important factors to a rabbit's good health is cleanliness. A clean environment means a healthy rabbit. A dirty environment means the potential for a rabbit with chronic health problems.

Of course, that's not the only reason to keep a rabbit's area sanitary. In the case of the indoor rabbit, your house suffers if you don't keep up after your rabbit's hygiene.

If you perform the following duties with the frequency specified, you shouldn't have a problem with your rabbit or your house:

Table 5-1		Cleaning Tasks
Task	*Frequency*	*What to do*
Litter box cleaning	Every 3 days	If your rabbit is litter-box trained, your cage-cleaning duties are much easier. 1. If you're using appropriate pelleted bedding with one litter box per rabbit, change the litter completely. The surface stays dry with a thick layer of pelleted bedding in the litter box. 2. Look for other areas in the cage where your rabbit may have gone to the bathroom (including the nest box) and clean those up, too. 3. Check the stools and urine daily to see if any abnormalities are present. If a rabbit is ill, use a small amount of litter and change it daily to observe any abnormalities. Changing the litter daily can be expensive. If you want to routinely change litter daily, use much smaller amounts in the box, such as one inch.

Task	Frequency	What to do
Cage duty	Daily	If you're feeding your rabbit a proper diet, you no doubt have some food to clean up inside your rabbit's cage. 1. Remove any fresh fruit and vegetables that your rabbit has left behind. (See Chapter 7 for more on feeding.) 2. Wash out your rabbit's food bowl and water bottle. 3. Remove any stray pieces of hay that have fallen from the hayrack.
Cage cleaning	Weekly	Give your rabbit's cage a good, thorough cleaning with a mild disinfectant. 1. Mix a solution of one part bleach to ten parts of water is effective against a wide range of germs. 2. Clean surfaces of debris. 3. Keep the solution in contact with the surface for 30 minutes. 4. Make sure that you rinse off the bleach solution and that it's thoroughly dry before placing the rabbit back in the cage. Food and water bowls/bottles can be soaked in this solution weekly for 30 minutes and then rinsed in a good disinfectant or put through a dishwasher, which has water that reaches high temperatures.

Never clean any animal-related items, particularly those containing fecal material or urine, in the kitchen sink where food is prepared for human consumption. Use the bathtub or the bathroom sink and rinse well afterwards.

Pooping on your plants

Rabbit droppings makes a great addition to your compost pile. Simply drop the goods on your heap and let it cook. For more on composting, check online at www.mastercomposter.com or go to www.bhg.com and search for "Composting 101." Tons of good books exist on this topic as well.

Chapter 6

Bringing the Hutch to Your Star(sky) Rabbit

Traditionally, domestic rabbits have lived outdoors. Although recent social trends have allowed rabbit owners to keep their pets inside (see Chapter 5), some people still prefer the outdoor approach when it comes to rabbit keeping.

If you want to keep your bunny outside, you need to find out the best way to provide a safe, comfortable, and healthy outdoor environment for your pet. This chapter can help you do just that.

Getting a Hunch about Hutches

For outdoor rabbits, their hutch is their home, the place where they spend most of their time. Rabbits depend on their hutches to provide them with security and comfort, a place that they can call their own. Your job as a rabbit mom or dad is to provide your pet with a good outdoor hutch that's properly situated in your yard and kept suitably clean and in good repair. The hutch must protect your rabbit from the weather and from predators and also provide him with enough room to move around.

A *hutch* is essentially a cage, often made of a wood frame and enclosed in wire mesh. Hutches usually stand on tall legs, although some are legless and can be placed on top of a table or other surface, or kept on the ground in milder climates.

You can buy an outdoor hutch for your rabbit or make one yourself. The choice is yours. Whichever route you take, be sure to provide your rabbit with the largest possible hutch that you can afford.

In addition to a hutch, a rabbit needs plenty of other amenities. Those you can find listed in Chapter 5.

Buying

Luckily for rabbit owners, commercially made rabbit hutches are readily available in pet supply stores, feed stores, catalogs, and on the Internet. They range in price from under $100 to several hundred. Figure 6-1 shows an example of a medium-size, fairly basic hutch.

Figure 6-1:
A hutch any bunny would be proud to call home.

Hutch styles vary considerably, and a design exists for just about every taste. Some basically look like big wooden boxes, but others resemble log cabins. Some have attached exercise runs (a great idea) while others have nest boxes built in.(See "Building a Bunny Run" in this chapter for more information on runs.) The hutch you ultimately choose depends a great deal on what you can afford, what you have room for, and what you think your rabbit can enjoy the most.

Aside from these considerations, you also need to ruminate on several other points.

- **Protection from weather:** The hutch you buy has to protect your rabbit from heat, cold, and dampness. So the hutch needs a waterproof covering and a well-crafted nest box (described in Chapter 5), if one comes as part of the design. It also needs good ventilation that can prevent hot air from becoming trapped inside the hutch where it can kill the rabbit.

- **Protection from chewing:** To keep your rabbit from gnawing away at the wood portions of your hutch, purchase or make one that has wire over the exposed wood sections.

- **Flooring:** While an outdoor hutch requires a metal mesh floor to allow the rabbit's droppings to fall through, you'll also need a portion of the floor to be a solid material. Rabbits who stand exclusively on wire day in and day out develop sore hocks and possible infections as a result. Make sure at least a third of the hutch floor is solid material, preferably not metal, which is poorly insulated from heat or cold. A wood floor safely treated to keep out moisture or covered with a no-wax flooring is preferable. See Chapter 10 for more on health.

- **Overall quality:** Just like with any other product, quality varies in outdoor rabbit hutches. When shopping for a hutch, look for quality workmanship and materials. If you're able to examine the hutch in person before buying it, check to make sure it's sturdy, and that the wire and wood aren't flimsy and poorly finished. Look for specifics in this chapter's "Materials" section.

Size

The size of the hutch you buy depends on several factors, the least of which is cost. The bigger the hutch, the pricier it will be. However, keep in mind that your outdoor rabbit can spend most of his time inside this hutch, so the bigger the hutch, the better for your rabbit.

In terms of a minimum size, you should use the following equation:

$$1 \text{ pound of rabbit} = 1 \text{ square foot of space}$$

A typical rabbit weighs around 6 pounds, and therefore needs about 6 square feet of hutch space (2 by 3 feet). Also, keep in mind that if you're buying a hutch for a baby rabbit, you should estimate how large your pet can grow up to be and do the math according to his full-grown size.

Of course, this is the absolute minimum. Your rabbit is much happier with even more space to call his own, and here's why:

✔ Rabbits who don't have enough space to move around often become bored.

✔ The less room a rabbit has for his living quarters, the less a rabbit exercises in general, the greater his chance is for obesity.

✔ Small spaces are quickly fouled with urine and feces, which creates an unhealthy environment for the rabbit.

In addition to room for your rabbit, your outdoor hutch also needs to be large enough to accommodate all the accessories that your rabbit needs to live comfortably. Chapter 5 lists all those necessary accessories.

If you intend to house more than one rabbit, you obviously need a bigger hutch. Double the one pound of rabbit per one square foot, using the combined weight of your rabbits. Make sure that your nest box is big enough to hold more than one rabbit, too. You should provide at least two hide areas; one can be larger and heated, but another can function as an escape if needed. See Chapter 3 for more information about housing multiple rabbits.

Design

In addition to size, you need to consider rabbit hutch design when determining your purchase. This is not just for aesthetic reasons but also for practical reasons, too.

Consider the following:

✔ **Height:** Rabbit hutches come in different heights, from short dwellings that lie close to the ground, to tall cages that require little bending when cleaning them or placing a rabbit in the cage or taking one out. Hutches low to the ground can be unhealthy for rabbits in the wintertime because cold air and dampness settles closer to the ground in climates with cold winters. In climates with mild winters, cages near the ground or on the ground are fine. (Rabbits prefer to be on the ground and the effect of having them elevated in a hutch is unknown. It may be stressful for them, but it's hard to evaluate.)

✔ **Ease of cleaning:** Don't forget that you'll have to thoroughly clean your rabbit's hutch on a weekly basis, as outlined later in the chapter. Some hutches are easier to clean as a result of their design. Look for a hutch design that allows easy access with more than one opening. The positioning of the doors should permit you to reach all parts of the hutch.

✔ **Rabbit security:** Hutches with secure hiding places that allow rabbits to hide from predators and feel like they're unreachable within the hutch are best for your bunny's well being. Opt for one of these hutches if it's within your price range. If not, give your rabbit several nest boxes to use for hiding places.

Materials

When it comes to materials, most hutches are made from wood and wire or strictly wire. Benefits exist to both, and the one that you get is a matter of personal choice. Table 6-1 shows some pros and cons of both.

Table 6-1:	Hutch Construction		
Material	**Typical construction**	**Pros**	**Cons**
Wooden hutches	The most popular type. These hutches usually consist of a wooden roof and several wooden side panels. Wire mesh covers the door, front, and some sides of the cage.	Wooden hutches are nice to look at and work well to keep a rabbit warm in the winter and cool in the summer, provided they're made from a quality wood (as opposed to press board).	The wood is more likely to rot and will not last as long as a wire hutch. Rabbits also love to gnaw on wood, and any areas of the hutch that aren't covered in protective wire will be chewed down.
Metal hutches	Unlike their wooden counterparts, metal hutches don't have a combination of wood and metal but are all metal. This means a metal frame, a metal roof, and a wire enclosure.	Metal cages tend to last longer than wood and are noticeably cheaper. They're also much easier to clean.	Metal hutches retain cold in the winter and heat in the summer, neither of which is good for your rabbit.

Whether the hutch you buy is wood or metal, it must meet certain specifications to be safe for your rabbit:

✔ **The wire:** All rabbit hutches have wire sides, which allow you to see in at your rabbit and allows your rabbit to see out. The type of wire used on your rabbit hutch is important because the rabbit comes into daily contact with this material.

Only buy a hutch that has wire mesh that's sturdy and smooth-edged. Chicken wire doesn't fall into this category and shouldn't be used for housing rabbits. Also, the mesh itself needs to be no larger than 1 by 2 inches in size. The reason for this is that larger mesh can entrap a rabbit's leg or head and cause serious injury. Larger mesh holes also enable predators, such as raccoons, to reach their paws inside the cage toward the terrified rabbit. Three of the four walls of his cage should be solid for protection from the environment and security. Nest boxes tend to have thin walls and afford little protection from the elements. Dwarf rabbits kept in cold climates may even need a heated area of the cage in the winter. Heating also helps to keep the water and food from freezing.

- **The floor:** Make sure that at least one third of the rabbit's hutch is made of solid, easy-to-clean flooring as a protection from the weather. The wooden floor should be free of splinters. Untreated wood isn't easy to clean. You may want to consider gluing or tacking a no-wax floor covering to the wood floor to make it easier to clean. This is warmer than a metal floor, which can be dangerously cold in winter to sit on. Wire floors alone don't produce foot disease, but wet floors, wire flooring that has too large of a space, thin fur on the bottom of the rabbit's foot, and obesity can lead to foot disease. The wire floor surrounding it should only be smooth, ½ by 1 inch, 14-gauge welded wire. This is the safest type of wire flooring for a rabbit.

- **The roof:** The roof of the hutch should be covered with a waterproof substance, such as heavy plastic or house-quality roofing material. Some experts suggest an overhang to the roof to protect the sides. It's okay for a portion of the cage to not have a roof to allow access to the sunlight, which is particularly welcome in winter. As long as at least half of the cage is roofed, that's sufficient. A complete roof is also okay but not entirely necessary. This is important because your rabbit needs to stay warm and dry in wet weather to avoid illness.

If you build it, he will hop

No one says that you have to buy a hutch. If you're handy with tools, you can probably build one for slightly less than you would pay. The benefits are you can design the hutch exactly the way that you want to and be sure your rabbit has access to the best quality materials.

You can purchase rabbit hutch kits over the Internet and through mail-order catalogs, or you can actually buy rabbit hutch plans from the American Rabbit Breeders Association through their Web site at www.arba.net. Figure 6-2 shows a simple design for those of you who are considering building.

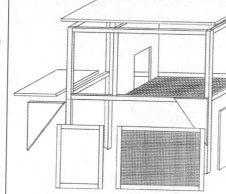

Figure 6-2: This gives you a general idea of the pieces needed to build your own hutch.

When preparing to build a hutch, keep these points in mind:

- Use the best materials you can afford. Exterior-grade plywood is a good choice because you can cut it easily and it comes in different thicknesses. A thickness of three eighths of an inch is the minimum you should use, but the thicker the better. Don't cheap out and use interior grade plywood because it won't hold up under harsh weather conditions.

- Screw the parts of the rabbit hutch together instead of nailing them. The hutch holdsup better this way and lasts much longer.

- Use quality wire for your hutch with a mesh no larger than 1 by 2 inches. The floor wire should be smooth ½ by 1 inch, 14-gauge welded wire.

- If you design your own hutch, make the doors big enough for you to comfortably reach toward the back of the cage when you need to clean it or extricate the rabbit. Also, design the doors to open toward you for the most ease.

- Be sure to include solid flooring in your hutch design. Your rabbit needs at least a third of the floor to be wood that has been sealed to keep out moisture or another material other than wire so there is protection from the elements and to prevent foot problems.

- Design the roof so it lays at a slight tilt. This will allow rain and snow to drop off rather than sit on it and melt. Use waterproof material to cover the roof.

If the hutch is elevated, you may want to put several inches of gravel under the hutch to allow for urine drainage to pass through. Some people put a layer of concrete for ease of cleaning. If you leave grass, the areas where the rabbit urinates may be burned permanently.

You know how it goes: Location, location, and location

One of the important tasks as an outdoor rabbit keeper is to keep your pet comfortable regardless of the weather. If you took the time to buy a good quality hutch that's both waterproof and well ventilated, you achieved half the battle. Your other task is to keep your pet safe from predators. In this section, you can find direction for doing both.

Weather

The biggest secret to keeping your rabbit comfortable in all kinds of weather is hutch location. By placing your hutch in just the right spot in your yard, you can help keep your pet warm and dry or cool and comfy, depending on what Mother Nature is doling out at any given time. Location is also important as it relates to your rabbit's general comfort and your convenience.

Rabbits, like most mammals, can withstand cold much better than they can withstand heat. Keep this important reality in mind when you're figuring out where you can place your rabbit's hutch:

- Pick a shady place in your yard for the hutch. Temperatures above 80 degrees are considered dangerous for rabbits. If you live in a cool climate and the morning sun hits the hutch for a short amount of time, then that may be okay. But generally speaking, the hutch shouldn't be exposed to direct sunlight for an extended time, especially during the hotter months.

- Rabbits can tolerate cold fairly well, and drafts aren't a cause for disease. Sudden and frequent temperature changes, however, are more dangerous. Select a spot for your hutch that's protected from cold, drafty air. If you live in a climate where winter temps go below 0 degrees Fahrenheit, provide a heater in your rabbit's cage.

- Constant (particularly cold) wind is bad for rabbits — especially small breeds under 4 pounds. Their small body mass makes it difficult to retain heat in a cold environment. (These breeds actually require heated cages in very cold climates.) Place your hutch in a spot that's protected from winter winds.

- Dampness is another unhealthy element for rabbits. Whether its cold dampness caused by rain or snow, or the dampness that results from heat and humidity, your rabbit should be kept safe from it. Make sure your hutch is waterproof and provide ventilation to the darker spots in the cage.

✔ On the topic of ventilation, clean, fresh air is important to all mammals. The fumes from the ammonia that comes from a rabbit's urine can be irritating to a rabbit's airways, but if the cage is clean, this shouldn't be an issue. A rabbit's respiratory system is *not* more sensitive than the respiratory systems of other mammals. However, they're close to the ground and in constant contact with ground odors. Place the hutch in a spot where plenty of fresh air is available.

✔ Although it may be tempting to keep your hutch inside a garage, this isn't a healthy place for a rabbit's home. The ventilation in most garages is less than ideal, and car exhaust and other fumes can make short work of your rabbit's health. In addition, the low lighting condition in a garage is unhealthy for your pet.

Quiet and convenience

Rabbits have a prey animal physiology and psychology and shouldn't be exposed to constant havoc and noise, which causes excessive stress. Likewise, you'll want your rabbit's hutch in a place where you can see it and where you can access it easily for feeding, cleaning, and other chores.

To keep your rabbit's nerves at ease, avoid putting the hutch in a place where plenty of activity takes place. For example, if your kids like to play basketball in the backyard, don't put the hutch in a place where the ball is likely to bang against the cage. Or if you have a motorcycle, don't put the hutch where your rabbit can listen to the engine start up every day (a great sound to you, but murder on a rabbit's sensitive ears). By using common sense, you can figure out the best spot in your yard from a rabbit's perspective.

Of course, you don't want to tuck your hutch away in a part of the yard where you may never see it, either. You also don't want to keep it where you have to climb over who knows what to gain access to it. If you can find a way to locate your hutch where you can view it from your back window or door, that would be ideal. Not only can this enable you to keep an eye on your rabbit, but it will also afford you the pleasure of seeing your bunny's activities when he doesn't know that you're watching.

Using your Hoover in the hutch

Even though your rabbit is outside and beyond the reach of your nose, you still need to keep his hutch spotlessly clean. The reason for this is that a dirty hutch is a breeding ground for bacteria, parasites, and disease. Chapter 7 has much more information on health if you're interested (and you should be).

But don't fret. If your rabbit's hutch is well designed, you shouldn't have too much trouble keeping it clean with minimum effort. Just use the following clean-up schedule:

- ✔ **Waste removal** (Daily): Your rabbit's droppings can accumulate quickly underneath the hutch and should be removed on a daily basis. Set up a compost area in your yard for the waste material or else designate a special covered trash can for your rabbit's waste. Keep a waste receptacle close by the hutch, along with a shovel, so it's easy for you to scoop the waste out from under the hutch and into the can without too much effort.

- ✔ **Food and water container cleaning** (Daily): To help keep bacteria to a minimum, wash out your rabbit's food bowl and water bottle on a daily basis. Use a biodegradable dish soap for your rabbit's health. These products are available in health food stores, as well as in many supermarket chains.

  Beware frozen water during winter. Keep the water in the heated box area, heat the water supply itself, or replace multiple times daily. You can use heat tape (as found in hardware stores to wrap around pipes) underneath a solid area where the water is to be kept. For this you need an outside outlet into which to plug the tape.

- ✔ **Nest box cleaning** (Daily): Most rabbits won't urinate or defecate in their nest boxes, but accidents do happen. Check the bedding in the nest box daily to make sure that it's clean. Remove soiled bedding when it's wet and replace it with clean, fresh material.

- ✔ **Hutch scrub** (Weekly): You need to thoroughly clean out your rabbit's hutch. Put your bunny in a safe place like his carrier or a rabbit-proofed room, and get a pail that has 1 part bleach to 10 parts water. Use a sponge to wipe down all the surfaces of the hutch and then scrub it with a bristle brush. This helps kill bacteria and other organisms that are building up inside your rabbit's home. Wait until the inside of the hutch is completely dry before putting your rabbit back inside.

Keeping Wolfie Away

Unfortunately, all kinds of predators would like to make a meal out of your outdoor bunny and preventing that from happening is your job. Most people think that cats and dogs are the only creatures they have to worry about preying on their outdoor rabbits, but this is not the case. Most cats find rabbits to be too big for hunting purposes (with the exception of the dwarf breeds, who are small enough for larger cats), and if your yard and hutch are secure, a dog probably won't be able to break in.

Predators who *can* go after your outdoor rabbit include raccoons, coyotes, foxes, mink, and weasels, to name a few. These critters often live in suburban and rural areas, and some of them are even found in urban sections of the country. And all of them are capable of scaling walls and fences, subsequently gaining access to seemingly protected backyards.

If your hutch is secure, it's unlikely that one of these animals will be able to break in and grab hold of your rabbit. However, a predator doesn't have to make contact with a rabbit in order to hurt or even kill it. Because rabbits are so easily frightened, the mere presence of a predator can literally scare a rabbit to death. At the least, a rabbit could injure its back, legs, or face while leaping around its hutch trying to escape.

If your pet lives outside, the danger from predators is inherent. However, you can take the following steps to limit the possibility that a predator can take your pet's life:

✔ Keep your hutch close to the house. The sound and smell of humans can discourage some predators from approaching the hutch.

✔ Use a sensor light to scare off approaching predators. Set up a motion sensor light near your rabbit's hutch. Predators are caught off guard when the light goes on as they come near the hutch.

✔ Surround your hutch with a fence enclosure. A chain link or even chicken wire enclosure with a roof can keep predators from being able to get close enough to the hutch to have access to your rabbit.

✔ Keep trash cans covered and avoid leaving pet food outside where the smell can attract predators to your yard.

Rabbit-proofing Your Yard

One of the nicest moments for an outdoor rabbit is when he gets to roam about the yard, investigating all the sights and smells that surround him. Of course in order for your rabbit to do this safely, you have to make sure your yard is safely enclosed and free from rabbit hazards. You also need to be sure that your yard is protected from your rabbit. Chapter 5 has a good illustration of this topic.

Protecting your rabbit

You should have a tall wall or solid fence around your yard, one that a rabbit can't jump over (5 feet higher or higher), through, or around. Because rabbits are notorious diggers, make sure your wall or fencing goes at least a foot into the ground.

Look at your yard from your rabbit's point of view (literally) to see any potential dangers. Figuring out what your rabbit sees can give you clues into the kinds of trouble he can get into. Look out for the following:

- Holes or gaps in fencing that are small enough for a rabbit to slip through
- Small nooks and crannies where your rabbit can get wedged
- Debris that may come toppling down on your rabbit should he climb over or under it
- Containers holding toxic materials such as paint cans, turpentine, and anti-freeze
- Objects with sharp edges
- Pesticides and other toxic garden products (snail and slug bait are particularly dangerous)
- Poisonous plants

Protecting your yard

Rabbits are pretty harmless in general, but they do have two good resources when it comes to doing damage: their teeth and their claws.

If you look around your yard, you probably notice objects that are vulnerable to gnawing and areas that are susceptible to digging. For example, your rabbit may love to sink his teeth into your really nice wooden deck. Your rabbit will probably want to dig a trench in your freshly planted vegetable garden and then snack on the veggies after they're ripe.

So how do you protect your outside stuff from your outside rabbit? Simple: by supervising while he's roaming around outdoors. Keep an eye on him and see what he gets into. If you see him starting to gnaw on your wood deck or furniture, cover those areas with bubble wrap or another heavy plastic. If your bunny starts digging in the garden, put a fence around the area so he can't get into it. You may want to provide him with a big box of dirt or sand that he can dig through to his heart's content or let him have an area of soft ground to excavate.

Try using the dog exercise pen idea for outside. It is a nice temporary exercise area, is moveable (so waste material doesn't burn the yard and you can put it in shade or sun), and folds up when not needed. It's a cheap, viable option for exercising the rabbit and keeping it away from the things in the yard you want to protect.

Avoiding poisonous plants

Rabbits love to graze on plants when they're spending time outdoors, but if you have poisonous plants in your yard, they may prove deadly for your rabbit. (For resources on more poisonous plants you should keep away from your rabbit, see this book's Appendix.)

If you have any of these more common plants in your yard, remove them or find a way to keep your rabbit from gaining access to them.:

- Jack in the pulpit, *Arisaema spp.*
- Common milkweed, *Asclepias syriaca L.*
- Boxwood, *Buxus microphylla*
- Oriental bittersweet, *Celastrus orbiculatus Thunb.*
- Poison hemlock, *Conium maculatum*
- Lily of the valley, *Convallaria majalis*
- Toadstools, *Crepidotus spp.*
- Jimson weed, *Datura spp.*
- Delphinium, *Delphinium spp.*
- Foxglove, *Digitalis purpurea*
- English ivy, *Hedera helix*
- Mountain laurel, *Kalmia latifolia*
- Lantana, *Lantana camara L.*
- Lupine, *Lupinus spp.*
- Daffodil, *Narcissus spp.*
- Oleander, *Nerium oleander*
- Azalea, *Rhododendron spp.*
- Black-eyed Susan, *Rudbeckia hirta*
- Black locust, *Robinia pseudo-acacia*
- Buttercup, *Ranunculus spp.*
- Castor bean, *Ricinus communis*
- Sumac, *Rhus coriara*
- American elder, *Sambucus canadensis*
- Nightshade, *Solanum spp.*

- Bird of Paradise, *Strelitzia reginae*
- Yew, *Taxus spp.*
- Arrowgrass, *Triglochin maritima*

Fitting Him with a Warm-up Suit

Being an outdoor rabbit doesn't automatically mean you get more exercise than your indoor counterparts. Quite the contrary! Outdoor rabbits spend more time in their hutches than indoor rabbits do in their cages, and that translates into less exercise.

For this reason, owners of outdoor rabbits need to make a conscious effort to provide their bunnies with exercise every day. This means turning your pet loose for supervised play for at least two hours a day — more if you can manage it. If they already live in a large pen with plenty of room, they may not need this additional exercise, particularly if the pen is on the ground.

Single bunnies need a little more motivation to exercise than do two rabbits. When you let your solo bunny out in the yard to play, he'll probably run around a bit, and then settle down to do some grazing on the lawn and investigating. To encourage your pet to stretch his muscles, you should provide him with some toys that he can amuse himself with. Such toys may include:

- A clean, empty bucket
- An empty paper towel roll
- An empty cardboard box
- Hard plastic balls (try large and small sizes to see which your pet prefers)
- A tube of some kind, big enough for your rabbit to hop through

You can also play with your rabbit yourself by letting him chase you or by dragging a toy on a string for him to chase. Refrain from chasing your rabbit yourself because the poor creature may think that you've gone into predator mode and will become terrified.

TIP

Building a bunny run

If you like the idea of leaving your outdoor rabbit outside for an extended period of time, but yet don't have time to sit and watch him, considering building your pet a bunny run. A bunny run is similar to a dog run, except not as tall. Like a dog run, it's made out of fencing materials — usually chain link fencing — and has five sides. The top of the bunny run can have a solid top or simply be chain link (if you have a larger rabbit whose face can't get through the links and the fence isn't plastic coated or galvanized), and the floor is usually grass.

When building a run for your bunny, keep these points in the forefront of your mind:

- The object is to build an enclosure that allows your rabbit time outdoors while still keeping him protected from predators. Don't skimp on the design or materials. The stronger and more well built your rabbit's run, the safer he is.

- The larger your run, the more exercise your rabbit gets. Make the run as big as you can.

- Provide your rabbit with shade. In fact, if you can build the run in an area where shade covers at least half the cage all day, this is best. Rabbits are susceptible to overheating, and direct sun can be deadly in the summer. Include a dish of fresh water, too.

- Provide a hide box for your rabbit. Should something spook your bunny while he's in his run, he'll be grateful for a hide box where he can duck for cover.

- Put some toys and a chew block or two in your rabbit's run to help give him something to do when he's out roaming around.

- Never keep your rabbit in his run at after the sun goes down because predators are more likely to lurk at dusk or evening. Remember, even if a predator can't get him choppers on your bunny, the presence of a predator can literally scare a rabbit to death.

- Make sure you're home when your bunny is in the run. Don't leave him in the run while you go off to work. If he gets into trouble (such as an encounter with a predator, gets a foot caught in the fencing, or whatever), you won't be around to help him.

Chapter 7

Stocking Up on Carrots

*T*hat old adage, "You are what you eat," doesn't just apply to humans. This truth applies to rabbits, too. Feed your rabbit a healthy and complete diet, and he'll be a healthy, happy-go-lucky bunny.

Providing a healthy diet for your bunny is much more involved than just dumping a cup of pellets in his food bowl every day. Rabbits need variety in their diet, just like humans do, and with just a little effort, you can provide all the vitamins, minerals and food energy that your rabbit needs.

Supplying Your Bunny with Belly Timber

Before you start feeding your rabbit, knowing that your rabbit is a *herbivore* is important. *Herbivores* only eat plants. Because rabbits are herbivores, everything they eat consists of plant material. So don't give your bunny a steak. Not only will his nose turn up at it, but the smell of it will probably scare the heck out of him. To get the proper nutrients a rabbit needs, your pet depends on you for good, fresh foods. Chapter 2 talks more about a rabbit's body and helps you understand why good diet's so important.

Grazing in the grass: Bunnies dig it

In the wild, rabbits are *grazers*, which means they spend a significant amount of time roaming from plant to plant as they nibble. In nature, rabbits have a wide variety of plants at their disposal and are thus able to get all the nutrients that they need from the many different plants in the environment.

Domestic rabbits have no choice in the matter of diet. They depend on their owners to provide them with variety of nutritious foods — fruits, vegetables, low-grade roughage, and only quality pelleted feed.

Watering your companion

Water makes up a substantial portion of the mammalian body, and rabbits are no exception. Rabbits drink up to half to two-thirds quart of water per day, depending on their size and diet. Without water, rabbits die quickly. Not only is water itself essential to keeping the vital organs working properly, but it's also important in the way that it aids digestion and keeps the rabbit's body cool in hot weather.

Rabbits must have *fresh* water at their disposal at all times. The water in their water bottles should be dumped and replaced with fresh water every single day, without exception. For outside rabbits, keep the water from freezing in winter. If you can provide your rabbit with bottled or filtered water, all the better. Rabbits, like humans, can do without the impurities present in most tap water.

Feeding Them Rabbit Food

Knowing the general rules of rabbit nutrition is good, but the details are what's most important. To keep your rabbit healthy, you need to provide the right blend of fresh foods and fiber.

Hay every day keeps the doctor away

When you look at the rabbit's gastrointestinal tract (see Chapter 2), you can see that having a high-fiber diet makes everything move more smoothly; fiber's essential in producing cecotropes, which are the nutrient-rich droppings your rabbit needs to eat. Rabbits being the grazers they are, make grass hay available all the time. You can put it in a hay rack (shown in Chapter 5) or in a box inside the cage or exercise area. When the supply runs low, keep replacing it.

The good news is you can provide fiber easily by feeding grass hay. In addition to the fiber, grass hays are rich in other essential nutrients. Several types of grass hay exist: timothy, oat, brome, Bermuda, and mixed orchard grass. Any is fine. In fact, mixing them is a gourmet treat. One type of hay to avoid using — alfalfa — is too high in calories and protein.

You can purchase hay at a pet store or feed store. Make sure the hay smells fresh and isn't damp or moldy. Some stores leave hay sitting for a long time, so find out how long it's been around. The fresher, the better. Try to buy only as much as you will use for about a two-month period and keep it dry. The grass hays are light brown-green and grass-like; alfalfa hay, which you want to avoid, is dark green with more tough stems. Grass hay isn't readily available in some areas but you can order online. The Appendix and Chapter 19 give Web sites worth checking out in this arena.

For those of you with allergies, use *timothy hay cubes* (avoiding alfalfa hay cubes). Although loose hay is preferred, these compressed cubes are the next best thing. If your rabbit eats cubes instead of loose hay, it's especially important for him to get a high-fiber pelleted food (see "The myth of pellets" in this chapter). If you can't find timothy hay cubes in your area, you can get them from the Ox-bow Web site listed in the Appendix.

Hitting the farmer's market

Wild rabbits eat plenty of fresh foods and your domestic rabbit should, too. Greens and fruit aren't only important to your rabbit's health but are also tasty treats that he'll undoubtedly enjoy.

Green vegetables, particularly the leafy type, are the most important fresh food, and he should have two or three kinds on a daily basis. Root veggies are also good. Give your rabbit at least this much

1 cup of greens daily = 3 pounds of bunny

Growing a garden

Rabbits love nothing more than to graze naturally. If you have a green thumb and want to give your rabbit a truly natural way for him to take in his daily nutrients, grow a bunny garden. Set aside a patch of your backyard and plant the seeds of some of the plants listed as good greens in this chapter. Use organic soil and avoid using pesticides or herbicides. When the plants mature, create a protective enclosure for your rabbit all around the garden and let him run loose among the plants daily if possible.

If you don't have a yard for planting, don't fret. Use as your garden a large tray you can keep on your balcony, fire escape, or window sill. Try to find a south-facing area or any area that gets plenty of direct sun. Once your plants have grown to maturity in the tray, give your rabbit access to it for a while so he can enjoy the fruits (and veggies) of your labor.

For example, if you have a 6lb rabbit, he should get 2 cups of greens every day. You can introduce them slowly to avoid the occasional soft stools that might develop. (See Chapter 9 for more info on soft stools.)

Before you feed greens to your rabbit, wash them thoroughly and check for any rotten areas. Be sure to cut those areas out before offering them to your pet, or better yet, skip these rotted greens altogether and offer some really fresh greens. You can buy chopped and cleaned bags of mixed greens sold for people salad, but please — no salad dressing! Where available, organic fresh foods are even better.

Check out the following list of good greens for rabbits:

- ✔ Arugula
- ✔ Basil
- ✔ Broccoli
- ✔ Brussels sprouts
- ✔ Carrot tops
- ✔ Celery
- ✔ Chard
- ✔ Chicory
- ✔ Clover (too much can cause soft stools, so feed in moderation)
- ✔ Dandelion greens
- ✔ Dark leaf lettuce (romaine is best; iceberg lettuce is low in nutrients)
- ✔ Endive
- ✔ Mustard greens
- ✔ Parsley
- ✔ Watercress

You can offer your rabbit other green leafy vegetables too and see if she likes them. Remember that rabbits are all individuals, and you may find that your rabbit doesn't like some of these greens but particularly enjoys others.

The myth of pellets

For years, pet rabbit owners have been giving their bunnies alfalfa-based, commercially produced rabbit pellets. This was considered a staple in pet rabbit diets for a long time. The result, according to many rabbit experts, has been a plethora of obese and unhealthy pet bunnies, which can be seen in Figure 7-1.

Figure 7-1:
Fatty, fatty,
two by four.
The top
rabbit isn't;
the bottom
rabbit is.

Bulging chest

Readily available, alfalfa-based pellets are convenient for rabbit owners, but they simply aren't good for indoor rabbits. New opinions on feeding rabbits have emerged of late, and dictate that if fed, pellets should be timothy-based, not alfalfa-based. Choose kinds that have 18% or greater fiber content.

Picking pellets

If you want a healthy, long-lived pet, search around for grass hay-based pellets, most of which are made from timothy. A few companies make this product, including Ox-Bow, Inc., which is mentioned in the Appendix. You can also opt to leave pellets out of your rabbit's diet, as long as you provide a constant supply of grass hay and plenty of fresh foods.

When shopping for timothy-based pellets, you'll notice that the larger bags of feed are the better deal, money-wise. But don't be tempted to buy a huge bag that lasts for six month because the pellets will lose their nutritional value over time. Buy only what your rabbit can consume in a month's time and keep them in a cool, dry place to prevent mold. Plop them into a container you can close tightly, which helps keep out mice and insects.

Chubby bunnies

A common problem vets see in pet rabbits is obesity. Rabbits who eat too many pellets and don't get enough exercise become dangerously overweight. (Figure 7-1 shows an obese rabbit, which you can identify by his bulging chest and big belly.) If your rabbit needs to slim down, you can help him by reducing his pellet intake or removing pellets altogether as long as he eats hay and greens instead. Restrict his diet to one-eighth to one-quarter cup of pellets for every five pounds of body weight. You can still give him treats but limit them to greens only. He can have as much grass hay as he wants. Timothy or oat hay is better than alfalfa hay, which is too high in calories.

Multiplying weight times age and then dividing by height . . .

The amount of pellets that your rabbit should eat depends on a few factors:

- **Adult.** The amount of pellets depends primarily on his weight, his health, and what other foods he eats. For rabbits that get all the grass hay they want and fresh greens daily, ¼ cup of timothy pellets per 5 pounds of body weight is a maximum.

- **Babies.** You can offer kits a higher volume of pellets (1 cup per 5 lbs of body weight) if they're not yet eating hay or greens. However, once they're eating hay and greens, cut back on the pellets to ½ cup per 5 pounds of body weight until they're 6 months old; when 6 months or older, cut back to ¼ cup per 5 pounds of body weight.

  Try to avoid feeding alfalfa-based pellets to babies because it may make it more difficult to change them over to timothy-based pellets as adults. If your baby is already on alfalfa pellets, try to switch him to timothy-based pellets as soon as possible. No emergency, but the sooner you can switch, the better.

- **Underweight.** If your rabbit' underweight or suffering from an illness that prevents him from eating hay and green foods, your veterinarian may recommend that you increase the amount of pellets. In some situations, the concentrated nutrients in the pellets may be beneficial to regaining strength, particularly after a disease that causes unhealthy weight loss. In these cases, please follow your veterinarian's recommendations. Chapter 9 talks more about illnesses and their signs.

- **Households with hay allergies.** If you or some other two-legged have hay allergies, you may have to leave the hay entirely out of the diet. In that case, continue feeding fresh foods as suggested, but increase the amount of timothy pellets to what's recommended on the food bag for your pet's weight.

TIP

Hopping on the scale

Not sure how much your rabbit weighs? And you can't get him to sit still on the bathroom scale? Use this simple method:

1. Stand on your scale and make note of your weight.

2. Pick up your rabbit and get back on the scale while holding your pet. Make note of the new total weight.

3. Subtract your weight alone from the weight of you holding the rabbit. This is your rabbit's weight.

REMEMBER

If your rabbit doesn't finish the pellets you provide him in a serving, throw them out before doling out the next serving. Don't pour the new pellets on top of the old ones, and don't forget to wash out the bowl on a regular basis to reduce the likelihood of bacteria or mold.

Treating your pet

Rabbits also enjoy fruits and yellow, orange, and purple vegetables. Although veggies can be fed a bit more liberally, sweet fruit shouldn't be overfed. Instead, use fruit as treats and offer them only in small quantities. In fact, a good general practice is no more than

REMEMBER

2 pounds of bunny or less = <1 tablespoon per day

5 pounds of bunny or more = <2 tablespoons per day

You can feed this all at once or throughout the day while training. With that in mind, the list that follows contains some treats your rabbit may enjoy:

- Apple slices without seeds
- Cantaloupe
- Honeydew
- Kiwi
- Nectarines
- Peaches
- Pears

- Plums
- Strawberries
- Tomatoes
- Watermelon

Popping pills

You may be wondering if you need to give your rabbit liquid or chewable vitamins and minerals in addition to her regular meal. If your pet is getting a balanced diet with grass hay and fresh foods at its core, you don't need to provide vitamin or mineral supplements. The rabbit makes his very own nutritional supplements in the form of cecotropes.

The exception to this would be if your rabbit is pregnant, nursing, recovering from an illness, or undergoing extreme stress. In these situations, check with a veterinarian first to see if you need to use supplements. Remember that when it comes to vitamins and minerals, you *can* have too much of a good thing. Over-supplementing certain vitamins and minerals can cause toxicity or severe illness.

Feeding mom

If you have a pet bunny, you don't have to do much more than give her unlimited grass hay, plenty of fresh foods, limited amounts of high-quality pellets, and an ample supply of water. But if you have a female rabbit *(doe)* who is expecting a litter of baby rabbits *(kits)* or nursing her young, you need to do a bit more to get her through her pregnancy and nursing. Chapter 13 offers detailed doe-feeding information.

Forbidden foods

Avoid foods high in carbohydrates (starches and sugars, for example). Many commercial treat foods contain high levels of starch and fat, and although a rabbit can eat small amounts without ill effect, he will start craving these foods (sound like a person?). Obesity and serious GI disease are just two of the resulting problems if his cravings are indulged. It's always easier to prevent than to treat a disease.

Avoid these at all cost:

- Beans of any kind
- Breads
- Cereals
- Chocolate
- Corn
- Nuts
- Oats
- Peas
- Refined sugar
- Seeds
- Wheat (and any other grains)

Don't let your bunny munch out of the cat or dog food bowl. Cat and dog food are much too high in protein and carbohydrates for your rabbit. If he eats too much of these foods the results can be fatal.

Chapter 8

Cleaning Behind Those Great Big Ears and More

Much like cats, rabbits are fastidious about their own bodies. They're constantly grooming themselves, making sure that every little hair is perfectly in place. Cleaning your rabbit's cage regularly can help your rabbit stay clean and healthy. A clean cage translates into a clean rabbit. Despite their self-grooming skill, however, rabbits need a little help from their human friends in this regard. As a bunny owner, you should provide regular grooming for your pet. This chapter shows you how.

Grooming your rabbit includes brushing, combing, clipping toenails, and examining your pet's entire body to make sure all is as it should be. This will take probably about an hour a week, depending on your rabbit's coat (longer coats require more care).

Stocking Your Toolshed

In order to properly groom your rabbit, you need the right tools at your disposal. You can purchase these items at a pet supply store, through a mail-order catalog or over the Internet. The appendix lists several helpful resources.

✔ **Pin brush:** A small pin brush, made for cat grooming, works great for rabbits. Pin brushes are made up of straight metal pins attached to a rubber base, and they're great at trapping loose hair within the coat. Pin brushes cost anywhere from a couple of dollars to $8 depending on the quality of the brush and where you live. The less expensive brushes do the job well, so don't feel compelled to spend a lot.

✔ **Flea comb:** A regular-size flea comb is a good tool. (Chapter 3 helps you determine which breed has short and which has long hair.) This smoothes out the coat, traps loose hairs, and helps you to find out if fleas are a problem for your rabbit. Flea combs trap fleas in their metal teeth. They also lift flea feces from the coat, which is an indicator that fleas are present. They're also good for removing mats from all types of rabbit hair. See "Running Down the Grooming Checklist" later in this chapter, for more about checking for fleas. Flea combs usually don't cost more than $3.

✔ **Wide-tooth comb:** Useful on rabbits with long coats, wide-tooth combs separate the hairs and prevent matting. You can use this tool after using the pin brush.

✔ **Bristle brush:** After you brush and comb your rabbit's coat, the bristle brush works as a finishing tool. Bristle brushes have soft nylon or hair bristles and can be used to give the coat a once over after you use the pin brush. The bristle brush picks up any remaining loose hairs and leaves your rabbit with a shiny coat, which is especially important if you're grooming your rabbit for a show.

✔ **Toenail clippers:** Guillotine-type nail clippers designed for small dogs and cats work best on rabbit toenails. These clippers are small and sharp and are less likely to split the nail than a human nail clipper.

✔ **Styptic powder:** In case a nail is cut too short, styptic powder tends to halt bleeding. It has an indefinite shelf life if kept dry. Although styptic powder is the preferred astringent, you can use crushed aspirin or cornstarch in a pinch.

Handling with Care

Rabbits are incredibly cute and everyone wants to hold them. The problem is that most rabbits aren't terribly thrilled about being held. Can you blame them? Their primary means of defense is being able to run away when they're in danger. When all four of their feet are suspended off the ground, they have no way to escape should something scare them. Further, when a predator captures a rabbit in the wild, that predator picks the rabbit up and carries it off. Given this reality, it's not hard to understand why being lifted and carried may be a scary sensation for a rabbit.

So does that mean that you can never pick up your rabbit? Of course not (although you should only carry him when necessary to move him from one place to another). But it does mean that you need to use patience, sensitivity, and the right handling techniques to reduce or eliminate fear in your rabbit.

Bunny trust has nothing to do with college

Before you attempt to start carrying your rabbit around, you need to gain your pet's trust. If your rabbit is a baby, you're in luck. If you start the handling process when your rabbit is young, your pet can grow up to be more comfortable being handled. If you have an adult rabbit that you're just getting to know, you need to do a bit more work to win your bunny's trust, especially if your new pet was mishandled in the past.

Building trust is a time commitment, but taking 15 minutes a day to work through the following numbered steps may speed the process:

1. **Sit on the floor with your rabbit or place your rabbit on a table.**

   Cover the table with a blanket to protect its surface and to secure the rabbit's footing.

2. **Get him used to the feel of your hands.**

   Pet your rabbit and talk to him while you do it. Then try giving him some treats. (See Chapter 7 for more on feeding treats.)

   Do this until you see that your rabbit is starting to trust you. See Chapter 10 for information about how to read your rabbit's body language. Signs of trust are when your rabbit

   • Approaches you on his own for touching (anytime)

   • Puts his paws on you

   • Shows relaxed body language during these 15-minute sessions

---

Beware of putting him on his back

You or your veterinarian may have cause to place your rabbit on his back for examination of some kind. I suggest that you avoid putting your rabbit in this position unless it's absolutely necessary. Rabbits may become extremely frightened when they're placed on their backs and restrained. They may cease to struggle, but the current thinking is that's only out of terror — not relaxation. Try to work with your rabbit by keeping his feet on solid ground. She'll appreciate you for it!

---

3. **Place your rabbit against your body.**

   While the bunny is on the table or on the floor, gently move him toward you. Keeping his feet on the ground, restrain him against your chest or legs. If you wish, you can gently hold him by the *scruff* (the loose skin on the back of his neck) with one hand while pressing his hindquarters against you with the other hand.

   Your rabbit may struggle at first if she isn't used to being restrained. Use a calm voice and patience to show her that she's safe despite the fact that you're restraining her. If your rabbit starts to panic and struggles wildly, let him go. Start over again with the trust-building sessions until he seems comfortable with your touch, then try the gentle restraint again. After your bunny seems comfortable being gently restrained against your body, it's time to get him used to being lifted.

4. **Lift your rabbit.**

   Make sure that you're in a quiet place where you won't be disturbed. Work from the table or floor area where you have been conducting your trust-building sessions because your rabbit feels safe here.

5. **Slowly place one hand under your pet's chest, just behind its front legs.**

6. **Slide your other hand underneath the rabbit's rump.**

   See Chapter 2 for an illustration of the rabbit's body. Always support the hind quarters to prevent injury to the spine. The most common injury is due to improper handling.

7. **Lift upward with the hand that's on the rabbit's chest and support the rabbit's body weight with the other hand.**

8. **Pull the rabbit's body toward you as you lift, pointing the rabbit's head toward the back of your elbow.**

9. **Slide your hand out from under the rabbit's chest as you press his forequarters against your side.**

   The idea is to carry the rabbit under your arm as you would carry a football, as shown in Figure 8-1.

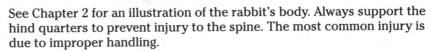

   If your rabbit begins to struggle, hold him more securely against you. If he starts flailing, place him gently back on the table or the floor. Don't drop your rabbit; you can seriously injure him.

   After your rabbit is comfortable with you, hold him this way for several minutes and increase the time that you spend handling him.

10. **When you can comfortably hold him like this for at least five minutes, you can start moving around with him tucked under your arm.**

    Be prepared that your rabbit may get scared when he feels you moving. If he starts to struggle, stop, and let him get comfortable again before you begin to walk again.

Figure 8-1:
Touchdown!
Holding your
bunny like
this will help
him feel
more
secure.

Running Down the Grooming Checklist

Grooming sessions provide an opportunity to examine your rabbit thoroughly for certain health problems. Catching these problems early increases the likelihood of being able to cure your pet. Chapter 9 tells you more about these diseases and what to look for.

When going over your bunny with a brush, make sure you mentally run through this grooming checklist:

✔ **Looking for parasites.** Rabbits are just as susceptible to these pests as dogs and cats are, especially if they live or play outdoors. When grooming, keep an eye out for fleas and ticks. Ticks appear as dark round protrusions about ⅛ to ¼ inch. Fleas are small, dark, and difficult to see. However, their feces (*flea dirt*) are readily visible, especially on a light-colored rabbit. They appear as small, dark flecks on the skin along the rabbit's back, neck, and especially rump. Talk to your vet if you find either one of these pests.

If you find parasites on your pet, contact your vet for information on how to safely rid your rabbit of these pests. Your vet can provide you with rabbit-safe products that can do the job. (More parasite and vet talk in Chapter 9.)

✔ **Seeking out lumps and sores.** As you go over your rabbit with a brush or comb, look out for any lumps or open sores on your pet's body. (The more familiar you become with your rabbit's body, the more you'll be able to notice such problems.) Lumps shouldn't be ignored. Scabs, sore, and crusty areas can be a sign of parasites or a bacterial infection. Sores on the feet and hocks can be the result of a damp or dirty environment and improper flooring.

✔ **Checking eyes and ears.** Examine your rabbit's eyes up close to make sure no discharge or swelling is present. Ears should be looked at for signs of parasites or bacterial infection, especially in lop-eared breeds (discussed in Chapter 3). There's more ear talk in this chapter's "Caring for Those Infamous Ears."

✔ **Feel along the jaw line for any lumps.** It should be symmetrical on both sides. Any obvious lumps or lack of symmetry should be examined by a vet.

Breaking Out the Brush

Rabbits are good at brushing their own coats and using their tongues to clean their fur and smooth it down. Rabbits left to do their own grooming are also notorious for leaving loose hairs around. If you have an indoor rabbit who hops around the carpet and on the furniture, the tendency to shed will become a nuisance.

The way to help remedy this loose hair situation is to brush your rabbit regularly. Brushing reduces the loose fur around the house, and it also gives you an opportunity to examine your pet closely for lumps, bumps, and other health problems. Grooming time also provides a great opportunity for bonding with your pet.

Keep in mind that you want to make grooming a pleasant experience for your rabbit, so brush your pet gently to avoid causing him any discomfort or pain. Rabbits have sensitive skin, and your bunny will come to dislike grooming time if you're too rough with him. Likewise, when you handle your rabbit for toenail clipping or any other grooming procedure, be patient and gentle.

Brushing short to medium coats

If your rabbit has a short to medium coat typical of most rabbit breeds, you need to set aside an hour a week for grooming.

Rex rabbit breeds have ultra short coats and care should be taken to brush gently to avoid damaging the skin. They, in fact, need very infrequent brushing.

Bypassing the bath

Unlike dogs, rabbits don't need regular bathing. In fact, it's best not to bathe a rabbit at all. The bath stresses them out terribly, and exposes them to injury because they'll struggle. In short, a bath is unnecessary. The only time a bath would be needed is if a rabbit came into contact with some kind of substance that could only be removed from its coat with a bath. If your rabbit needs some help keeping clean on occasion, you can do some spot cleaning. If your bunny stepped in something sticky or irritating to the skin, it would be wise for you to remove it right away.

Pet supply stores sell waterless shampoos, which can be sprayed directly onto your pet's coat. Simply saturate the area with the waterless shampoo product and follow the directions on the label.

If your rabbit develops soft stools or the fur is stained with urine as a result, wash his bottom to help him stay clean:

1. Fill two containers or a double sink with lukewarm water.

2. Dip the rabbit's rear end in the water.

3. Use a wash cloth, soft brush, or your hand to loosen the material.

4. Take the rabbit out of the water, apply a very small amount of shampoo (suitable for cats), and thoroughly massage the area with your hands.

5. Dip him into the clean water of the other container and rinse off the soap and debris.

6. Towel dry him, getting as much water out as possible.

7. Put him in a cage with towels on the floor to absorb water. He'll finish grooming himself.

If you need to repeat or rinse more, you can let the rabbit take a break on some towels, change the water and rinse again.

It can be incredibly difficult to remove matted feces and urine if it has accumulated; the skin underneath may be very sore and irritated. In fact the skin may even tear if you try too hard to remove this material. It may be necessary to have a veterinarian do a thorough cleaning to your sedated rabbit. The hair can be clipped at this time to aid in future cleaning should it be necessary during the treatment of the illness. If in doubt, have a vet check it out!

---

1. **Find a comfortable place to sit while grooming your pet.**

2. **Assemble your grooming tools within reach.**

   See the "Stocking Your Toolshed" section.

3. **Hold your bunny securely in your lap.**

   Chapter 9 gives you instructions on how to do this properly. You can use a secure surface instead of your lap if the rabbit is calm.

4. **Brush your rabbit with the pin brush, moving in the direction that the coat grows to minimize breakage of the hair (as shown in the color insert).**

If you notice many loose hairs in your brush after a few swipes on his coat, and it's spring or fall, your rabbit may be molting. (See the "I'm gonna molt that hair right offa my bod …" sidebar, later in this chapter.)

Don't brush his face, feet, ears, or tail. It's best to stay away from these areas because they don't have a lot of hair. When brushing your rabbit, be sure to be gentle and talk to your pet in a quiet voice to reassure him. If he's reluctant to be brushed, try offering him some healthy treats to nibble on while you're brushing. This will distract him and help him associate grooming time with something pleasant.

5. **Go through your rabbit's coat with your flea comb.**

   Check for fleas that may get caught in the comb. Check also for black specs on the teeth of the comb, which could be flea feces. If you're unsure, place these specs on a paper towel and place a drop of water on them. If the wet area of the towel turns red, your rabbit has fleas. If you're still not certain if your rabbit has fleas, ask your veterinarian to make a diagnosis.

6. **Comb out any hair matting.**

   Flea combs work well for these.

7. **Give him the once over with the bristle brush if you have one.**

   This will pick up any loose hairs you missed and help give the coat a nice shine.

Brushing long coats

If you have an Angora, Jersey Wooley, or other longhair rabbit breed (see Chapter 3), you need to brush your pet on a daily basis, regardless of the season. These rabbits are extremely prone to hair matting. The hair is not only long but fine textured.

1. **Find a comfortable place to sit while you're grooming your pet.**

2. **Assemble your grooming tools within reach.**

   See "Stocking Your Toolshed."

3. **Situate your rabbit comfortably in your lap.**

4. **Start with your pin brush.**

5. **Part sections of your rabbit's coat and brush from the area where the hair attaches to the skin outward, in the direction the hair is growing.**

   Be sure to loosen any areas that appear to be matting. If you do this every day, you'll eventually weed out all the mats, and your rabbit's coat won't have a problem. As mentioned, flea combs can be great for getting out mats if you have enough space between the mat and the skin to get the comb started.

6. **Move onto the wide-tooth comb and bristle brush.**

   Gently comb in the direction that hair grows with both of these tools. Start with the wide-tooth comb and finish up with the bristle brush. After this, move on to ear cleaning and toenail clipping.

If you aren't comfortable caring for your longhair rabbit's coat yourself or simply don't have time, you can take your rabbit to a professional groomer for grooming or shearing. Make certain the groomer you go to works on rabbits regularly, because these delicate creatures need special handling to prevent them from getting injured during the grooming process.

Another option is to trim your longhair rabbit's fur yourself. Using a pair of sharp scissors, you can cut the hair back to a couple of inches in length so that it's easier to maintain. Don't cut your rabbit's fur all the way to the skin. Not only is this dangerous because you may accidentally cut your rabbit, but your rabbit does need to have some fur on his body. His coat acts as a natural insulator against heat and cold.

If you come across mats in your rabbit's fur, you can cut these off. First try to remove them with a flea comb or fine-toothed comb before cutting them. Do not pull up on your rabbit's fur as you cut the mat because you will cut too close to the skin. If the mats are severe, get help from a groomer or your veterinarian.

Clipping It Not Quite In the Bud

Rabbit toenails grow constantly, just like human fingernails, and so need to be clipped regularly. If you don't clip your rabbit's toenails, they will become excessively long and your pet will soon have trouble walking. He'll also be in danger of catching a long toenail on his cage wire or on your carpet and could possibly tear the nail right out of his paw.

I'm gonna molt that hair right offa my bod ...

Rabbits shed like dogs and cats, and seem to drop their fur most often during spring and fall. However, because we keep rabbits indoors under all kinds of lighting and temperature conditions, they can shed all year round. During the heaviest shedding times, brush your rabbit more often, especially on the rump area where the most loose fur seems to accumulate. Should your rabbit ever shed to the point where bald patches appear, contact your veterinarian. This loss of hair could be a sign of hormonal abnormalities, parasites, or a disease.

You need a manicure

As a child, I volunteered to be a rabbit carrier at my local 4-H club rabbit show. The rabbits flailed their paws against me as I carried them from their cages to the judge's podium. By the end of the day, my stomach was completely covered with scratches. Rabbit toenails can be sharp, and when a bunny becomes insecure and starts to struggle, human skin usually pays the price. To prevent your stomach and arms from being torn to bits when you handle your rabbit, take the following precautions:

✔ **Trim your rabbit's nails.** If you keep your rabbit's toenails trimmed, you're less likely to be scratched should your pet struggle when you're carrying him.

✔ **Train your rabbit.** By slowly acclimating your rabbit to the sensation of being carried, you reduce the likelihood that he'll start to flail when you're holding him.

✔ **Wear safe clothes.** Never carry a rabbit while your arms or torso is uncovered. If your rabbit panics, you'll find out first hand just how painful rabbit scratches can be.

✔ **Monitor children.** Kids love to carry their bunnies, but if they don't do it right, they can end up covered in scratches. Prevent younger kids from carrying rabbits (especially large ones), and teach older kids the proper way to do it.

Another good reason to keep your rabbit's nails trimmed is for your own protection. Whenever you handle your rabbit, you come into contact with those nails. Should your pet become insecure and start to kick and struggle, long nails may do a good amount of damage to your skin. (See Chapter 9 for details on the proper way to handle your rabbit.)

You can tell if your rabbit's nails are too long because the nails extend beyond the edge of the fur on the rabbit's foot. If you're not sure, have your veterinarian take a look at your bunny's feet to let you know if he needs a trim.

The good news is that you don't need to clip your rabbit's toenails every time you groom him. Simply evaluate the length of the nails whenever you sit down to groom him. If they're starting to get long, then it's time to get out the clippers.

Rabbits, like most pets, don't enjoy having their nails trimmed, so it's best for you to start doing this with the aid of another person. This helper, preferably an experienced person, is the one to hold your rabbit while you do the actual nail clipping. Sources for experienced people are rabbit breeders, other experienced rabbit owners (find out through rabbit organization), veterinary staff, and pet stores and groomers that care for rabbits.

1. **Have your helper position the rabbit on her lap with the rabbit's rear resting against the helper's lower abdomen.**

   Make sure both you and the handler are wearing long-sleeved shirts of heavy material because the potential for getting scratched is high with this grooming procedure.

   The helper should have a secure grip on the bunny without hurting her. Chapter 9 shows this restraint.

2. **Gently grasp one of the rabbit's front legs.**

3. **Turn the leg so the *dewclaw* (the nail on the inside of the foot) is visible.**

4. **Examine the nail to determine where the quick is.**

   The *quick* is the vein that extends from the toe to nearly the tip of the nail. This appears as a dark line in the nail. You want to clip the tip of the nail that does *not* contain the quick, as cutting the quick makes the nail bleed. If you're having trouble locating the quick or have a rabbit with black nails, get a flashlight and shine it through the backside of the nail toward you. The vein will become visible.

   In the event that you should accidentally cut into your rabbit's vein, making the nail bleed, don't panic. Just dab a bit of styptic powder (available at drug stores) onto the nail and the bleeding will stop.

5. **Cut the tip of the nail off, as shown in Figure 8-2.**

   Do this for each of the five nails on each of the rabbit's front feet.

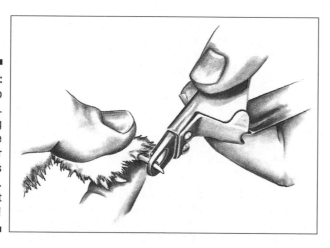

Figure 8-2:
Clippity do da . . . Clipping should be painless for all parties involved. Mind that quick!

6. **Relax for a while.**

7. **Have your helper hold the rabbit again, so you can start working on the hind nails.**

   This time, your helper should grasp the rabbit in the way described earlier in this chapter and shown in Figure 8-1. This will make the back paws accessible to you. Make certain that your rabbit is comfortable in the position that she's placed. Otherwise, she'll struggle and make clipping her nails impossible.

8. **Proceed with the back nails in the same way that you did with the front.**

   You may find that the back nails are a bit tougher to cut than the front because they're thicker. So be prepared to use a little more force to clip those hind nails.

If all this sounds too overwhelming to you as a first-time rabbit owner, you can always take your rabbit to the veterinarian, pet store, groomer, experienced rabbit owner or rabbit breeder for nail clipping. Ask your vet to show you how to do it yourself, so you can incorporate nail clipping into your regular grooming routine and won't have to go to the vet's office every time that your bunny needs nail clipping because this may prove to be a hassle, and it gets expensive, too.

Caring for Those Infamous Ears

A rabbit's ears are his great showpiece, so you want to help him keep them clean. You can do this during your bunny's regular grooming time, checking the ears for cleanliness at least once a week. (Don't worry, your lop ear won't get hurt if you check him out; his ears are soft and floppy.)

Whenever you groom your rabbit, thoroughly check his ears for waxy build-up, dirt, or a foul smell. If you see some debris in your rabbit's ears, ask your veterinarian for a solution that you can use to wipe the ears clean using a cotton ball or a cotton swab (as shown in the insert). Don't routinely remove the wax from a rabbit's ears. It has a protective purpose. Don't stick Q-tips down into the ear canal at any time.

Chapter 9

Nipping and Gnawing Common Health Problems in the Bud

. . . .

In This Chapter

▶ Spaying or neutering helps

▶ Recognizing that your rabbit is ill

▶ Understanding what diseases affect rabbits

▶ Knowing what to do before getting to the vet

. . . .

You may not be surprised to discover that your rabbit, like all creatures, can easily become sick or injured if he's mishandled or improperly cared for. In fact, rabbits can get sick even if you take really good care of them. Of course, a rabbit who's well cared for is less likely to become ill, but it can happen. The key to keeping your rabbit healthy is to watch him closely for signs of illness because rabbits are good at hiding their illness — a trait that's frustrating for rabbit owners but valuable in the wild. Rabbits instinctively hide their illness so that predators are unable to detect their vulnerability.

Most illnesses are more successfully treated if they're caught early. Familiarize yourself with your rabbit's normal behavior so that you'll notice when something is wrong — before it's too late.

If your rabbit gets sick, taking him to a veterinarian who specializes in treating rabbits is vital. After you locate a good veterinarian, bring your rabbit in for annual checkups.

Paging Dr. Doolittle

No matter what kind of pet you own, finding a good veterinarian is imperative. A small animal vet who treats only cats and dogs is not a good bet when it comes to treating a rabbit since rabbits have a unique physiology that's very different from more common pets (as shown in Chapter 2).

In the world of veterinarian medicine, rabbits are considered *exotics,* and are grouped together with rodents, reptiles, birds, and other less common pets. Most veterinarians who have a special interest in treating these kinds of animals advertise themselves as exotics practitioners. They not only have special training in this area, but also a certain level of experience.

Not only must your vet know rabbits inside and out, but she must also be good at what she does. Just as with any profession, the skills and attitudes of veterinarians differ from individual to individual. You need to find a vet who is good at handling rabbits, excellent at diagnosing them, and an ace at treatment. Finding someone who has a good bedside manner with human clients isn't a bad idea, either.

In most areas of the country very few veterinarians have specific training or extensive experience with exotic pets. For example, people who live in rural areas won't have the selection that city dwellers have. Therefore, you may have to deal with a small animal vet who's willing to work with you and learn about your pet.

Putting out the feelers

So how do you find a veterinarian to treat your rabbit? You can use a number of different options:

- ✔ **Personal referrals.** Getting a referral from a fellow rabbit owner is the best way. Talk to other rabbit owners and find out which vets they use. Ask them what they like about each, and get details of the situations where they've used them. By listening to these stories, you'll get a good sense of who each doctor is and whether you want to give her a try.

- ✔ **Club referrals.** Contact a local rabbit club to get a referral to a local exotics veterinarian. A local rabbit club could be anything from a *breed club* (which specializes in breeding a particular breed) to a 4-H rabbit project group. Call, e-mail, or write a letter to someone in your area, asking for a referral.

- ✔ **Local and state veterinary associations.** Look in your telephone directory under veterinarians and you'll probably see a local or state association for vets. If not, contact your local animal shelter and ask them for the number. Then contact the association and ask them for the name and number of a vet in your area who treats rabbits.

- ✔ **Rabbit breeders.** You can meet rabbit breeders at shows or contact a local rabbit group. You can even find breeders on the Internet. Contact a breeder in your area (one who shows rabbits) and ask for a referral. Chapter 13 has more breeding information.

Evaluating the vet

Once you find a vet or two that you think you might like to use, contact the office by telephone and ask the following questions:

✔ **How long have you been treating rabbits?** The answer should be at least two years, preferably longer.

✔ **What kind of special education or experience do you have treating rabbits?** You want a vet who has training in this area, or at least has a significant amount of experience to make up for lack of formal training. Continuing education courses and programs are a good sign that this vet is serious about treating rabbits.

✔ **Do you take after-hour emergencies?** If not, where are they sent? If your vet closes at 6 p.m. and can't be reached for emergencies that take place after hours, she most likely refers patients to an 24-hour emergency clinic. Ask questions about this clinic (where it's located, the clinic's experience with rabbits) and visit it to make sure it meets your requirements.

✔ **May I visit your clinic to look at your facilities?** The answer should be a resounding Yes. Please respect the fact that an appointment may be necessary so as not to interfere with the services given to clients during the day.

Once you've narrowed your search, pay a visit to the clinic. While you're there, look for the following:

✔ **Clean environment.** You want to patronize a clinic that looks and smells clean. The exam rooms and reception areas should be neat and tidy, and the personnel should be well groomed. Such cleanliness is indicative of a good attitude to animal care.

✔ **Friendly, knowledgeable staff.** The receptionist and technicians you meet should be nice, friendly, and willing and able to answer your questions.

✔ **Skilled vet.** You probably won't get to see the vet in action until you make your first appointment. When you're there, observe how she handles your rabbit. The vet should be gentle but firm and patient. She should also be willing to answer your questions, admit when she doesn't know the answer to something, and be friendly and a good listener.

✔ **Fees you can afford.** With veterinary care, you often get what you pay for. Don't expect to get great care for dirt-cheap prices. On the other hand, make sure you can afford the services offered. Ask for a fee schedule, which should show what the clinic charges for examinations, lab fees, and spays and neuters.

Being a good client

You want a veterinarian who's skilled and compassionate and will take excellent care of your rabbit. You can do a lot to make sure you are a good client too, by following these guidelines:

✔ If you are happy with your vet, be sure to stick with him or her. Don't jump around from clinic to clinic trying to save money.

✔ Pay your bills on time. If you are having trouble paying, be honest with your vet and try to work out a payment arrangement.

✔ Follow your vet's instructions thoroughly regarding your rabbit's health.

✔ Be honest with your vet about your rabbit's care and condition.

✔ Ask questions if you don't understand explanations, diagnosis, or treatment plans.

✔ If you have a complaint with the veterinary staff, bring it to their attention first so that there's an opportunity to get it cleared up to your satisfaction.

✔ Never be afraid to get a second or even third opinion. A responsible veterinarian won't feel threatened if you seek other ideas.

✔ Be a proactive pet owner and do research as needed to help your pet. Bring any information to your veterinarian and discuss your findings.

Going for an exam

Unlike dogs and cats, rabbits don't get annual inoculations (except in the U.K. with myxomatosis and hemorrhagic viral diseases). However it's an excellent idea to take your rabbit to the vet for an initial exam, even if he appears healthy. The vet can check him to make sure he's in good health and can discuss your rabbit's diet, plans for neutering, and other health-related issues.

The initial exam gives you the opportunity to get to know your veterinarian, and gives the doctor a sense of who your rabbit is. If your pet gets sick and needs immediate care, the vet will already have information on file and have a good sense of how you're caring for your bunny.

Following that initial exam, annual exams are a good idea. These annual exams are invaluable in keeping ahead of disease problems and in communicating any changes in care. As they become *geriatric* (7 years of age and older), get an exam every 6 months.

Counting backwards from ten

If your bunny needs surgery or a certain diagnostic procedure requiring that he be anesthetized, you may be worried. Is it safe to put bunnies under anesthesia? Can their sensitive systems handle the chemicals required for surgery or diagnosis?

The answer to these questions is yes. In fact, other than the obvious need for anesthesia during surgery, it's often better to sedate the rabbit for stressful diagnostic procedures. Doing so eliminates your pet's fear or discomfort. A safe anesthetic gas (sometimes in combination with other injectable drugs to manage

pain) is used for general anesthesia, which produces complete unconciousness. If lighter sedation is needed, a variety of injectable drugs can be used. Sometimes a local anesthetic alone is all that's needed (for instance in eye exams or small skin biopsies).

If your bunny needs surgery for spaying or neutering or some other medical procedure, take your pet to a veterinarian with rabbit experience. The vet can determine the safest method of anesthesia to minimize discomfort and stress for your pet.

Spay It, Don't Spray It

Plenty of good reasons exist to *spay* your female rabbit (having her uterus and ovaries removed) or *neuter* your male rabbit (having his testicles removed), including improved behavior (see Chapters 12 and 13) and the elimination of the potential for more unwanted rabbits in the world (see Chapter 1). But one of the best reasons is for the health of your rabbit.

Spayed and neutered rabbits are less prone to a variety of diseases and tend to live considerably longer than their counterparts — rabbits who haven't been spayed or neutered. For more details on illnesses common to rabbits who haven't been spayed, see Chapter 14. Male rabbits who haven't been neutered are also inclined to spray strong smelling urine around the house and get into other kinds of trouble. You'll be much happier with your male rabbit if you have him neutered.

Rabbits can be spayed or neutered as soon as they reach reproductive maturity: about 4 months of age or later. Females should be spayed before two years of age to lessen the chance of developing uterine cancer. (See Chapter 13 for more on that topic.) Both procedures are fairly routine in the hands of a veterinarian experienced with rabbits.

No bun in the oven

Another reason to spay your female rabbit is to avoid false pregnancies. Female rabbits are so geared toward pregnancy that those who aren't bred can act as if they're pregnant anyway. Even though she isn't carrying any new baby bunnies, milk production and other characteristics associated with pregnancy appear. The female may become aggressive as part of this condition. To learn more about problems that can develop with unspayed rabbits, see Chapter 13.

The cost for these procedures varies depending on many factors, including the area of the country in which you live and the age and health of your pet. The spay procedure takes considerably longer than a castration to perform and requires abdominal surgery, therefore the cost for spaying a female may be two or more times the cost of neutering a male. Many veterinarians require presurgical laboratory work to make sure your pet is in good health prior to the procedure. Please discuss with your vet any questions you may have. This one-time cost is well worth it, however, since a spayed or neutered rabbit lives a longer, healthier life.

Keeping the Cooties Away: Infectious Diseases

The best defense against all diseases is a good, healthy immune system. Help your rabbit achieve this state of health with the proper environment (Chapters 5 and 6) and diet (Chapter 7).

Infectious diseases are illnesses that rabbits catch from each other in a variety of ways, depending on the organism responsible for the disease. Diseases that affect rabbits respond to various treatments, depending on the cause, such as those that follow.

- **Bacteria:** One-celled microorganisms that can be often be killed with antibiotics.

- **Protozoa:** A single-celled microorganism that's the smallest form of animal life. The treatment for protozoal infections depends on what tissue in the rabbit's body they've invaded. Some tissues can be easily medicated while others are nearly impossible to treat.

- **Viruses:** A minute parasitic microorganism. Antibiotics don't work against viruses.

- **Fungi:** A multicellular organism that reproduces by budding or by spore production. Topical or oral antifungal medications clear infections.

If your rabbit is diagnosed with an infectious disease, or you suspect that he may have one, be sure to

- Isolate him immediately from other rabbits.

- Disinfect everything with a solution that's nine parts water and one part bleach (especially before another rabbit uses his cage, food bowl, or other items).

Myxomatosis

Myxomatosis is a disease caused by several strains of poxvirus. Insects serve as transmitters. This virus was spread intentionally in Europe during the nineteenth century to destroy large rabbits populations that were considered vermin at the time.

The disease still exists in Europe today in both wild and domestic rabbits. In its most severe form it can be fatal. The United States tends to see a milder form of the disease, particularly along the California and Oregon coast. It's suspected that mosquitoes are the carriers in those areas. The version of myxomatosis seen most often in both wild and domestic rabbits in the United States is the appearance of skin tumors, particularly on the extremities. However, occasionally the more severe form can also be seen. The symptoms to look for are

- Fever

- Lethargy

- Discharge from eyes

- Swollen, red genitals

- Red, swollen, and watery eyes

- Facial swelling (occurs last)

A variety of different insects can transmit the disease. If you live in an area of Europe where the disease is found in wild rabbits, keep your pet rabbit indoors. If you live in a high-risk area, discuss the possibility of vaccinating your pet with your veterinarian.

Signs of pain

Chapter 10 talks in depth about your pet's body language and what he does when he's in the world of hurt.

- Abnormal hunched appearance when sitting
- Alert but reluctant to move
- Moves slowly or with effort
- Depression/lethargy
- Limping
- Unusual or sudden aggression
- Loss or decrease in appetite or water consumption

- Tooth grinding
- Hiding when it's not usual behavior, facing the corner
- Shows no interest in the surroundings (loss of curiosity)
- Crying or grunting when moving/defecating/ urinating or being handled/examined
- Coat is unkempt due to loss of interest in grooming
- Taking a long time to eat
- Dropping food out of the mouth

If your rabbit shows any signs of the disease, contact your veterinarian immediately. If your vet makes a diagnosis of myxomatosis, your vet will give your rabbit appropriate supportive care (primarily intravenous feeding and fluids) in the hopes that the bunny can fight off the virus on its own.

Venereal disease

A *venereal disease* is one spread through sexual contact. Rabbits develop a form of syphilis caused by a bacteria, but it's not the same disease as seen in humans.

Rabbits transmit syphilis through breeding. To keep your rabbit from contracting syphilis, inspect the genitals, lips, nose, chin, and eyelids of the rabbit with which you intend to breed your pet. Although this won't guarantee that your rabbit won't come into contact with the disease, it certainly reduces your rabbit's chances.

Affected rabbits develop crusty sores on their genitals, lips, nose, chin, and eyelids. If your rabbit has been bred and develops these symptoms, contact your vet right away. Antibiotic treatment is recommended and usually works quickly to clear up the problem.

Respiratory ailments

Rabbits can develop a number of different respiratory diseases. The common term of any upper respiratory infection in a rabbit is *snuffles*. Conditions that make a rabbit more susceptible include a dirty environment, particularly one that's wet, poor air circulation, and high humidity or heat. Many types of bacteria can cause respiratory disease in rabbits, but the two most common are *Bordetella bronchiseptica* and *Pasteurella multocida*. Rabbits may also develop other problems such as heart disease or tumors in the chest that can mimic some respiratory disease signs.

Bordetellosis

The Bordetella bronchiseptica bacteria causes a condition known as *kennel cough* in dogs, but can also affect rabbits. It's transmitted through the air. The incidence of infection with this bacteria increases as the rabbit ages and not only can cause its own damage to the air passageways, including irritation to the nasal passages, bronchi, and lungs (pneumonia), but can make it easier for other bacteria such as *Pasteurella multocida* to take hold. If your rabbit has bordetellosis you may see

- ✔ Labored breathing
- ✔ Nasal discharge and sneezing
- ✔ Matted fur on the inside of the front legs (from wiping nasal discharge)
- ✔ Lethargy
- ✔ Loss of appetite

Rabbits displaying signs of respiratory disease should get veterinary attention as soon as possible. Your vet may do a culture to determine the cause of the infection and a chest X-ray to see the extent of disease. Since this is a highly contagious disease, your pet should be isolated from other rabbits. Guinea pigs in particular are susceptible to developing pneumonia from infections with *Bordetella,* so don't house them with rabbits. Also, if your pet dog is diagnosed with kennel cough, keep him far away from your bunnies until he's healed.

Pasteurellosis

Pasteurella multocida is a bacteria that can be found in the respiratory tract of many rabbits without any outward signs. There are many strains, some more prone to cause disease than others. In addition, this bacteria can take hold if the environmental conditions are poor or the rabbit's immune system is compromised. Usually it causes *upper respiratory disease* (infecting the nose, trachea, and bronchi) but can on occasion cause ear infections, pneumonia, and abscesses in many areas of the body. Like *Bordetella,* it's transmitted primarily through the air. The following are signs you might see in a pet with pasteurellosis:

- Sneezing and nasal discharge
- Matted fur on inside of the front legs
- Difficulty breathing
- Lethargy
- Loss of appetite
- Lumps or masses anywhere on the body
- Head tilt or head shaking

Rabbits transmit the *Pasteurella* bacteria to each other via sneezing or direct contact, so keep affected rabbits away from the healthy ones. If you see your rabbit sneezing or coughing, contact your vet right away. As with bordetellosis, your vet may do a culture to determine the cause of the disease and an X-ray to determine its extent before devising a treatment plan.

Ringworm

Ringworm is the common name for a disease caused by one of several fungi that can affect rabbits, people, cats, dogs, horses, and other animals. The disease is also known as *dermatophytosis.* It's not a common disease in rabbits, but can occur in young rabbits or those exposed to other animals with the disease. The disease is transmitted by contact with the fungi's spores, which can travel through the air and stay active in the environment for long periods of time. The common signs are

- Dry, crusty skin
- Itchiness
- Fur loss in a circular patches, usually on the head, feet, and legs

Some rabbits can recover from ringworm on their own, but the fungus stays in the environment to infect other rabbits, other pets, and even people. After your veterinary makes the diagnosis your pet may be treated with both topical and oral medications and you need to clean the environment thoroughly.

Disinfecting the rabbit's environment — cleaning the cage with a dilute bleach and water solution — is important, especially if your rabbit has ringworm.

Antibiotics are anti-bunny?

Antibiotics are one reason taking your bunny to a veterinarian who specializes in rabbits is so important. Some antibiotics commonly given to dogs and cats (like oral amoxicillin) can be fatal for rabbits. These drugs can kill off the healthy bacteria in a rabbit's GI tract as well as the bacteria that's causing disease. This disruption can lead to enteritis (see "Enteritis" in this chapter). However, many safe antibiotics can be used in rabbits *orally* (given by mouth), *topically* (on the skin), or by injection. An experienced veterinarian will know which of these is safe to use.

Viral hemorrhagic disease

In 2000, the first case of _Viral Hemorrhagic Disease_ (VHD) was diagnosed in rabbits in the United States. Since then, this deadly disease has been recorded in several areas of the country, prompting great fear among rabbit owners and breeders.

Caused by a *calici virus,* VHD affects 70 to 80 percent of rabbits exposed to it, and in rabbits that develop signs of the disease, it's 100 percent fatal. Oral contact with contaminated feces transmits the disease. VHD is also known as _Rabbit Hemorrhagic Disease_ (RHD), _Rabbit Calicivirus_ (RCV), and _Rabbit Calicivirus Disease_ (RCD).

VHD affects major organs and causes severe hemorrhaging. The virus has a short *incubation* period (the amount of time an organism needs to become numerous enough to cause disease), and rabbits often die within a few days of exposure to the disease. The symptoms of VHD can include

- High fever
- Lethargy
- Loss of appetite
- Spasms
- Spontaneous bleeding from the mouth or rectum
- Sudden death

VHD is an insidious disease with no cure. However, a vaccine is available in areas of the world where the disease is endemic. The United States Department of Agriculture (USDA) is keeping close watch on the spread of VHD. If your rabbit shows VHD symptoms, rush him to a veterinarian immediately. Because this is a reportable disease, your veterinarian will contact the USDA.

The best prevention is to

- Keep your rabbit from coming into contact with other groups of domestic rabbits. (Keep a new rabbit separated for at least 30 days to ensure he is healthy before you expose him to your other rabbits.)

- Avoid using grooming tools, cages, and other objects that strange rabbits have used.

- Wash your hands and clothes after handling rabbits at a show, shelter, or rabbitry.

The good news is that because death occurs so soon after the onset of the disease, rabbit owners are thus immediately alerted to its presence. If action is taken right away, then you can at least minimize the spread of the disease between rabbitries.

Banning Pesky Parasites

Just like dogs and cats, rabbits can be bothered by *parasites* — organisms that feed off your rabbit's body — that can make them pretty darn miserable. Keeping those nasty parasites at bay is your job as a rabbit mom or dad.

Baylisascaris

Baylisascaris is a roundworm common in the intestines of wild raccoons. When the raccoon leaves its droppings, usually on logs, decks, and the like, they contain roundworm eggs. These eggs can remain infective for up to a year. If your bunny is exposed to raccoon feces in the backyard or in contaminated hay, she can ingest the eggs, which then hatch into *larva* (baby roundworms). Instead of going to the intestine as they would in a raccoon, they migrate to various areas of the rabbit's body, including the brain, where they cause inflammation and tissue damage.

This parasite can affect a wide variety of animals including dogs, cats and humans. The signs of infection with this parasite include

- Abdominal pain
- Blindness
- Head tilt
- Loss of balance
- Loss of muscle coordination

- Paralysis of one or both sides of the body
- Sudden lethargy
- Coma
- Sudden death

This disease is difficult to diagnose because it can mimic other diseases. Your veterinarian can perform a variety of tests to try to pinpoint the problem. Some rabbits recover from mild cases, while others may have permanent neurological damage. Antiparasitic drugs are ineffective against this parasite.

The best way to avoid this serious disease is to avoid areas that raccoons frequent. They prefer to leave their feces in open areas, particularly on wood, like decks and logs, in open areas of barns, and on top of hay piles. If you find raccoon feces that need to be removed, dispose of the material in the garbage, not a compost pile, and wash your hands thoroughly afterwards. In addition, only buy hay from reputable sources who keep their product under sanitary conditions.

Ear mites

Settling in the rabbit's ear canal, *ear mites* cause itching and a dark, crusty discharge in the ear. Frequent head-shaking and ear-scratching are common signs.

A veterinarian, examining the discharge from your rabbit's ears under a microscope, can diagnose ear mites. An injection or topical application of an antiparasitic drug can successfully treat ear mites. Infected rabbits need to be separated from other rabbits until the infection has cleared up because ear mites are highly contagious between rabbits. Also, even though the mites that affect cats are different from rabbit ear mites, cats can carry the parasite that affects rabbits and pass it along to them.

Encephalitozoonosis

Encephalitozoon cuniculi is a nasty protozoan parasite that can disable your bunny. *Encephalitozoonosis* is shed through the urine and can be passed along to other rabbits who come into contact with infected urine. This most likely happens between the doe and her babies around the time of weaning. In addition, mother rabbits can pass the parasite along to their babies through the placenta.

This disease affects the brain, spinal cord, kidneys, heart, and possibly other organs of the rabbit. Its effects on the brain and spinal cord can cause the rabbit to develop

- ✔ Head tilt and clumsiness
- ✔ Inability to use the hind legs
- ✔ Wobbling when walking

Encephalitozoonosis is difficult to diagnose. There are blood tests that look at the rabbit's immune system response *(titer)* to the parasite. A high titer along with clinical signs is suggestive of encephalitozoonosis, but is not 100 percent accurate. Your veterinarian will evaluate the situation with this information, rule out other disease, and make a decision on supportive treatment.

So far no cure has been found for this disease. Usually by the time the signs are present, the parasite has done its damage. Keeping infected rabbits away from healthy bunnies is important. Never breed a rabbit that shows signs of this disease.

The good news is that many rabbits exposed to this disease never develop any problems. Rabbits who are best able to keep disease at bay are those that are well cared for and stress-free.

Fleas

Yes, rabbits get fleas — the exact same fleas that drive your cat and dog crazy, too. In fact, if your indoor rabbit becomes infested with fleas, your dog or cat are most likely to have spread these parasites to your bunny.

To see if your rabbit has fleas, observe your pet to see if she's scratching herself a great deal. Chapter 8 gives the lowdown on finding and getting fleas out of her hair. If after reading this information you're still not certain if your rabbit has fleas, ask your veterinarian to examine your pet.

The best way to treat fleas is with a topical application (no flea dips or shampoos, please!) available from your veterinarian. Products applied once a month to your rabbit's skin are most effective, making flea reproduction impossible. All your other mammal pets need to be treated as well, including cats, dogs, and other rabbits.

Be aware that these products aren't FDA approved for use on rabbits at the time of this writing but are generally considered safe if applied in conjunction with the advice of a veterinarian. Ask your vet is she has used the product she recommends and what the results were.

Flies

Flies just annoy people, but they can be dangerous for your rabbit, especially an outdoor rabbit. Some species of flies like to lay their eggs on the rectal area of a rabbit, especially if the area is moist and dirty. (See Chapter 8 for information on keeping your rabbit clean and well groomed.) They also like to plant their eggs on open sores anywhere on a rabbit's body. The resulting maggots burrow into the rabbit and feed on her flesh. Disgusting for sure.

You can keep flies from doing their dirty business on your outdoor rabbit by

- Making sure that both your rabbit and her cage are clean. (See Chapter 8 for more information on rabbit grooming.)

- Checking around your rabbit's rectal area and keeping it clean and dry. Keeping the rectal area clean is especially important if you have a long-hair rabbit because feces, trapped in the long wool, attract flies.

Contact your veterinarian immediately if you notice

- Fly eggs and/or maggots on your rabbit

- Matted fur

- Wet, irritated skin

To kill the fly larvae, your vet needs to treat your rabbit by removing the larvae and dead tissue from your rabbit. Your veterinarian then prescribes supportive treatments to help with healing.

One species of fly known as *Cuterebra* has a different habit than the flies that leave hundreds of their offspring on dirty, moist areas of your bunny. The *Cuterebra* fly lays a single egg, often in the neck area where the skin is thinner. The egg hatches and the single larva takes up residence under the skin in a snug little pocket where it continues to grow. Eventually an oblong lump with a small hole becomes visible on the rabbit's skin; this is the larva's breathing hole. This condition is also known under the common name of *warbles*.

Eventually, when the larva is mature, it enlarges the breathing hole, emerges, drops to the ground. There it forms a pupa and eventually hatches into an adult fly. It is important not to try to remove this larva by yourself because if it ruptures inside the sac, it can release dangerous toxins into the rabbit's system. Take your pet to a veterinarian who can easily remove it with a minor surgical procedure.

Fur mites

Fur mites are tiny spiderlike parasites *(Chelyletiella parasitovorax)* that can be seen with mild magnification. Also known as *walking dandruff,* fur mites can cause

- Clumps of hair to fall out
- Dry, flaky skin
- Red, crusty, and itchy patches of skin particularly along the spine and rump

Your veterinarian will examine a sample of the skin debris under the microscope. The treatment for this parasite can include topical or injectible antiparasitic medications as well as a thorough cleaning of the environment.

If the population of mites is low, signs of their presence may be nonexistent for a long period of time. (It can be for many months.) However, rabbits can still transmit the mites to other rabbits during this time. These mites can be transmitted to dogs and cats in the household as well (and back again). Treating all the mammal pets in the household as well as the environment is important because the mites can live off the pets in bedding, carpeting, and around cages for several days.

Intestinal parasites

Intestinal parasites include roundworms, pinworms, protozoa and tapeworms. Signs of a heavy parasite infestation include

- Distended abdomen
- Poor coat condition (dry, unhealthy looking hair)
- Worms in the litter box or near the anus
- Loss of weight even though the pet is eating well

Your rabbit may have a light worm infestation without showing any obvious outward signs. Your veterinarian can diagnose intestinal worms in your pet by examining a stool sample. (You can get this by putting a few pieces of your rabbit's stool in a plastic bag.) Treatment consists of a deworming agent, administered orally or by injection to your rabbit.

To prevent your rabbit from becoming infested with intestinal parasites:

✔ Avoid letting your rabbit graze in areas where wild rabbits may have been, particularly where you see their droppings.

✔ Keep your bunny away from outdoor areas where dogs and stray cats may have defecated.

Montezuma's Revenge

Rabbits can develop a number of gastrointestinal (GI) tract problems. The most common underlying cause of most of these disorders is an inappropriate diet.

Therefore, the best thing you can do to prevent disease of the GI tract is feed a healthy diet high in fiber and low in carbohydrates. By following the dietary suggestions in Chapter 7 you reduce the likelihood that your rabbit will develop digestive problems. In the event that your rabbit does feel under the weather as a result of digestive tract disease, you and your vet can hopefully step in and get her back to normal.

Diarrhea in rabbits is characterized by the excretion of large amounts of dark brown to blood-tinged stool in the absence of any normal stool. This is a different condition than soft stools, which is a mixture of soft pudding-like stools mixed with normal stool. Diarrhea can be the result of several different diseases, but is always an emergency signal. This is a life-threatening situation. Seek veterinary attention immediately if you observe diarrhea in your rabbit.

Enteritis

The rabbit GI tract, particularly the cecum, contains a complex population of bacteria, protozoa, yeast, and other organisms that make it possible to digest high-fiber foods. (See Chapter 2 for a description of the rabbit's GI tract.) Any change in this thriving population can lead to a disruption of normal digestive ability and in some cases to life threatening disease.

Enteritis is an infection or inflammation of the intestines and has a number of causes. Rabbits suffering from enteritis may have

✔ Stools ranging from occasional soft stools to outright diarrhea

✔ Bloated abdomen

✔ Teeth crunching

✔ Protruding eye(s)

 ✔ Restlessness

 ✔ Lack of appetite

 ✔ Weight loss

By far, the most common cause of enteritis is feeding your pet the wrong diet, particularly one that is low in fiber and high in carbohydrates. (See Chapter 7 for what bunnies should eat.) Other causes include the use of antibiotics that are inappropriate for the rabbit, exposure to high levels of stress, and exposure to certain bacteria. (See the "Watch out for antibiotics" sidebar in this chapter for more information.) Really, anything that causes a serious change in the normal population of healthy microorganisms in the rabbit's gut will allow "bad" bacteria to overgrow leading to disease. If your rabbit is showing any abnormalities in his stools, you should contact your veterinarian as soon as possible.

The most important thing you can do to safeguard your rabbit from enteritis is to feed a healthy high-fiber diet, as well as providing a clean, stress-free environment. Chapters 5-7 help you do this.

Tyzzer's disease

A bacteria called *Clostridium piliforme* causes *Tyzzer's disease*. Depression and profuse, watery diarrhea are symptoms of Tyzzer's. This disease can be fatal, particularly in rabbits that were recently weaned. Older rabbits with this illness may develop a chronic wasting disease, where the rabbit refuses to eat and slowly wastes away.

A low-fiber, high-carbohydrate diet, along with poor hygiene and stress can predispose a rabbit to Tyzzer's disease. If your rabbit shows signs of depression and diarrhea, take him to a veterinarian right away. The most important part of treatment for Tyzzer's is a high-fiber and low-carbohydrate diet.

Enterotoxemia

The most serious disease caused by a disruption of the GI tract's normal bacteria is *enterotoxemia*. This condition occurs with the overgrowth of certain bacteria, particularly *Clostridium* species or *E.coli*.

When these bacteria proliferate, they produce dangerous toxins absorbed into the blood stream and they poison the rabbit. Enterotoxemia is seen most often in young weanling rabbits (see Chapter 13 for weanling information), but can be seen in any rabbit that has had a severe disruption of the normal GI tract flora due to the conditions mentioned under enteritis.

Signs of enterotoxemia include

- Profuse diarrhea that's brown or bloody
- Loss of appetite
- Weakness
- Sudden death

Medicating your rabbit

If your bunny is diagnosed with an illness, chances are she'll need medication. This may be in the form of a pill, liquid, or eye or eardrops. Ask your vet to show you how to administer the medication before you take your bunny home. Before you begin, take a deep breath and resolve to be patient. Rabbits can be uncooperative when being medicated, so be prepared.

Your rabbit may just eat a pill or drink the liquid medicine out of a bowl. You can also try disguising the pill: Mash it up and mix it with applesauce, mashed banana, fruit juice, or veggie or fruit baby food — whichever your bunny likes best. If it is mashed up well enough, it might even go through a syringe. Give that a try first. If not, you'll need to restrain your bunny regardless of the medication type you're giving. The best way to restrain your rabbit is to

1. Have the medication all measured out and ready to go.

2. Wrap her in a towel.

3. Stabilize the bunny against your body. Keeping your rabbit from struggling so much that she hurts herself is important.

   Talk to her in a soothing voice and try to help her calm down while you administer the medications.

Your method of administering medicine to your rabbit will depend on the form of the medication. For oral medications remember that rabbits have a nice space between their incisors and molars where there are no teeth; it serves as a perfect space in which to insert the piller or syringe. Here are tips on how to give a variety of medication types:

- **Pills:** You can use a *piller* (available from your veterinarian), which is a long stick of sorts that allows you to place the pill far back in the rabbit's mouth so he'll swallow it more readily.

- **Liquid medication:** You can put this in a syringe (without the needle) and place it in the space between the incisors and the molars on the side of the mouth. Slowly inject the liquid, letting your bunny swallow it. Don't put the rabbit on her back because she may inhale the medication into her lungs if you do that.

- **Eyedrops or ointment:** You can pull down the lower lid of the eye and place the drops or ointment in the pocket between the eyeball and the lid. When the rabbit closes her eye, the medication spreads around the surface of the eyeball. Be careful not to touch the eye with the applicator.

- **Eardrops:** Simply place the medication into the rabbit's ears, then gently massage the base of the ear to get it worked down into the ear canal. Expect plenty of ear-shaking and scratching. (Having something cold and wet running down your ear canal feels weird!) Be sympathetic toward your bunny and be sure to help her wipe her face clean if the ear medication musses her fur.

If you suspect that your rabbit is suffering from enterotoxemia, contact your veterinarian right away because this condition is rapidly fatal if left untreated. It's better to prevent this serious disease altogether with a high-fiber diet.

Soft stool

Soft pudding-like stools present along with normal round, dry stools are a sign of a disruption of the delicate balance in the rabbit's intestinal flora. This condition is not life-threatening, but needs to be treated before it progresses to more severe disease.

Rabbits normally produce two types of droppings. One is the round hard stool you find in great profusion in your rabbit's cage and the other is the nutrient-rich *cecotrope* produced from the cecum and is eaten directly by the rabbit to be digested. (See Chapter 2 for more information on rabbit GI physiology.)

Normally you never see the cecotropes and if, on occasion, you do, they should be soft but formed in small, oblong pellets. When there's a mild disruption to the normal flora of the cecum, the cecotropes come out unformed in mucous-coated blobs or pools of thick pudding-like stool. (Sounds appetizing doesn't it?) This isn't true diarrhea because the rabbit can still produce the normal round droppings. These soft cecotropes get stuck to rabbit's fur and are deposited to dry into an almost concrete-like substance in the cage and exercise areas. The rabbit can't eat the cecotropes because they have no form and these sticky clumps can eventually cause not only a cleaning headache, but an impaction of stool on the bunny's rear end.

The most common cause of soft cecotropes is a high-carbohydrate, low-fiber diet. Other, less common causes are cancer, internal abscesses, partial intestinal obstruction, and other systemic diseases, such as liver or kidney disease. It's best to have your rabbit examined by a veterinarian to make sure there is no underlying disease. Since the majority of cases are caused by an inappropriate diet, all that's usually necessary for treatment is a switch to a high-fiber diet low in concentrated carbohydrates. See Chapter 7 for details on feeding your rabbit a healthy diet.

If a rabbit doesn't produce any stool for 24 hours, he's in need of immediate medical attention. The most common cause is a complete or partial obstruction to the gastrointestinal (GI) tract or a complete shutdown of the GI tract caused by a chronic GI motility problem. These conditions are fatal within 48 hours if left untreated. Chapter 18 has more information on this topic, including symptoms that may accompany this lack of stools.

Urinary tract disease

Rabbits are prone to a number of *urinary tract diseases,* ailments that affect the bladder and kidneys. Each of these maladies is serious and requires immediate veterinary treatment.

Cystitis

An infection of the bladder, *cystitis* is somewhat common in rabbits. Signs of the condition are the same as urolithiasis. (See the list in the "Urolithiasis" section.)

Because these symptoms are similar to that of urolithiasis, taking your rabbit to a veterinarian immediately for diagnosis is critical. Cystitis may be cured with long-term antibiotic treatment.

Rabbits who develop cystitis often have recurring bouts of the condition, so watch them closely for recurrences.

Kidney disease

Kidney disease (also called *renal disease*) can occur, particularly in older rabbits. Kidney disease can be caused by bacterial infection, parasites, toxins, or cancer. See if your rabbit has any of the following signs of kidney disease:

- ✔ Anemia
- ✔ Depression
- ✔ Poor appetite
- ✔ Weight loss
- ✔ Excessive water consumption
- ✔ Excessive amounts of urine

Kidney disease is a serious condition. The sooner treatment takes place, the better your pet's chances for survival. If you see any of these signs, take her to a veterinarian right away.

Urolithiasis

Urolithiasis, also known as bladder stone, is seen in rabbits. Rabbits, unlike dogs, cats, and humans, normally excrete any extra calcium from their diet through their urine, which can give normal rabbit urine a cloudy look. Humans, dogs and cats excrete extra calcium through the stool.

Occasionally, rabbits can develop bladder stones or bladder *sludge* (thick material not yet formed into stones). The causes can be many, including long-term inadequate water intake (leading to more concentrated urine), underlying bladder infection and genetic predisposition. The high calcium level of some foods has often been blamed entirely for this disease, but this alone won't cause bladder stones. Inadequate water intake can occur when the water is not changed frequently, is frozen, or is not easily accessible.

Colorful urine

Normal rabbit urine can be quite colorful and range from light yellow to a deep orange-red (a rusty color). This could be scary if you didn't know it was normal. The colors are produced either by pigments that pass through the system from some food, or from normal pigments called *porphyrins*, produced by the bladder itself. Beets, for instance, produce a urine that's magenta in color like the beets.

So what about when the urine is red? Bright red color to the urine is usually an indication of blood coming either from the urinary tract or in the case of an unsprayed female, from the reproductive tract (see Chapter 13), and is definitely something to pay attention to. Sometimes it can be hard to differentiate red from the rusty (which is more orange) color of plant pigments. It is easy to tell the difference by having your veterinarian test a fresh urine sample. If you see red in your rabbit's urine, particularly if she strains to urinate or acts abnormal in any other way, seek veterinary attention as soon as possible.

Rabbits suffering from urolithiasis show the following signs:

- ✔ Straining to urinate
- ✔ Frequent small amounts of urine produced, often outside of the normal toilet areas
- ✔ Small stones or blood present in the urine
- ✔ Depression
- ✔ Abdominal pain (hunched posture)

If your rabbit shows any of these signs, take her to your veterinarian immediately for diagnosis and treatment. Surgery may be necessary in the case of large stones. Sludge and small stones can often be flushed out of the bladder under anesthesia.

The best prevention for bladder stones is making sure your rabbit

- ✔ Takes in sufficient amounts of water daily.
- ✔ Eats a healthy diet including high-moisture fresh foods, which adds water to his system.
- ✔ Has available water changed daily and that the bottle is working properly so your pet doesn't have to work too hard to get a drink.
- ✔ Exercises. You can get ideas for how to do this in Chapter 15.
- ✔ Has a clean toilet area. This encourages urination, which keeps the bladder contents flushed. Rabbits that aren't exercised or have unclean toilet areas may tend to hold their urine for much longer periods of time.

Various and Sundry Body Woes

Rabbits can develop a whole slew of other diseases and conditions besides the ones already mentioned. Some of these problems are specific to rabbits, but others are difficulties that all mammals face — including people. If you know how to recognize these ailments, you'll respond quickly, calling the vet and getting appropriate treatment. The more quickly that you respond, the better the chances of effectively eliminating any disease or discomfort that's afflicting your rabbit.

Dental disease

Dental disease is fairly common in pet rabbits. Nature designed your bunny to eat a variety of plant materials that includes some tough, abrasive material. In order to keep your rabbit's teeth from wearing down to the point where he can't eat, nature arranged it so that rabbit teeth are always growing.

If a rabbit's teeth are improperly aligned, the teeth won't wear down properly. The result is teeth that grow too long, making it difficult for the rabbit to chew (a condition known as *malocclusion,* which is shown in Figure 9-1). Either the *crown* (the top) of the tooth can overgrow or the *root* (bottom of the tooth under the gum line).

If the crown overgrows, sharp edges form, which can cause sores on the tongue and the inside of the mouth. If the root overgrows, it can cause deformities of the jaw bone, leading eventually to abscesses. If the upper incisor roots grow too long they can pinch off the tear duct, so tears can't flow. This leads to spilling of tears on the face and a chronically wet and matted facial fur.

Figure 9-1: The rabbit on the left suffers from malocclusion. The rabbit on the right is a-okay.

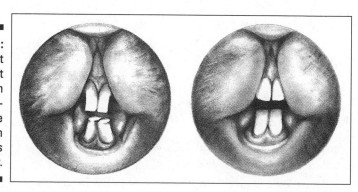

Dental disease is caused most commonly by a diet low in abrasive materials, genetic malocclusion of the teeth, or facial trauma. Check your rabbit for the following signs of dental disease:

- ✔ Being picky about foods (particularly unable to eat pellets or hard vegetables)
- ✔ Bulging eye(s)
- ✔ Dropping food from the mouth
- ✔ Excessive salivation
- ✔ Loss of appetite
- ✔ Nasal discharge
- ✔ Tearing eyes
- ✔ Excessive teeth-grinding
- ✔ Lumps along the jaw or under the eye

If your rabbit has any of these signs, take him to a veterinarian immediately. Dental disease that's just starting may show no outward signs, so it's important that your veterinarian perform a thorough mouth exam at least once a year on even outwardly healthy pets. Early detection is key to treating dental disease in rabbits.

Heatstroke

Your bunny is capable of tolerating cold much better than heat. Rabbits who become overheated are susceptible to heatstroke, which can be fatal. Temperatures of 80 degrees Fahrenheit are dangerous to rabbits.

Rabbits on the verge of heatstroke lay in a stretched-out posture and pant, breathing rapidly and sometimes foaming at the mouth.

Heatstroke is an emergency situation. Before you transport your rabbit to the veterinarian, take measures to bring his body temperature down.

1. **Get him out of the sun and into a cool place.**

2. **Put a cool, wet towel around his ears.**

   The wet towel around his ears cools the blood that's flowing through his ears. Then that blood circulates throughout the rest of his body, thus helping to lower overall body temperature.

3. **If he's conscious, offer him fresh water.**

4. **Rush him to the veterinarian for immediate treatment.**

   The vet will give the rabbit fluids intravenously and other appropriate medications.

To avoid heatstroke:

- Keep your rabbit in the shade on hot days,

- Provide plenty of water.

- If temperatures get particularly high, fill a soda bottle part way with water, place it in the freezer, and put the frozen bottle in your rabbit's cage or hutch. Or better yet, bring him inside into the air conditioning.

Head tilt

Head tilt (also called *wry neck* or *torticollis*) is a sign of any one of a number of problems including inner ear disease, or disease of the vestibular (balance) area of the brain such as cancer, trauma, stroke, or parasitic infection.

If your rabbit is tilting his head to one side, take him to your veterinarian right away for a diagnosis. Your vet may be able to treat the problem, depending on the cause. The earlier it's treated, the greater the chances for a cure, so address this condition as soon as you notice it.

If the condition is irreversible despite treatment and your pet is still active and eating well, you can opt to let your rabbit live with this condition. Many rabbit owners have found that their "tilted" rabbits are able to live relatively normal lives.

Inflammation of the feet

Pododermatitis (also known as *sore hocks;* see Chapter 2 for more information) occurs when the area below the *hocks* (the joint closest to the paw on the hind leg) develops ulcers and becomes inflamed. A bacterial infection is usually present.

Obesity, a dirty, wet environment, or a lack of space within which to move around can set the stage for this condition. Rex rabbits are particularly prone to this problem because their feet lack the thick furry padding that other rabbits have. Your veterinarian can treat sore hocks with a wound cleanser and an antibiotic. You can also

✔ Keep the cage floor dry and clean. If your pet has an all-wire cage floor, provide an area off the wire to sit, like a box with shredded or flat newspaper in it (in addition to the litter box).

✔ Put your rabbit on a diet.

✔ Provide more room and more exercise time for your rabbit. Cages that are too small can aggravate the problem. Chapter 6 talks more about hutch size and how to calculate the right size for your pet.

To avoid having to deal with this problem in the first place, keep your rabbit fit and healthy and provide him with a clean, good-size cage. Chapters 5 and 6 offer more cage information.

Obesity

Obesity is a common health problem among pet rabbits. An obese rabbit is at increased risk to develop other health problems. It's vital to prevent this condition.

You can keep a handle on your rabbit's weight by feeding him properly and weighing him regularly to make sure he's not gaining too much weight. (See Chapter 7 for information on proper diet and on how to weigh your rabbit.) He'll be weighed at his annual veterinarian visit and your vet can tell you if he is tipping the scales too far.

Some of the health problems that obesity can contribute to include

✔ Difficulty grooming

✔ Foot inflammation

✔ Inability to ingest *cecotropes,* rabbit-produced pellets that contain essential nutrients (see Chapter 2)

✔ Sluggish, unhealthy digestive tract

✔ Shortened life span

✔ Stress on the heart and vertebrae

Rabbits become obese the same way that people do — too many calories and not enough exercise. Among rabbits, excess calories often come from eating excessive amounts of alfalfa-based commercial rabbit pellets.

Rabbits who eat fresh foods and hay as a primary diet and get regular exercise are less likely to develop obesity. If your rabbit is obese, place him on a diet with the advice of a veterinarian. If your rabbit needs slimming down, talk to your vet about creating a new diet for your pet. (For more on diet and exercise, see Chapters 7 and 15, respectively.)

Paralysis and hind limb weakness

Rabbits are prone to several conditions that can result in weakness or paralysis of the hind legs. These include arthritis and fusing of the spinal vertebra, intervertebral disc disease, trauma, parasites, toxins, stroke, bacterial infections, cancer, and systemic disease.

Since the conditions that cause hind limb weakness or complete paralysis are so variable, you could see a variety of other abnormalities such as loss of appetite, pain, or lethargy. However, any noticeable weakness of the hind quarters is abnormal even in the absence of other signs and your pet should get veterinary attention as soon as possible. Some conditions are reversible if treated immediately.

If your rabbit has any of these signs, take him to the vet for an evaluation and treatment. Many diligent rabbit owners have been able to make life livable for paralyzed bunnies with special care and support. (If you're living with a paralyzed rabbit and need help, contact your local House Rabbit Society for information. See the Appendix for contact information.)

Breaking Out the Bunny Cane

With the right care, your rabbit can live to be 10 years of age or even longer. And of course, the better the care is that you give to your pet, the healthier he'll be in his old age. (See the rest of Part II for information on how to provide the best basic care for your pet.)

However, rabbits, just like the rest of us, start to develop some problems as they get old. If you have a senior bunny in the house, watch out in particular for signs of kidney disease, hind leg weakness, arthritis, and dental disease.

Making some adaptations to his environment can make life easier for your older bunny:

- ✔ Be especially careful to give him a good, healthy diet.
- ✔ Cut down the side of his litter box to give him easier access.
- ✔ Provide him with plenty of soft places to sit.
- ✔ Reduce stress in his environment as much as you can.

Postmortems

It's unpleasant to think about your bunny undergoing a *postmortem examination* (also known as *necropsy*, it's an internal examination of the organs and tissue performed by a veterinarian after the rabbit has died). However, if you lose your beloved rabbit to illness or you don't know the cause, think about having your vet perform a postmortem.

The reason for this is simple: By helping your veterinarian learn about the problem that took your rabbit, you're contributing to your veterinarian's knowledge of rabbit medicine. This information can help your vet successfully treat other rabbits in the future and may actually save lives. In addition, if you have other rabbits in the household you can find out if the condition that caused the death puts your other rabbits at risk. Chapter 14 offers more information about how to deal with a rabbit's loss.

Part III
Holing Up With Your Companion

The 5th Wave   By Rich Tennant

"What I don't understand is how you could put the entire costume on without knowing the rabbit was inside."

In this part . . .

When you know how to care for your bunny in terms of feeding and housing, you can take on more intricate parts of your relationship. Here you understand what your rabbit means when he acts a certain way and what you can do if he's acting up. Training can be a fun part of your life together and this part tells you how to approach this, step by step. If after working with your rabbit extensively you find you're interested in breeding rabbits, this part tackles this tough issue head on. And finally, the toughest issue of all: losing your pet. This part tells you how to handle it.

Chapter 10

Reading Your Rabbit

· ·

In This Chapter

▶ Communicating with your rabbit

▶ Discovering the rabbit mind

▶ Relaxing your rabbit

· ·

*O*n the surface, rabbits may seem like simple creatures who just want to eat, sleep, and play, but they're actually much more complicated than that. You don't survive as a species for millions of years if you don't have much going for you besides the basics.

Rabbits are excellent at reading humans' body language, communicating silently (and quite loudly), and figuring out what has changed and why. They're also experts at detecting danger. If you want to communicate effectively and live harmoniously with your domestic bunny, take heed of the following bunny wisdom.

Speaking the Lagomorphs Language

The first step in communicating with your rabbit is being able to figure out what the heck he's trying to tell you. For the most part, rabbits speak with their bodies — that is, their movements and postures. This is how they talk to each other, and this is how your rabbit communicates with you.

To understand what your rabbit is saying to you, you need to pay close attention. Observe your pet in different situations and be able to recognize the following messages:

✔ **This is my turf!** Does your rabbit ever rub his chin on the corners of the furniture, on the edges of his nest box, or on your hand? If so, you are witnessing a display of territory marking called *chin rubbing*. When your rabbit rubs his chin on something, the scent glands located on the underside of his face leave an odor detectable to other rabbits, letting them know that this territory belongs to the owner of the scent. Let your rabbit do this all he wants because it makes him feel safe to be in an environment he has carefully marked as his own territory. And don't worry; the scent your rabbit leaves behind is undetectable to the human nose.

✔ **Watch out!** If you saw the movie "Bambi," you probably remember a little rabbit named Thumper, who got his name by repeatedly stamping his back leg on the ground. This wasn't just cartoon behavior. Real-life rabbits thump their hind legs on the ground to issue warnings, too. If you see your rabbit do this, he is probably alerting you to a variety of circumstances.

✔ **I don't want you to see me.** In the wild, rabbits are masters of camouflage. They can flatten their bodies and blend in with the brush to avoid being seen by predators. Pet rabbits do this, too. If your rabbit gets nervous when being approached by someone he doesn't know, or by another animal, he is likely to lower himself to the ground in a behavior called *flattening*. He holds his ears tightly against his head, and his eyes bulge out, as shown in Figure 10-1. In this position, your rabbit is trying to tell you that he is scared. Remove him from whatever situation is frightening him, and let him know that everything is okay.

✔ **I'm comfortable and secure.** Some people confuse the body position of flattening with the body position of squatting. However, these two positions are polar opposites. Flattening expresses fear, whereas *squatting* (which means what it says) expresses comfort. Rabbits who are squatting, one of which is shown in Figure 10-1, have a distinctly more relaxed appearance. Their muscles don't appear to be tight, nor do they seem to be holding their ears tightly against their heads. Instead of a frightened look in the eye, your bunny shows a relaxed expression.

Figure 10-1:
The squatter's on the top, the flattener on the bottom.

- **I'm pooped out.** A rabbit lying on its side with its legs extended is feeling tired yet secure. A rabbit in this position needs to be left alone so he can sleep. Some rabbits have a variation on this position: They lay on their stomachs with their legs stretched out behind. This position is rather amusing to see. Try to stifle your laughter, though. Your bunny is trying to rest!

- **Ick, I don't like that.** If you rabbit gets a whiff or taste of something he doesn't like, or if he wants you to leave him alone, he may give his ears a good shake to let you know what he's thinking. Called *ear shaking,* this cue indicates that your rabbit isn't happy at the moment.

    Frequent ear shaking can be a sign of a medical problem and should be assessed by a veterinarian. Chapter 9 details other health problems and their potential signs.

- **Get me out of this position!** If you're holding your rabbit and he starts to kick violently, he is letting you know that you aren't holding him in a way that helps him feel secure. You need to reposition your rabbit so he doesn't feel that he needs to kick himself free of your grasp. (You may also see your rabbit kick when playing. This is a different kind of kicking and basically means "Yippee, I'm having fun!") Chapter 8 tells you how to properly hold your rabbit so you can avoid this type of language.

- **I don't like what you're doing.** A gentle nip is a rabbit's way of saying "Okay, I've had enough." Unless the biting is chronic and painful, take it at face value and give your rabbit a break from whatever you are doing. Chapter 11 gives training tips.

- **Hey, let's cuddle.** If your rabbit sidles up to you and snuggles against you, he isn't just trying to get warm. He's letting you know that he enjoys your company and wants to be close to you. He may also be trying to get your attention.

- **I love you.** If your rabbit kisses you in the form of a lick on the hand or face, he is telling you that he loves you. Rabbits usually reserve this show of affection for each other, but special humans are also graced with rabbit kisses on a none-too-infrequent basis.

Doing Animal Imitations: Rabbit Talk

Although rabbits primarily communicate with body language, they also have the ability to make sounds. You may hear your rabbit make some of the following sounds:

- **Hissing:** Your rabbit may make this sound likely in response to another rabbit. Hissing is an aggressive sound that basically sends the message "Take another step and you're toast!"

- **Purring:** Like a cat, a rabbit purrs when content. Unlike the feline purr, however, the rabbit purr comes not from the throat but from the teeth.

- **Clucking:** This is the rabbit version of "Oh, that was yummy!" A rabbit cluck sounds sort of like the cluck of a chicken, but very faint.

- **Whimpering:** Rabbits who want to be left alone sometimes whimper in hopes that you won't pick them up. Pregnant females are especially likely to make this sound.

- **Tooth grinding:** You may hear two types of tooth grinding:

  - Loud grinding: He is in pain. Get your rabbit to a veterinarian right away.

  - Soft grinding: He's expressing happiness.

- **Snorting and growling:** An angry rabbit snorts and/or growls at whomever has made him mad. In most cases, this behavior is reserved for other rabbits that are perceived as a threat of some kind. A bite or charge usually follows the sounds of snorting and growling, so if it's directed at you, get out of the way!

- **Screaming:** You never want to hear this sound. When a rabbit is truly terrified for its life, it lets out a scream that is almost humanlike in nature.

Thinking Like One of Them

Of course, it helps to put rabbit body language and vocalization into context. Exactly how do rabbits think? What goes on in those fuzzy little heads?

When trying to understand rabbit psychology, it's most important to realize that rabbits are *prey* (versus predatory) animals. They are close to the bottom of the food chain, so they basically exist to provide meals for other animals. Of course, rabbits exist within their own right, and they're just food for cougars and hawks. But their lot in life of being a primary dinner source for other animals has made a significant impact on the rabbit's collective personality.

Preying for safety

Imagine that you're always being hunted. Everyone wants to make a meal out of you. Does this make you a bit paranoid? I would think so. Now think about how rabbits must see the world. Although they somehow manage to enjoy life, they're always waiting for some big scary creature to make a play for them. The result? A very wary creature with quick reflexes and a strong propensity to run first and ask questions later.

If you want to live with a rabbit, you need to realize how much the prey mentality factors into her personality. Rabbits are surprisingly happy-go-lucky, despite their lot in life, but they're always on the lookout.

Don't assume that just because your rabbit is cuddling with you one minute that he won't suddenly be afraid of you the next. If you've ever watched nature documentaries on TV, you've no doubt noticed that zebra herds will calmly graze within close vicinity to a lounging pride of lions. The zebra seem to have no fear of the lions because the lions aren't acting like predators at that moment. But the minute the lions start making quick, aggressive movements, the zebra heads go up, and the herd heads out.

It's the same thing with your rabbit. Human companions must work hard not to be mistaken for predators. If you act calm and friendly, your rabbit sees you as friend. If you start getting loud and making fast, aggressive moves, your rabbit becomes afraid of you, thinking that you've turned into a hungry predator.

Showing others who's boss

In this book, you see mentioned time and again the rabbit's penchant for being a social creature. In fact, without this aspect of the rabbit's disposition, rabbits wouldn't be the terrific pets we have grown to know and love.

When left to their own devices, rabbits live in complex social groups with a distinct hierarchy. A *king buck* and *queen doe* rule the colony's warren with a collective iron paw, and more submissive bunnies play different roles within the group. In the case of domesticated rabbits, these rules of hierarchy are applied to humans, fellow domesticated rabbits, and even other household pets. An example of a dominant and submissive rabbit is shown in Figure 10-2. And just as within the world of wild rabbits, different bunny personalities exist in captivity that determine which rabbits will be king and queen and which will be subjects.

To understand this relationship, think about human beings. Some people are naturally more assertive than others. Some are natural leaders, but others prefer to follow. Our individual personalities ultimately determine where we end up in life, and the same goes for rabbits. The tougher, more assertive rabbits rise to the top of the pecking order, while the ones with meeker personalities take a more subservient role.

Figure 10-2: The dominant stance is shown in the rabbit on top; the submissive rabbit is the one on the bottom.

It won't take you long to figure out what kind of rabbit personality you're dealing with. If you have a rabbit who's on the bossy side, always nipping at you to get out of the way or pushing your other pets around, you have a bunny who would probably be the king of the warren had he been born a wild rabbit instead of a domestic one. On the other hand, if you have a quiet, gentle soul who complies easily, never gets aggressive, and seems a bit on the timid side, you have a rabbit who'd happily let others rule were he a wild rabbit living in the social hierarchy of a *colony,* or group.

Either type of rabbit — and all those in-between — have much to offer. Assertive rabbits can be entertaining to live with, but the softer personality types surely steal your heart.

Coexisting peacefully with Fido and Fluffy

One of the neatest characteristics of rabbits is their propensity to get along with other pets. They're genetically programmed to find a way to live with others — even if those others are members of a different species.

Of course, the rabbit's status as a prey animal puts it in an awkward position when trying to get along with some of the other domestic animals bunnies often encounter in our human world.

Parrots and ferrets can be a challenge. Even though rabbits and these animals don't have a history of animosity toward each other, parrots can have problems with the idea of a rabbit in the house. Aggressive parrots should be kept away from rabbits, which is not too difficult to do. Ferrets, on the other hand, are likely to want to make a meal out a rabbit and so are best kept at a safe distance.

Fresh fruit makes a great treat for rabbits. It's important not to overfeed sweet fruit, however, because of its sugar content.

It's important to teach children the right way to hold a rabbit. Proper handling ensures the safety of both the child and the rabbit.

Crock-style bowls make the best food dishes because they are chew- and tip-resistant.

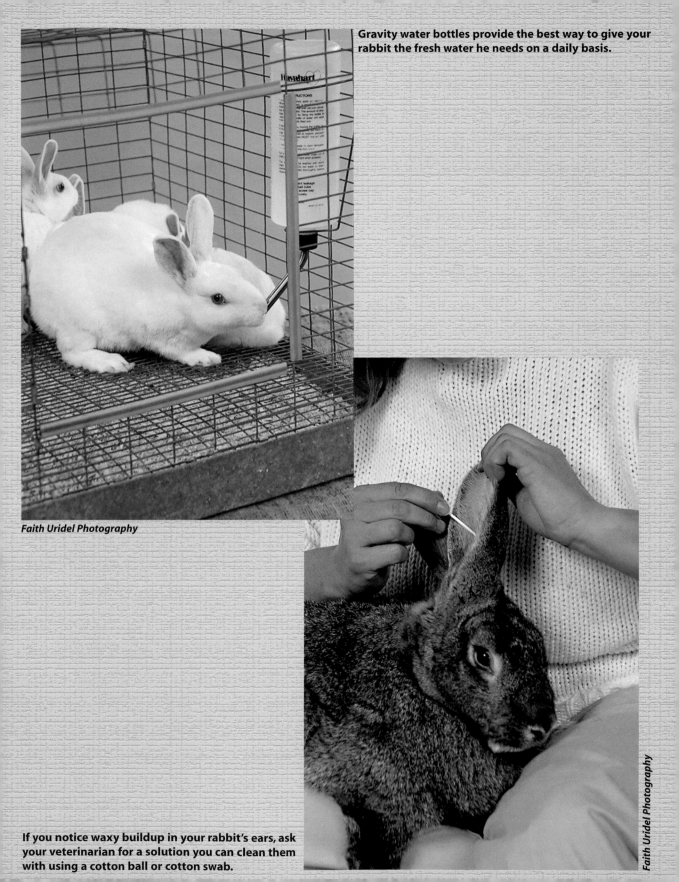

Gravity water bottles provide the best way to give your rabbit the fresh water he needs on a daily basis.

Faith Uridel Photography

If you notice waxy buildup in your rabbit's ears, ask your veterinarian for a solution you can clean them with using a cotton ball or cotton swab.

Faith Uridel Photography

An experienced tattooer inks rabbits exhibited at ARBA shows. The rabbits registration number is shown on the ear.

Faith Uridel Photography

A rabbit's front incisors grow continuously throughout its life. Problems with dental disease can be a result of misaligned teeth.

Eric Ilasenko Photography

Litter boxes designed to fit in the corner of your rabbit's cage are often a good choice.

The Jersey Woolly is a diminutive breed with long, soft hair.

Rabbit shows are fun events that give you an opportunity to see up close all the recognized rabbit breeds.

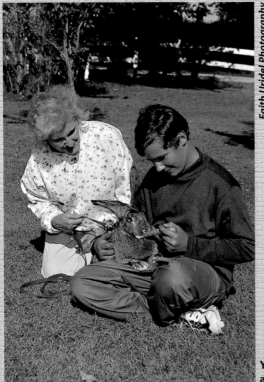

You can take your rabbit outside on a harness and leash provided the area is safe from dogs and other predators.

Mother rabbits need a secure nest box to keep and raise their young.

Eric Ilasenko Photography

Eric Ilasenko Photography

...therland Dwarf is one of the smallest of the domestic rabbit breeds.

It's important to groom your rabbit at least once a week using a pin or slicker brush. This not only removes loose hair, but also gives you a chance to examine your rabbit.

The Holland Lop is a dwarf breed of lop rabbit that was developed in the 1960s.

Although cats and rabbits have been on opposite sides of the chase for a long time, the sheer size of today's domestic felines makes the situation much less uncomfortable for rabbits. Most cats and rabbits are virtually the same size, and no cat in its right mind would take on an average-size rabbit. Dogs are the greatest challenge because their wild relatives considered rabbits a prime source of food. In fact, if you research the history of dogs and rabbits, you'll see that the dog and the rabbit have long had a strained relationship, as far back as the Ice Age. If you have a dog or a cat, take note of these tips on determining whether your pets can get along.

Dogs

If you have a dog and plan to get a rabbit, you need to take care. Most dogs have a strong instinct to chase and even kill rabbits, and some have gotten into the habit of running after wild rabbits in an attempt to annihilate them. If you're going to keep both of these species as pets, stay constantly aware of this inherent tension between the two creatures.

Think about your dog's

- **Personality:** Is your pooch a mellow old coach potato who's hard pressed to chase or get excited? Or is she a more active dog?

- **Age:** Older, calmer dogs usually do better with rabbits and are less likely to harass them. If your dog is young and excitable, it may work out, but only if you're able to reliably control your dog. If your dog ignores you when you call her and basically marches to her own drummer, you have a problem.

- **Breed:** Many terriers, some types of hounds and a number of other breeds have been bred for hundreds of years to hunt rabbits. If your dog comes from one of these hunting breeds, one look at your new rabbit could trigger previously dormant hunting instincts in your dog. Unless you have a young puppy — preferably under 6 months old — it's going to be tough to train your dog of this type not to harm the rabbit.

Before even attempting to introduce a rabbit to your household, take your dog to obedience training. Obedience training helps your dog to listen to you and to respect you as an authority. This recognition of you as the *pack leader* can enable you to show your dog *not* to harm a rabbit.

After you decide that your dog is controlled enough to officially meet your rabbit, and your rabbit has had time to get used to his new home, follow these steps to introduce the two:

1. Put your dog on a leash and put someone the dog respects in control of the leash (an adult only).

2. Allow the dog to approach the rabbit's cage slowly, in a quiet manner.

If the dog starts to act up, correct him by saying "No" and quickly jerking the leash. Do this consistently. When the dog approaches the rabbit quietly, even for a moment, praise him with pats and verbal kudos.

Your rabbit will probably be scared the first time that she sees your dog and is likely to hide in her nest box. This is a good way for the rabbit to feel secure when the dog's around. If the dog is calm and nonthreatening, the rabbit will probably become braver, even curious. You'll know that the rabbit is curious if the bunny comes out of her nest box when the dog is around. When the rabbit seems comfortable with the dog in the same room and the dog is calm and quiet around the rabbit, you may assume that the two have reached a truce.

Don't assume that just because your dog seems disinterested in the rabbit that you can safely let the two loose together. Your dog can never be trusted with the rabbit. Don't take chances with your rabbit's life. Keep your dog and your rabbit separated by a cage or other barrier at all times. Some dogs, no matter how hard their owners try, can avoid chasing a rabbit. Their predatory instincts are simply too strong. In these cases, you have to keep the dog permanently separated from the rabbit or return the rabbit to its breeder or to a foster home.

Cats

Although dogs and rabbits are often a tricky combination, cats aren't usually a problem when it comes to cohabiting with a rabbit. Even though cats are predators and may be inclined to chase rabbits, they're less capable of doing damage. It's rare that a cat will be so aggressive toward a rabbit that the two can't be housemates, especially if the rabbit is a large one. Of course, you may even have to watch out for your cat. Some rabbits are so bossy that they make life miserable for the kitty of the household.

You can get a good sense of how your cat and rabbit behaves toward each other when you introduce them. If your cat begins to stalk your rabbit and treats it like prey, don't allow the two together unless your cat is on a harness and leash, as shown in Figure 10-3. If your rabbit is the same size or larger than your cat, let the cat approach your rabbit and permit the rabbit to put the cat in his place. Your rabbit will probably try to bite and kick your cat, and you can be sure that your cat will never attempt to stalk the rabbit again.

Follow these steps to safely introduce your cat and your rabbit:

1. **Trim your cats claws using a nail clipper.**

   If your cat's nails are trimmed, he is less likely to be able to scratch your rabbit should he decide to take a swipe at your bunny. If you aren't sure how to do this, see the nail trimming section in Chapter 8. Cat nails are trimmed essentially the same way as a rabbit's.

2. **Begin the introduction with the rabbit in her cage.**

   No need for the cat to wear a harness during this stage. Your cat and rabbit will probably stare at each other and seem nervous. That's because they are! Your rabbit may dive into the nest box, and your cat may arch his back and even hiss. This is normal behavior.

3. **If your cat approaches the rabbit slowly and isn't aggressive, reward the kitty with praise and a treat. If he hisses and runs away, ignore him.**

   Eventually, his curiosity will get the best of him and he'll come back to take a closer look. In time, your cat will get used to the rabbit. Should he get too interested and stick his paw through the bars of the rabbit's cage, squirt the cat with a water pistol from a distance. This is a message to your kitty that aggression toward the rabbit is not okay.

4. **When the cat and rabbit start to take each other's presence for granted, you can move to the next step: face-to-face introduction.**

5. **Let your rabbit out of her cage in a rabbit-proof room.**

   See Chapter 5 for more on rabbit-proofing.

6. **Put your cat in a harness with a leash attached and let him be in the same room with the rabbit, while you're holding the leash.**

7. **When your rabbit starts moving around, your cat may want to follow her. Don't allow this to happen.**

   Keep the cat in place and allow him to watch the rabbit hop around the room. When the rabbit hops, the cat may make moves toward her as if to chase her. Don't allow this. Instead, keep the cat still and let him watch the rabbit move around the room.

   In the event that your rabbit behaves aggressively toward your cat, let your cat run away from the rabbit. If your cat feels cornered, it may attack in self-defense. If your rabbit continues to behave aggressively toward the cat, the cat finds out that he needs to stay away from the rabbit, which is fine. Your rabbit should be allowed to call the shots in this situation. In the unlikely event that your rabbit starts seeking out your cat just so she can attack the poor feline, you can discipline your rabbit with a squirt of water to the body and a firm "No!"

8. **Repeat these sessions regularly until both your cat and your rabbit are comfortable with each other.**

   It will probably take time before the two start to ignore each other (or even become friends), but it's worth the effort.

If you have one of the smaller breeds of rabbits or a baby bunny, take care if you have a cat who wants to stalk your rabbit. Make sure to always keep the two separated because your cat may actually be able to do some harm to a smaller bunny. You can read more about breeds in Chapter 3.

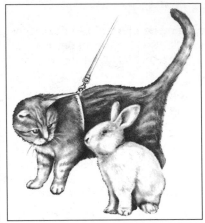

Figure 10-3:
Harness
that
potential
predator!

Pairing humans and rabbits

If you want your rabbit to see you as a friend and not a foe, you need to act more like a rabbit than a predator. Getting into your rabbit's mind and viewing the world from his perspective can help you do this. To gain your rabbit's trust, convince him that you have no intention of turning him into a meal.

To help gain and deepen your rabbit's trust in you, you can take the following steps:

- **Speak softly.** When you're around your rabbit, talk in a quiet, gentle voice. You can talk and coo to your bunny all you like, but do it at a low volume in a soft and non-menacing way.

- **Move slowly.** Quick, jerky movements are the movements of hungry predators. Move slowly and deliberately when you're around your rabbit. And whatever you do, don't chase your rabbit. If your bunny is being resistant about being caught, try luring him to you with a favorite treat. If you run after your rabbit, you'll suddenly seem like a predator with something unpleasant on your mind.

- **Feed at the right times.** Rabbits tend to prefer eating in the early morning hours and at dusk. The reason for this is that these are the safest times to avoid predators. By giving your rabbit his main meals at these times of the day, you help cater to his instinctual need to eat at a safe time. This makes for a more generally relaxed rabbit. Chapter 7 talks about food.

You're grounded, mister

Just about every species of mammal has its adolescent years, and rabbits are no exception. Just like human teenagers, rabbit "teens" are coping with raging hormones, newfound independence, and moving from youth into adulthood. And just like human teenagers, rabbit adolescents feel the need to test their boundaries to see what they can do. They're trying to establish their social order within the group, and because humans are part of the "group," they're included in the aggressive, "testing" behavior. This is normal and healthy behavior.

Consequently, teenage bunnies tend to be mischievous and may be a bit hard to handle. Spaying or neutering before the behaviors become deeply entrenched can provide some measure of relief for the situation, as can a bucket load of patience. (Chapter 9 talks more about spaying and neutering.) Just keep reminding yourself that like your child, your rabbit will indeed grow out of this phase. However, it's important to handle them properly during this period. Rough handling during this period can cause irreparable damage to the bond you have with your pet.

✔ **Never use harsh discipline.** Rabbits aren't like children or dogs. They don't understand harsh discipline, and bunnies interpret any kind of yelling or striking to be the maneuvers of an enemy. Use positive reinforcement to teach your rabbit how to behave. You can get help for this in Chapter 11.

Kids and rabbits

Children and bunnies are an adorable combination. The sight of a cute kid cuddling a cute rabbit is almost too much to bear. But in order to keep both creatures safe in each other's company, parents need to be aware of potential problems.

Rabbits fascinate kids. Whether it's those giant ears or nonthreatening demeanor that attracts them, children tend to become obsessed with their bunnies. If you have a kid or two and an indoor rabbit, your children will no doubt spend plenty of time with the rabbit. This is fine as long as you keep the following in mind:

✔ **Children must be taught how to handle a rabbit properly before they're allowed to interact.** Young children shouldn't be permitted to lift a rabbit because both child and rabbit may get hurt in this situation. Older children may lift smaller rabbits safely, as long as they're taught the proper technique (see Chapter 8).

✔ **Let your kids know that rabbits have sensitive ears and don't like loud noises.** Teach them to keep loud play to a minimum when they're in the vicinity of the rabbit. When kids are feeling rambunctious and want to scream and run around, they should do it outside or at least in a different room from where the rabbit is kept.

✔ **Rabbits need their quiet time.** Unlike most dogs, they're not always up for playing. Teach your kids to give the rabbit some space. If you need to, set aside a section of the day as the rabbit's quiet time when no one is allowed to bother him.

✔ **Children enjoy feeding time with rabbits in particular.** Let your children feed treats or dinner to your bunny, but show your children that they should sit quietly if they want to watch bunny dine. The rabbit shouldn't be touched or disturbed while eating.

Chapter 11

Putting Boxing Gloves on Your Rabbit: Training

Yes. You can train your rabbit, both for fun and to help you control some of his behaviors. Of course, you can't train them to sniff for drugs, guide the blind, or roll over on command, but you can train them to take actions that are appropriate for rabbits. For example, you can show a rabbit how to use a litter box, follow a few basic commands, and behave somewhat properly in the company of human companions.

Training a rabbit can take as little as a few days or as long as several weeks, depending on the rabbit and what you are trying to teach him. Any rabbit that is old enough to interact with you is old enough to train. Even senior bunnies can learn new tricks.

Choo Choo: Training Yourself

Following these general rules is important when training a rabbit to respond to a command:

✓ **Taking the time to bond.** Know that your rabbit trusts you before you attempt any kind of training.

✓ **Training your rabbit in a quiet safe place.** Your bunny needs to be able to concentrate on you.

- ✔ **Being consistent.** Always use the same command; don't change or add words. If you want to teach your rabbit to jump up on the couch and want "hop up" to be your command, always use that phrase when you ask him to come up.

- ✔ **Using rewards.** Give your rabbit his reward immediately after he executes the command. The best rewards for rabbits are food treats. (See Chapter 7 for details on healthy food treats for rabbits.)

- ✔ **Being firm.** Don't give your bunny the treat if he doesn't follow the command. Doing so only encourages him to ignore you.

- ✔ **Being patient.** If your bunny is having trouble catching on, figure out another way to teach him. Never use harsh words or punishment of any kind.

- ✔ **Going back to square one if you need to.** If you're having success with your rabbit's training but then hit an impasse, your rabbit needs a refresher course. Go back to square one and start the training process all over again.

- ✔ **Keeping training sessions short.** Take no more than ten minutes at a time and always end on a positive note. In other words, stop right after your rabbit does it *right,* not after he does it wrong.

When Littering Is Good: The Litter Box

One of the reasons that rabbits make such good indoor companions is that you can train them to use a litter box. Their denning instinct, inherited from their wild ancestors, is the reason behind this behavior. Rabbits prefer not to go to the bathroom where they eat and sleep, and venture out of their dens to relieve themselves. Not unlike toddlers who are going through toilet training, some bunnies are easier to train than others when it comes to using the litter box. With these holdouts, you need to expend more time and patience.

When training a rabbit to use the litter box, being consistent and praising your rabbit is important. Never scold your rabbit for not using the litter box because this only frightens and confuses her.

To teach your bunny to use the box, start in his cage and gradually work your way up to larger spaces until he is using the box even when he has the run of the place.

To begin preparing for your bunny's litter box training, first purchase an appropriate box and litter. You can read more about litter boxes — what they look like, what to put in them, and how to clean them (and see a picture) in Chapter 5.

When your rabbit is first discovering how to use the litter box, don't clean up after her too often. If her box is too clean, she may forget why it's there. Clean it a couple of times a week, and that's it.

Encouraging your bunny to go in her cage

You can start your bunny's training within a small area. Starting litter training in your rabbit's cage is best because this provides your bunny with plenty of opportunities to use the box.

1. If your rabbit already has a corner of the cage where she likes to go to the bathroom, place the box in this area. Putting some of her fecal pellets and urine-soaked paper in the box can help her get the idea.

2. Attach the box to the side with a clip or twistable wire for removal when cleaning.

3. If she doesn't start using the box right away, put a nice bunch of grass hay in it to attract her attention.

4. If you see her go to the bathroom in the litter box, give her a treat and some gentle verbal praise. With consistent reward, your bunny should get the idea in no time.

If your rabbit takes to sitting in the box and just hanging out there or chewing on the hay that you put there, don't be concerned. Rabbits often eat and go to the bathroom at the same time. Rabbits won't eat soiled hay, so don't worry about that. But munching on the clean hay stimulates your rabbit's digestive system and causes her to use the box in the way that you intended.

If you find that your rabbit is sleeping in her litter box instead of using it as a toilet, you should provide her with a more attractive bed than the one that she has. You can do this by using a different bedding material or giving her a more private nest box, which you can read about in Chapter 5.

When you see your rabbit regularly using his litter box (which can take anywhere from a week to a month or more), you can give him more room to roam without worrying too much about him going potty outside the box. Follow the next set of instructions to see how.

Providing 1.5 bathrooms

If your rabbit is using her litter box in her cage every day, then train her to use a litter box in other areas of the house.

TIP

Cleaning up

During this process, accidents are inevitable. Cleanup is easier if you protect the area under and around the litter box with newspaper or a heavy plastic carpet protector pad. Have litter boxes deep enough to contain the urine; rabbits urinate horizontally out behind them, not downwards like a cat or dog.

Clean up after your pet; pick up fecal pellets with a tissue and wash urine marks on carpeting with a mixture of vinegar and water. You can use one of the enzyme pet accident cleaners on

the market. If your bunny urinates on wood flooring, use gentle dish soap and water or cleansers made for hardwood floors.

If she does her business in the box on a regular basis, you can give her more room. Move the entire operation to a bigger space, such as the living room or a bedroom. Eventually, you should be able to let your rabbit have access to all the rabbit-proofed rooms in your house (see Chapter 5 for more on proofing the house) and count on her to use the litter box every time.

1. **Set up a special room for your bunny.**

   A kitchen, bathroom, or hallway are acceptable places. Make sure they're small, low-traffic areas.

2. **Use a baby gate to section off the area.**

   Also remember using the dog exercise pen to set up an area of exercise. Chapter 6 has more information about this.

3. **Put the litter box in the corner of the special area.**

   Rabbits often like to pick their own areas. You can put the box in the corner they select.

4. **Place your rabbit's food, water, and bedding in another part of the room.**

5. **Keep an eye on your rabbit to make sure that she uses the litter box on a regular basis.**

6. **If you see her go to the bathroom in the litter box, give her a treat and gentle verbal praise.**

   If she goes outside the box, she wasn't ready for this step in the training process. You can go back to keeping her in the cage so she develops a stronger habit of using the litter box or provide a smaller amount of space and more than one litter box.

TIP

If your rabbit starts making mistakes at any point in this process, you may have

- ✔ **Placed her in a bigger space too soon.** If this happens, the best approach is to start over. Put the box back in your bunny's cage and get her accustomed to using the box in her cage as she did before.

- ✔ **Not given her enough litter boxes.** Buy a few more litter boxes and place them strategically around the house. You can put more than one in a room or put a box in each room that your rabbit frequents. With so many litter box options to choose from, chances are that your rabbit will get it right.

  If you don't want to keep that many boxes around the house permanently, you can try removing them one by one. See if your rabbit seeks out the closest box, even if it's in the next room. If so, you have probably successfully trained your rabbit to use the litter box.

If you have more than one rabbit in your household, make sure you provide at least one more litter box than the number of rabbits in the room. Some rabbits won't use a litter box if it has been used by a more dominant rabbit.

Tricks and cute behaviors are not all you should show your rabbit. Bunnies should know how to behave properly around humans. This means no biting or attacking, and listening when they're told not to do something. Chapter 12 gives you the information you need to do this.

Giving a Command Performance

Training a rabbit is *not* like training a dog. Dogs are socialized to humans and are anxious to be accepted. Rabbits, on the other hand, hop to a different drummer. Even though rabbits are creatures that like company as well, they are not as closely bonded to humans as dogs are and obeying your every command is down low on their list of priorities. When that becomes a real problem, refer to Chapter 12 for more behavioral information.

I've got the TTOUCH

You won't find many training schools for rabbits out there, but if your rabbit has training and behavioral issues, you may find a method called Tellington-TTOUCH Training helpful. First developed for horses, this method is being used more frequently for rabbits. It has also been adapted for other companion animals.

TTOUCH employs a gentle, nonforceful way of helping your rabbit deal with whatever is troubling him. Using circular movements of the fingers and hands over the rabbit's body, as well as other related methods, TTOUCH practitioners help rabbits discover new ways to deal with problems. Issues, such as excessive fear and aggression, are addressed through this method.

To learn more about this type of training or to find a TTOUCH rabbit practitioner in your area who can help you, visit the TTOUCH Web site at `www.lindatellington-jones.com/ttouch.htm`.

Using treats and praise, you can convince a rabbit to follow a few select commands and even perform a few cute behaviors to impress your friends.

When training use short sessions of no more than 5–10 minutes at a time; rabbits have short attention spans. Save one trick for each training session. In fact, it's a good idea to teach your rabbit one thing at a time so he doesn't get confused. For instance, once he knows to come on command, you can move on to jumping on command.

Here, Fluffy: Coming when called

If you let your rabbit run in a large area of the house, you may want her to come when you call her name. It will allow you to find her if she's hiding and you're concerned for her welfare.

Rabbits can be trained to come when you call them, provided that you always give them a good reward when they do what you ask.

The best way to get a rabbit to come when you call him is to find out what her favorite treat is. Whether it's a piece of tomato or a chunk of melon, use this as your lure. (Chapter 7 gives you more ideas on what a good treat entails.)

1. **Get down on the floor close to your rabbit.**

2. **Offer the treat.**

3. **"[Say your rabbit's name], come!"**

   Your rabbit will see or smell the treat and will come toward you to get it. She doesn't know that you called her because she hasn't figured out this part yet, but if you repeat this routine over and over, she'll start to associate hearing you call her name and "Come!" with getting her favorite treat.

4. **After your bunny consistently comes to you from this close distance, start to work from farther away.**

   Instead of being so close, squat several feet away from your pet. Offer out the food and call your rabbit's name and "Come!"

Some rabbits catch on more quickly than others, but within a few weeks, your rabbit should come to you just about every time that you call her. You may even be able to get her to come to you from another room.

Making like Van Halen: Jumping

Another fun behavior that you can drill is jumping up on a piece of uphol-stered furniture on command. (Unupholstered furniture can be too slippery!) Of course, that's if you *want* your rabbit on the couch. If you'd rather bunny keep all four paws on the floor, you may want to skip this one.

To train your bunny to jump up on the couch on command,

1. **Hold the treat on the couch when your rabbit is having her free time in the house and is hopping around on the floor.**

2. **When she approaches the couch, make sure she sees the treat.**

   You can do this by holding it in a spot where she can reach the treat just standing on her hind legs with her front paws on the couch cushions.

3. **"[Say your rabbit's name], hop up!"**

   Or if you prefer, just pat the top of the couch with your other hand as a signal.

4. **Even though she's on her hind legs at the edge of the couch and hasn't jumped up on the couch, give her the treat so that she associates a treat with the couch.**

5. **When Fluffy responds to you without fail, hold the treat farther back onto the couch.**

   That way, your rabbit has to really reach to get the morsel.

6. **Repeat steps 1–5.**

   Eventually, she'll jump up on the couch to get it, provided it's not too high for her. If it is, you may want to skip this trick or provide a small stool for your rabbit to hop up on to make her way to the couch.

Make sure that you have given the command just before your rabbit makes her attempt to get the morsel. You want her to associate hearing her name and "Hop up!" or a hand patting the couch with the action of coming on the couch and getting the treat.

7. **When your rabbit finally jumps up on the couch, gently praise her, and scratch her on her favorite spot while letting her dine on her reward.**

Eventually, you may eliminate the treat because the command or a pat on the cushion should be enough to get your rabbit to join you on the couch. Your rabbit can jump down alone. Helping her might be more detrimental!

Working on the abs: Sitting up

Another good trick (and one that will impress visitors) is sitting up on command. This trick is pretty easy because rabbits naturally sit up on their hind legs all the time.

1. Start when your rabbit has all four feet on the floor.

2. Put your hand above her head with the treat in your fingers.

3. "[Say your rabbit's name], sit up!"

4. When your rabbit rises up on her hind legs to get the treat, give her the treat and some verbal praise.

5. After she rises up consistently in response to your command, start eliminating the treats.

Wean her away from the treat gradually — one time, she gets the treat, the next time, she doesn't. Pretty soon, all you'll have to do is say her name and "Sit up," and your bunny will rise up in that adorable position.

Depending on how trainable your rabbit is, it can take anywhere from just a few training sessions to a couple of weeks before she's trained to sit up on command.

Cozying up in his cage: Go in

Your rabbit can be trained go into his cage or into his travel carrier on command. If you want to train your rabbit to go into his travel carrier, make sure he's already comfortable with being inside it. See Chapter 18 for details on how to make your rabbit feel okay about being in his travel carrier.

This can be a handy trick for your bunny because it will spare you the trouble of pursuing him when you want to put him away for the night or in his carrier for a trip to the vet. (You should train for this behavior at times when you don't need to have your rabbit in his cage for a trip or bedtime. This allows for more flexibility in the training process.)

1. **Get a piece of your rabbit's favorite treat.**

2. **Put your bunny close to the opening of his cage or travel carrier.**

3. **Say "Go in!" as you lure him into the opening with the treat in your hand.**

   Make sure your rabbit sees you put the treat inside, so he knows it's in there.

4. **After he's inside the cage or carrier, give him the treat.**

   After your rabbit gets the idea, you can place the treat in the carrier and then say "Go in!"

If he doesn't go in and retrieve the treat after you give the command, don't put him inside or give him a treat anyway. He needs to associate getting the treat with actually going into the cage or carrier.

Taking a walk on the wild side

Do you have a bold bunny who likes to explore new places? Take your rabbit to a safe place, such as a friend's fenced backyard. You can walk your rabbit on a leash that's attached to a harness. A *harness* restrains the pet around the chest and shoulders, instead of by the neck, as a collar would. (Chapter 10 shows an example of such a harness. In Figure 10-3, however, the cat is in the harness.) This is a good way to take your rabbit outside while still having control over him.

Do not use a collar on a rabbit, since your rabbit's neck could be seriously injured if your pet resists.

However, you should be careful about where you walk your rabbit. Dogs and disease are two serious dangers that rabbits can encounter in unprotected areas.

Also, most rabbits are uncomfortable in strange surroundings and may not enjoy outings to new places.

Adjusting to the harness

Your rabbit first must get used to having his harness on.

Don't leave it on for long periods of time because a rabbit can chew off the harness, and the pieces of leather, plastic, or metal belt buckle can cause intestinal obstructions.

1. **Buy a harness.**

   You can get a cat harness at your local pet supply store or one especially made for a rabbit from a catalog or Internet retailer.

2. **Put the harness on the floor near your rabbit when he's hopping around.**

   Let him get used to seeing it.

3. **Place some treats around it to encourage him to get close to it.**

   This helps him to associate the harness with treats and to realize that the harness is harmless.

4. **Lay the harness gently on your rabbit's back to get him used to the feel of it.**

   You don't want to actually put it on him or buckle it at this point. The idea is to let him adjust to the weight of it on his back before you put it on him.

5. **When he seems comfortable having the harness on his body, buckle it on him and let him hop around the house under supervision.**

6. **After he seems at ease wearing the harness, snap a leash on to it and walk around the house with him.**

   If your rabbit panics when wearing the harness, go back to square one and start getting him used to it all over again. Don't leave the harness on when not using it, as the rabbit will probably chew it off.

On the walkabout

When your rabbit is comfortably walking in his harness indoors, try taking him outside. Let him explore your backyard or to a friend's house on lead, but do not walk a rabbit around the neighborhood unprotected by a fence.

After you have the leash on the harness, it's important to remember that

✔ Rabbits can't be taught to *heel* or do most of what leash-trained dogs do. Instead, your rabbit will hop around, and you'll basically follow.

✔ Be gentle with your rabbit while walking him. If you need to get from one place to another while he's on the leash, pick him up and carry him.

✔ Take care not to allow him to eat any unknown plants or walk through areas that may have been sprayed with pesticides or visited by dogs.

✔ Your pet is vulnerable when he's outside of his home. You need to keep a close watch for loose dogs who could attack your pet. (If you see a dog approaching your rabbit, pick your rabbit up and hope the dog doesn't try to snatch him out of your arms. Consider carrying pepper spray to protect your rabbit from an attacking dog.) Also, never leave your rabbit unattended or tied up because he could become tangled in his leash and might panic.

Chapter 12

Reckoning with a Bad Bunny

- -

In This Chapter

▶ Understanding your bunny's misbehavior

▶ Training your rabbit to react on command

▶ Saying "No!" to biting, chewing, and fighting

▶ Changing your little devil into an angel

- -

*N*o pet is absolutely perfect, and rabbits don't wear wings either. Despite their innocent appearance, rabbits can be terribly naughty and nasty, but that doesn't mean that your "bad" bunny has to hold you hostage.

If you realize that your rabbit doesn't think or see the world the same way you do, being patient with him is easier. Then you can work on changing his behavior. He doesn't recognize that certain objects have value or that urine smells bad to people. When your rabbit acts in a manner that you find offensive or unpleasant, he is only acting upon his rabbit instincts and learned behavior from living in household. Sometimes, rabbits "retaliate" or try to control the other creatures (including people) in the household.

Take the time to understand why your rabbit is misbehaving, have patience, and apply the knowledge you gain from this chapter. You may be surprised at how successfully you can turn your mischievous bunny into a real sweetheart.

Behaving Thy Furry Self

Not all rabbits are aggressive, but more dominant bunnies behave this way toward human companions. If your rabbit is an adolescent or hasn't been spayed or neutered, your pet may behave aggressively. You can gently show your pet that this behavior is unacceptable. (If you're not sure whether your bunny is being sweet or ornery, read Chapter 10 on rabbit body language.)

Bossy bunnies

Not all rabbits are inclined to get aggressive, but some more dominant bunnies can start behaving this way toward human companions. An adolescent bunny or a bunny that hasn't been neutered or spayed can exhibit aggressive behavior. Most bossy bunnies are either

- ✔ Adolescents finding their way in the hierarchy of the household (and trying out the dominance theme).

- ✔ Established as dominant. This can happen when they've gone unchallenged during the establishment of dominance. In other words, people stopped handling him during his adolescent testing period. Thus, the rabbit learns that he's at the top on the social heap.

You can gently show a bossy bunny that this behavior is unacceptable. (Not sure whether your bunny is being sweet or ornery? Read Chapter 10 for rabbit body language information.)

Dominance

Rabbits are programmed to establish a hierarchy in social groups, and your domestic bunny is no exception. Just as with people, some rabbits are more aggressive and pushy than others.

If you have a rabbit who nips for no apparent reason, such as when you're watching TV, making dinner (ankles are the usual target), or simply moving around in his vicinity, you probably have a dominant biter.

The object of the dominant biter is to get you to move over, get out of the way, stop whatever you're doing, or to get some food. Recognizing this and refraining from rewarding the biter by giving him what he wants is important, because rewarding him just reinforces his biting behavior.

Try these approaches to help curb rabbit nips:

- ✔ When the rabbit bites you, let out a screech. Then reach down and gently push your rabbit's head to the floor and hold it there for a couple of seconds. This is rabbit speak for "I'm the dominant one here, not you." Hopefully, your rabbit will get the message over time and stop trying to push you around.

- ✔ If you rabbit nips you for food, don't give him any. Trying screeching to discourage him, and offer him food later on when he is being nice.

- ✔ If your rabbit keeps biting you and acting obnoxious, put him gently into his cage for a time out. He may soon discover that challenging you means his freedom is restricted, and he will cease and desist.

Just say "No!"

By saying "No!" to your rabbit, you can train your rabbit to quit undesirable behaviors. Training your rabbit to respond to this verbal command is invaluable, especially if your rabbit is about to do something that could harm him. If your bunny is digging up the carpet, chewing on an electrical cord, stealing some of the cat's food, or getting into some other kind of trouble, you can say "No!" to get your pet to stop it immediately.

To train your rabbit to respond when you say "No!" to your rabbit,

1. Keep a squirt gun or spray water bottle handy when your bunny is loose in the house.

2. When you see him doing something he shouldn't, say "No!"

3. Squirt water at him immediately afterward.

   Aim for his body, not his head or face.

Rabbits don't like being squirted with water, and after going through these preceding steps a few times, he'll start to catch on that "No!" is followed by a shower. Soon enough, you'll only have to say "No!" to get your rabbit to stop whatever he's doing. You can then retire the spray bottle or squirt gun.

Biting the Hand That Feeds You — Literally

When a rabbit bites you, it hurts. Those incisors are designed to shear off pieces of tough plant material, and when they're directed at human skin, it's pretty darn painful, not to mention just plain upsetting.

Rabbit bites rarely break the skin, so you probably won't have to do much to your wound other than lament over it. If your rabbit does make you bleed, wash the area with plenty of water and soap; then check with your doctor to see if further medical attention is needed.

Rabbits usually bite because they feel a need to

- Assert dominance
- Defend their food
- Protect their bodies

If your rabbit is a biter, you first need to figure out which of these situations you're dealing with. Then you can figure out how to solve the problem.

Food aggression

In the wild, rabbits must compete with one another for food. Because bunnies live in large social groups, someone is always trying to snag the best patch of grass. The rabbit who is good at defending his food source is the one most likely to survive, especially in the wintertime when food is scarce.

If your rabbit gets nippy when you feed it, you have a rabbit with food aggression. Understanding this behavior is difficult for people because you're the one giving the rabbit the food in the first place. So why is he attacking you like you're going to take it away from him? You're the one who is providing it.

Actually, bunnies are pretty logical. From the bunny's perspective, food is present and so are you, and you may take it away if he doesn't defend it by biting your hand. Also, the fact that your hand places the food down and then moves away mimics the actions of another rabbit, who may come into close contact to investigate a food source, and then retreat.

Solving this problem can be tricky because in most cases, it's a product of your rabbit's inherent personality. However, you can try the following actions to thwart this inappropriate rabbit behavior:

- ✔ Instead of placing your rabbit's food in the same place every time you feed him, relocate his bowl to different parts of his hutch, cage, or your home. Relocating his food discourages your rabbit from viewing his food bowl as being within a specific part of his territory that needs defending.

- ✔ Help your rabbit make the connection between the presence of your hand and the giving of a food item. Do this by feeding him outside of his cage or hutch, and holding onto a food object while your rabbit eats it. Use a carrot, piece of hay, or something long at first so your hand isn't in close proximity to the bunny's teeth should he decide to nip you. After feeding him out of your hand becomes routine, and your rabbit is comfortable eating from your hand, move the procedure to the inside of his cage or hutch and continue it.

- ✔ Place food items all around your rabbit's cage or hutch so that he associates food with being all around — not just in the food bowl. If you disperse food in this way, then your rabbit can't be quite so territorial about food that's spread out.

Self-defense

Rabbits prefer to use running away as a means of self-protection, but in situations where they can't run, they resort to biting, lunging, snorting, or attacking (lashing out) with their front feet. If your rabbit bites you when you approach him or put your hand in his cage, he's most likely nipping you out of fear.

Consider taking the following actions to alleviate this problem:

- **Avoid approaching your rabbit from below eye level.** If you have a tendency to put your hand in front of your rabbit's face to make contact with him or you reach under his face to scratch his chin, this could be the problem.

- **Reach down into his cage through a top door.** If your rabbit bites you when you reach into his cage to remove him, he is reacting defensively to your approach. This usually happens if you reach in through a side door in the cage. Instead of taking this route, reach down into the cage through an opening in the top door. Your rabbit is less likely to back into a corner and force you to approach from the front if you reach down to get him.

- **Back off from mother-to-be or nursing mother.** If you have a pregnant doe or one that's nursing a litter or experiencing a false pregnancy (a condition where the rabbit's hormones make her feel like she is pregnant, when in reality she is not), you can expect some maternal aggression on her part. Your rabbit is attempting to keep you away from her nest (before giving birth) or away from her young (after birth). Either way, try to cut her a little slack. This is normal behavior and shows that your rabbit is a good mother. (See Chapter 14 for more information about rabbit moms and their kits.)

Taming Bandit

Another example of how to deal with an aggressive rabbit comes from Marinell Harriman, an experienced house rabbit caregiver. In her book "House Rabbit Handbook: How to Live with an Urban Rabbit," she tells the story of a bunny named Bandit who was so dominant and aggressive, he attacked her whenever someone entered the room. Instead of punishing him, Harriman's approach was to give Bandit a rub down, brushing (which he loved), or scratching behind his ears. Eventually, Bandit's aggressive greetings became loving ones, and he would meet people with excitement and bunny kisses.

Busting Loose: Kicking

Finding a rabbit owner who has never been kicked is hard. It sort of goes with the territory. Rabbits most often kick their owners while being held, and they do it because they're trying to escape. Remember to always provide support to your pet's hindquarters and hold him against your body to provide the greatest amount of security.

When your rabbit kicks you while you are carrying him, your pet isn't deliberately trying to hurt you. Kicking is a rabbit's way of flailing and trying to get his feet underneath him. If your rabbit is repeatedly kicking you when you are carrying him, you're not handling your pet correctly. Review Chapter 8 and work on your bunny-carrying skills.

If your rabbit doesn't kick you but seems to be scratching the heck out of your child, then you need to work with your son or daughter to help foster his or her rabbit carrying skills. Remember that young children aren't strong enough to handle most rabbits, and so only allow your young children to interact with bunnies while all the rabbit's feet are squarely on the floor.

Chowing Down

Rabbits chew on plant material that ranges from abrasive to soft. They don't chew on dead wood because it has little nutritional value. They do strip bark off young trees, however, but because it has nutritional value in the living tissue. Both outdoor and indoor pets need to have exercise and healthy materials for their teeth. In domestic situations, however, the strong urge to chew can create huge problems for both the rabbit and his owner.

If you have an indoor rabbit who is making short work of your wooden furniture legs or electrical wires, you have a problem. Fortunately, this is a common problem that's easily solved. Chapter 5 has information about rabbit-proofing, protecting your property, and supervising your pet.

Digging In

Pet rabbits love to dig. This goes back to their days as wild bunnies when they had to excavate their own homes. By digging their little hearts out, wild bunnies create their very own dens located safely underground.

But when domestic bunnies get that urge to dig, it causes problems. Their owners get angry because the digging ruins the carpet, destroys the garden, and turns the lawn into what looks like a mine field. If your bunny is a merciless digger, causing damage and destroying your house and yard, you can take some steps to eradicate the problem. Chapter 5 tells you what those steps are.

Duking It Out

Rabbits have a reputation for being gentle and peace-loving creatures; so many new rabbit owners are shocked to find out that bunnies can be real hooligans when it comes to interacting with other rabbits.

This penchant to brawl goes back to the rabbit's strong sense of territory and social hierarchy. In wild rabbit *colonies* (rabbits living together in dens), each bunny has to get along with the crowd yet also maintain his own space, territory, and place in the group. Because rabbits aren't big on conversation, much of this is done through body language. Fighting is body language taken to the extreme. (For more on rabbit body language, see Chapter 10.)

It's not okay to let your rabbits fight because it can result in serious injury or even death to one or both bunnies. In situations where rabbits are closely confined and don't get along, they can even fight to the death.

Fighting is usually a problem in households where more than one rabbit resides. In single-bunny households, fighting is sometimes a problem between rabbits and other pets. Although in most cases, the other pet backs down quickly and that's the end of it. If you have more than one rabbit, and are encountering a number of bunny battle royales, you need to take a close look at the situation to figure out what's going on:

- **Sex:** If your rabbits aren't spayed or neutered and they're fighting, then the fact that they're not spayed or neutered is could be the problem. Intact males, in particular, like to fight and may even try to castrate each other. Either have your rabbits altered or separate them. Two males that haven't been neutered will fight with each other. In many cases, females that haven't been spayed will also fight with each other, too.

- **Dominance:** Two dominant rabbits who refuse to back down to one another won't be able to live together peacefully. Keep these kinds of bunnies in separate cages and limit their exercise time together. Avoid feeding them while they're together because the presence of food can often trigger a fight.

✔ **Personality conflicts:** Rabbits who normally get along well sometimes get into fights with each other. Pay close attention to the circumstances that led up to the fight and try to eliminate the situation in the future. A favorite toy, a certain treat, or attention from a special person can start a fight between bunny friends. If necessary

- Separate the rabbits when offering special things so they won't fight over them.

- Make sure you have sufficient hide areas and litter boxes available when the rabbits are together. Have at least as many hide areas and litter boxes as you have rabbits. If space permits, one more space than the number of rabbits is preferred.

- Establish extra feeding areas on opposite sides to avoid "discussion" at feeding time.

Pee Marks the Spot

Dogs and cats aren't the only critters who can urinate around the house and make a huge mess. Rabbits can be guilty of this, too. Just like dogs and cats, rabbits use their urine to mark their territory. When a rabbit urinates on something, such as your carpet, or possibly even you, he's making a statement. In the case of an inanimate object, the statement is "This is part of my territory." If your rabbit is spraying you, he's claiming you as his mate!

You can take one significant step to eliminate the problem of inappropriate urinating: Spay or neuter your pet. The rabbits who are most guilty of this behavior are intact males, who are committing this act as a result of raging hormones. Females who haven't been spayed are also prone to the behavior of urine-marking for the same reason.

If you don't want to neuter or spay your rabbit, so you can breed him, then you have to live with the urine-marking problem or keep your bunny from running loose in the house.

Chapter 11 has information on how to clean up messes. Other factors that contribute to inappropriate urination include

✔ Not enough litter boxes. This can be the case per number of rabbits or not enough litter boxes for the space the rabbit is exercising in. If your rabbit has the run of the house, one box is not enough.

✔ Medical problems. If your rabbit was housetrained and suddenly he's urinating outside his litter box (especially if he's going in multiple places with small amounts of urine), call the vet.

✔ **Behavioral factors.** For example, rabbits object to changes in the household and their caregiver's schedule, and the introduction of new animals or people. Rabbits urinate inappropriately in response to situations that are stressful to them for whatever reason. These problems need to be addressed and are seen with some regularity.

Realize that rabbits, particularly intact males, urinate (spray) on vertical surfaces. Females can do this but usually to a lesser degree. Even if neutered, male rabbits tend to direct the urine outwards instead of downwards. They tend to urinate along a border, wall, or corner. In order to prevent inadvertent accidents in the litter box, make sure the litter box is deep enough to have a side to confine the urine and put newspaper or plastic carpet protector under litter boxes that are outside the cage to catch any urine that goes over the edge for easy cleanup.

Barbering

Do you have a rabbit who is pulling big chunks of fur from his coat? *Barbering* refers to hair pulling or hair chewing (not pulled out but chewed off). Rabbits can do this to themselves or to each other. If you see this happening, it's not because your rabbit is pulling his hair out in frustration or trying to make a rabbit fur jacket for your next birthday.

Actually, one of several things is going on:

✔ Your female is pregnant, preparing to give birth, or suffering from a false pregnancy. Pulling fur from her body to line the nest she's preparing for her kits is normal, so if she's pregnant or thinks she is, it's not something you need to worry about. Chapter 9 has more info on false pregnancies.

✔ When two or more rabbits are pulling each other's fur, it's usually a sign of boredom or dominance behavior. The behavior may not stop until they're separated or given a larger space and more things to do

✔ Someone is sick. If your female is spayed or you have a male rabbit who is pulling fur, take your rabbit to the vet. Parasites, such as fleas and mites, as well as irritating skin disorders, or internal pain can motivate a rabbit to pull out its fur. Chapter 9 offers more health information.

Shaking in His Bunny Boots: Fearfulness

Being the owner of a nervous, fearful rabbit is frustrating. Although rabbits tend to be flighty in general because of their nature as prey animals, some rabbits never seem able to relax. No matter how comfortable you make their surroundings, they seem to hop around in constant fear.

Like people, rabbits are individuals, and some individuals are more nervous than others. Factors can include

- **Breed:** For more information on what breeds tend to be nervous, read Chapter 3. Smaller rabbits tend to be more high strung than larger breeds.
- **Genetics:** Some rabbits come from genetic lines that are more fearful than others within their own breed.
- **Socialization:** Poor socialization as a youngster can make for a distracted adult.
- **Stress:** A stressful environment can put a rabbit on edge.

If you have a rabbit who has a nervous personality, think about which of these preceding factors may come into play. If it's breed or genetics, you can't do much about it except to create a calm, relaxing atmosphere for your pet. If your pet's environment is to blame for your rabbit's nervousness, the situation needs some reworking.

The following checklist can determine if you can make improvements to your rabbit's environment:

- **Good climate:** Don't expose your bunny to temperature extremes, especially heat.
- **Privacy:** Your rabbit must have a nest box where he can go when he feels the need to hide from the world.
- **Proper diet:** Give your pet access to unlimited amounts of grass hay and fresh green foods daily.
- **Proper handling:** Your pet needs to be handled in a way that helps him feel secure; lift him only when necessary.
- **Protection from other pets:** Don't allow your dog or cat to bother or terrorize your rabbit.
- **Quiet surroundings:** Don't expose your bunny to repeated loud noises and activity.

Chapter 13

Making the Pick of the Litter: Breeding Bunnies

Rabbits are known for being reproductive champions. Expressions such as "breeding like rabbits" come from the fact that rabbits breed quickly, easily, and often. If you enjoy your pet rabbit, you may be thinking about breeding him or her. This chapter helps you determine whether to take on this responsibility and gives you the tools to make an educated and responsible decision. If you decide that breeding your rabbit is the right move, this chapter also provides you with advice on how to do it right.

Taking on a Mountain of Responsibility

On the surface, breeding your rabbit may seem like an easy, fun pastime that the whole family can enjoy. The reality is that rabbit-breeding is a serious, time-consuming activity with practical and moral issues to consider before you embark.

Tackling a moral issue

Believe it or not, deciding whether to breed your rabbit is a moral decision. Why?

Population: Way too many

The first answer is simple: Thousands of rabbits are destroyed at animal shelters every year because they don't have homes. Many volunteers who work hard to find homes for abandoned rabbits don't believe that rabbits need to be bred at all for any reason. If you breed your rabbit, you contribute to the rabbit overpopulation problem. This is true even if you can find good homes for all the baby bunnies that you bred.

The homes that those babies end up in may have provided a chance in life for other homeless rabbits waiting for adoption. (See Chapter 4 on rabbit adoption and shelters.) In addition, the bunnies you breed will probably reproduce — bringing even more rabbits into the world. This is true whether you breed a female rabbit for babies, or allow your male rabbit to be used as a stud for a female.

According to House Rabbit Society statistics, within two generations, some of your rabbit's descendants will end up dead at an animal shelter. The Appendix offers House Rabbit contact information if you want to find out more.

Parents are always parents

If you decide to take on the responsibility of breeding rabbits, you're obligated to take the best possible care of your doe and the resulting babies.

And even after you place your babies in homes, you're responsible for them. Good breeders take back a rabbit they bred at any point in that rabbit's life. In other words, if the people who you sold the baby rabbit to can no longer keep the animal, it's your responsibility to take the rabbit back.

It's also your job to sell your rabbits to responsible owners. You should screen people who want to buy your babies and make sure they're prepared to give them a good home.

You can't say you gave at the office: Contributing to the breed

Some people in the world of purebred rabbits think that purebred rabbits of *high quality* (excellent examples of their breed) can be bred if the rabbit's owner is knowledgeable and responsible as a breeder — that is, the breeder is involved in the show world and knows a lot about rabbits and how to care for them.

Will your rabbit contribute to the quality of her breed? If you have a purebred doe and want to breed her, it's imperative that you

> ✔ **Get involved with the rabbit-showing world first.** Have you shown her? Has a judge told you that she's a good example of her breed and worthy of breeding? (See Chapter 17 for details on how to get involved with rabbit showing.)

> ✔ **Find out everything you can about your rabbit's breed.** (See Chapter 17 for details on how to get involved with purebred rabbits.)

> ✔ **Determine that she is healthy.** Certain health problems can be passed along genetically. *Malocclusion* (improper alignment of teeth) is one of these. (See Chapter 9 for more information on this dental problem.) Don't breed rabbits suffering from malocclusion because they're likely to pass along this terrible problem to their offspring.

> ✔ **Find out all about how to place those babies in good, responsible homes.**

Eating up your cabbage: Money

Some rabbit owners are under the impression that they can make money by breeding rabbits. This is far from the truth. If you take proper care of your rabbits, the money you spend surpasses any amount of dough that you may make selling baby bunnies: Veterinary expenses, extra food and litter, and caging all add up. This is especially true if your rabbit isn't a purebred. Mixed-breed baby rabbits are hard enough to give away, never mind sell!

Dealing with complications

Don't assume that raising a litter of bunnies is a piece of cake. It sometimes works that way but not always. Any of the following circumstances means extra work:

> ✔ Problems after the birth may lead to the mother's or the babies' deaths.

> ✔ The litter may have to be bottle-fed.

> ✔ The mother may not accept her babies, meaning she won't nurse or care for them. (See "Feeding by hand" in this chapter.)

> ✔ Does who aren't spayed face health issues. Female rabbits who have their reproductive organs intact are susceptible to a variety of illness. (See the "Fighting Female Trouble" section, later in this chapter, for more information.) They can also be less well-behaved than their spayed counterparts. (Unneutered bucks spray strong-smelling urine even outside of the cage and around the house and may be difficult to litter box train.)

TIP

Is it a boy or girl?

Before you can breed your rabbit, you need to be certain of its sex. Trying to get a litter of babies out of a male may be tricky. Another good reason to be sure of your rabbit's sex is because you'll want to keep males apart from females, even when they're babies. Rabbits as young as 4 months old are capable of reproducing. If after this test you remain unsure about the gender of your bunny, ask your veterinarian or an experienced rabbit breeder to take a look for you.

To determine your rabbit's sex

1. Gently place the rabbit on his back in your lap. (If the rabbit panics when you try this, let him rest a minute and then try it again. If he continues to resist, ask your breeder or vet to assist you.)

2. Using your thumb and forefinger, spread apart the hair on the area just beneath your rabbit's tail.

3. Push down gently in this area, and the vulva of a female or the penis of a male becomes visible. You can see the difference in the accompanying figure. The male is on the left; the female is on the right.

Mature males (over 6 months) have under the tail scrotal sacs with testicles. They can pull the testicles up into the body at times, but you can still see the wrinkled area of the sacs.

You can perform this procedure on rabbits as young as a few weeks. The older the rabbit, however, the easier it is to tell whether you're looking at male or female reproductive organs.

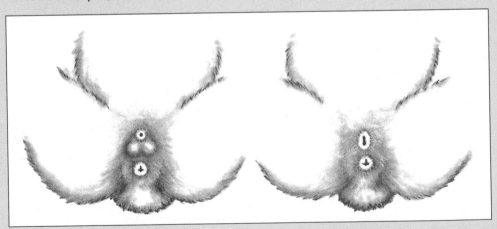

Ask yourself the following questions to help determine if you should breed your female rabbit:

- ✔ Is my rabbit an excellent example of her breed, as confirmed by a rabbit judge?

- ✔ Is my rabbit free of health problems, particularly those that can be passed along to the next generation?

✔ Am I actively involved in the purebred rabbit world? Have I studied my rabbit's breed, and feel ready to make a contribution to the breed by becoming a serious breeder?

✔ Do I have the money, patience, and dedication to raise a litter of rabbits and find good homes for them?

✔ Is my primary motivation for breeding to contribute to my rabbit's breed, and not to make money?

✔ Have I looked into the potential for homes for babies before breeding? Good breeders evaluate the market before breeding their rabbits.

If you answered yes to all these questions, then you may be ready to take on the responsibility of breeding.

Sporting a Stethoscope: You're a Rabbit Ob/Gyn

If you've already bred your rabbit or your doe became pregnant accidentally (if accidental, talk to your vet about having her spayed after she has weaned her kits), the following sections can help you care for both mother and babies in the best way possible.

Doe-ing the best you can

Taking care of your female rabbit both before and during her pregnancy is vitally important if you want to keep her healthy and produce babies that are in good physical shape.

Pre-breeding

Although rabbits can breed as young as 4 months of age, wait until your female is at least 6 months old before you put this kind of strain on her body. On the other hand, if you wait too long to breed your female, she may not be interested in mating or may not conceive. It's best not to breed does older than 5 years. Even though these older females are capable of reproducing, the demands of pregnancy and motherhood put a strain on their body that can ultimately reduce their life span.

Breeding at around 6 to 12 months of age for the first time is optimal.

This is a good time to evaluate your doe's facilities. Make sure she has a safe, comfortable cage with a spacious nesting box filled with clean litter. See Chapter 5 for more information on providing your indoor doe with housing, and Chapter 6 for details on housing if your rabbit is kept outdoors.

Afternoon delight

Unlike dogs, cats, and even people, rabbits don't have ovulation cycles that consist of short periods of time when they're fertile.

Rabbits are *induced ovulators* (they release the eggs when they're bred, not automatically during specific cycles, such as people, dogs, or cats) which means that they're actually ready to breed most of the time during the appropriate times of the year. Instead, does are willing to breed just about all the time in the winter, spring, and summer. If they're kept indoors where light is plentiful, they will breed year round. The act of breeding itself causes them to ovulate, which makes them fertile.

You can tell if a female rabbit is willing to breed if she is accepting of a male rabbit's advances. If she acts hostile toward him, she is not ready to breed; the season may be wrong for her. During this time, if they're bred, the mating causes the female to ovulate: She produces multiple eggs for fertilization.

The best way to bring the pair together is to take the doe to the buck. Take your female to the male rabbit's cage and observe the two. The male may chase the female around the cage for a bit and then mount her. If you bring the male to the female, she'll probably become territorial about her cage and give the poor guy a hard time. The likelihood of a breeding in this case is remote.

After you see the pair mate at least twice, you can put the female back in her own cage. If the male and female start fighting, separate them. They may not be a good match, personality wise, and are unlikely to mate.

Buns in the oven

How can you tell if your rabbit is pregnant? About 20 days after the mating, her abdomen becomes noticeably larger. If you don't see enlargement in this area or you just aren't sure, your veterinarian can *palpate* (feel) your doe's tummy to determine if baby rabbits are inside.

Female rabbits take 28 to 32 days to gestate, meaning that it takes about a month between when the doe is bred and when she produces her litter. During this time, feed your doe a good diet, rich in nutritious greens, timothy pellets, and fresh hay, along with an ample supply of fresh water. Chapter 7 has more detailed feeding information. Don't forget to give your mama rabbit opportunity to exercise. Give her at least two hours a day of free roaming time — even more, if possible. Chapter 15 has exercise information. A couple of days before she's scheduled to *kindle* (give birth), the doe cuts back on how much she eats.

Nesting time

About 25 days after your doe has been bred, give her a place where she can nest and kindle.

The best kindling boxes are snug and cozy four-side enclosures — only a bit bigger than the doe herself. You can buy one of these from a pet supply store specializing in rabbit products or you build one (but don't paint or stain the wood). If you build a box, make the sides about 4 inches high. Be sure no nails or sharp areas are exposed.

Place your rabbit's nesting box in her cage and fill it with straw or shredded white paper. The doe also pulls fur from areas of her body to add to the box. In nature, the female fur provides warmth for the newborn kits. (See Chapter 9 for more information about fur pulling.)

At some point during her pregnancy, your rabbit may start acting aggressively toward you. This is normal for a pregnant doe and is nothing to worry about. She'll still be a bit temperamental even after she delivers her babies, but she'll go back to normal after her stint with motherhood is over.

Kits are coming!

Your rabbit is usually ready to give birth early in the morning, probably while you sleep. Signs of impending labor include restlessness, frantic digging in the nestbox, and rearranging the nesting material. If you're lucky enough to witness the birth, be quiet and don't do anything to stress the doe. If she gets upset, she may go so far as to cannibalize her babies.

You'll see the newborn kits come out head first or feet first; either way is considered normal. Birthing usually takes a few hours to complete, although some does take as long as an entire day, or even two, to produce all the babies.

The average litter size for rabbits is seven kits. Some rabbits have as few as one baby, but others have many more than seven.

If your rabbit displays one or more of these signs, she may be experiencing a difficult birth that requires veterinary intervention. Contact your veterinarian for advice.

- Appears to be struggling to give birth and nothing is happening over a period of several hours.
- One or more kits have come out, but the rabbit continues to strain for hours with no results.
- A kit is stuck in the birth canal and won't come all the way out.
- Doe appears weak, lethargic, or unable to stand.
- Excessive bleeding from the birth canal with or without kits.

Kit-ting around

Baby rabbits are born deaf, bald, and blind (because their eyes aren't open). This makes them completely helpless and dependent on their mother right after birth.

Mom's job

Your mother bunny knows how to take care of her young instinctively, nursing and cleaning her new kits. You can help, though. Keep a close eye on the new babies, but at the same time, avoid disturbing the mother rabbit too much.

To the amazement of many, a mother rabbit won't reject her young if she smells human scent on them. So handling the babies is okay. Keep them grouped together for warmth. If any of them wander off away from the crowd, put the individual kit back with the rest of the litter. Getting involved is a good idea if this happens because the stray baby needs to stay close to his siblings in order to survive. On the other hand, don't over handle the babies or you'll stress the mother rabbit. Hold the kits only when necessary to move them back into the nest or examine them if you suspect a problem.

Keep an eye on how your mother rabbit cares for her babies. Don't be alarmed if she isn't in the kindling box with them all the time. She isn't supposed to be! Mama rabbit doesn't need to stay in the kindling box to keep the babies warm. The fur she pulled from her body before kindling helps do that, and the babies' bodies provide additional warmth for one another.

In the wild, sitting on her nest all the time would draw too much attention to her helpless young. She produces nutrient-rich milk, and the babies have stomachs large enough to hold plenty of milk for 12 hours.

Mom is going to need plenty of good food to nurse these babies, so provide her with unlimited grass hay, greens, and timothy pellets (see Chapter 7) while she's nursing. She only nurses twice a day, probably when you aren't watching, during the night.

If you're worried that the babies aren't being fed, you can weigh them each day to make sure they're getting food. Use a postage scale, which you can buy at an office supply store. Babies that are underfed will cry all the time and have sunken appearing abdomens, rather than round little bellies. They also become weaker and weaker.

Growing like a weed

Within a few days of being born, kits develop a fuzz over their bodies. Over the next couple of weeks, the rabbits' ears start to look like normal bunny ears, and their bodies grow. At 20 days, the babies start to open their eyes, usually one eye at a time. they can see, they begin exploring, wandering away from the kindling box and searching through the cage or hutch. Any noise or disturbance sends them hightailing it back to the safety of the box. As the babies get older, they spend more time outside the next box. At 2 to 3 weeks of age, they start to nibble on hay and solid food.

You won't need to clean the entire cage during this time. The mother rabbit cleans up after her babies and keeps up the nesting box. Just do daily cleaning of the mother's litter box (if she has one; see Chapters 5 and 6 for information on cleaning up after your indoor or outdoor rabbit).

Wean on me

Your mother rabbit starts to *wean* the babies at 4 weeks of age, which means she is starting to get them more used to solid food and less reliant on her milk. She nurses them less often, and the babies start to show more interest in solid food. Provide them with plenty of fresh grass hay, fresh greens, and timothy pellets while they're growing, as described in Chapter 7. After the babies have reached 6 to 10 weeks of age, you can separate them from their mother.

Going home

At 10 weeks, they're ready to go to new homes.

If you are involved with showing rabbits — as responsible rabbit breeders are — you can let your friends in the rabbit-showing world know you have a litter available. With the assistance of an experienced rabbit-showing friend, determine which babies are *show quality* (will do well in the show ring) and which are best sold as pets. You can then sell the show-quality rabbits to people who want to show (or keep them yourself for showing), and sell the other bunnies to people who want a purebred rabbit for a pet.

Your experienced rabbit friend can also help you determine the right price to charge for your breed, in your area. This varies considerably by breed and region, so have someone in the know advise you on this.

After you determine which rabbits will be sold, screen potential buyers. Ask them these questions:

- ✔ **Is it legal to keep rabbits where you live?** Make sure your buyers can keep rabbits where they live. Some areas forbid rabbit ownership.

- ✔ **Have you ever had a rabbit before?** If the answer is no, but you think the person still has good owner potential, recommend books (like this one) for a reference guide.

- ✔ **Where do you plan to keep the rabbit?** Be certain the buyer doesn't plan to keep the rabbit loose in the yard, or in a dark garage or basement.

- ✔ **Why do you want a rabbit?** Make sure the buyer isn't looking for a rabbit to eat or to irresponsibly breed.

Run free, wee bunny!

I'll never forget the time that I rescued a wild baby bunny from the jaws of a barn cat at the stable where I ride. The bunny was tiny — maybe 6 inches long — and seemed incredibly helpless to me. His ear was sliced, and he was bleeding, so I took the baby to a local vet who specialized in wildlife care. After gluing the baby's ear back together, the vet gave the baby back to me. "What do I do with him?" I asked. I expected to be told to bottle feed him and take care of him until he was fully grown. "Just turn him loose near where you found him," the vet said. "He's old enough to take care of himself." This experience taught me that although wild baby bunnies may appear tiny and helpless, unless they're newborn, they're able to fend for themselves in the wild.

If you come across a baby bunny whose eyes are open, has fur on his body, and is hopping around on his own, he's probably fine and better if left alone. Wild cottontails are weaned at 3 weeks of age and can fend for themselves early on.

If you find a nest of newborn baby bunnies, leave it alone. The mother is probably somewhere nearby. If you aren't sure, you can check on the newborns for the next couple of days, being careful not to disturb them or loiter around enough that you scare away the mother. If the babies are crying constantly or are developing sunken-in stomachs, they're probably orphaned. The best approach in this situation is to find a qualified wildlife rehabilitator in your area and turn the bunnies over to the rehabilitator. (Call your vet or local animal shelter for a referral.) *Hand-raising* (nursing a baby animal with a bottle) wild rabbits is difficult, and an experienced rehabilitator is the only person for the job.

Paying Attention to Potential Problems

Unfortunately, several matters can go wrong shortly after kindling. Being prepared for any difficulty that may arise can help you cope with these situations.

Inexperienced mother rabbits are usually the ones that have the most problems with their new responsibilities, so if your rabbit has never been bred, keep an eye out for trouble.

The stomachs of baby rabbits who are doing well are obviously full. Healthy kits move around and show obvious growth and development. However, if you see that your kits exhibit any of the following, contact your veterinarian immediately:

- Blue coloration
- Brown urine
- Cold to the touch

- Diarrhea
- Discharge from nose
- Excessive crying
- Eyes stuck shut after ten days or showing discharge
- Lack of movement
- Sunken abdomen

Scattered litter

Sometimes, a mother rabbit is confused about what to do after she gives birth to her first litter of kits. Their reaction to this confusion is to kick the contents of the kindling box all over the cage — including the newborn rabbits inside. She also acts disinterested in the babies and won't nurse them or take care of them.

If your mother rabbit scatters her litter, you need to intervene. Otherwise, the babies will die from lack of warmth and starvation.

1. Pick up the scattered babies and warm them up in your hand until they start to move around.

2. Place them back in the kindling box, along with the mother's pulled fur and straw bedding.

3. Take the mother rabbit out of the cage and keep her separated from the babies for about an hour.

4. Wait until the babies seem warm and comfortable before you put the mother back in the cage.

5. Keep a close eye on her; she may do it again.

   If she does, you'll have to remove her from the cage and hand raise the babies as you would orphans. (See "Naming them Annie: Orphaned kits" for help with this.)

Cannibalism

One of the worst things a mother rabbit can do, from a human standpoint, is eating her young. As a child in 4-H, I bred my Florida White, Doey, and experienced firsthand the tragedy of a cannibalized litter — a breeder's worst nightmare. It's an awful thing to expect to find a litter of kits in the morning and instead see just your doe looking at you as if she had never been pregnant in the first place.

If your rabbit is obviously pregnant one day and not the next, with no sign of any baby rabbits, your doe probably cannibalized her litter. Mother rabbits commit this deed for one of three reasons:

- Genetically prone to the behavior.
- Have a poor diet.
- Severely stressed.

You need to examine your doe's particular situation to determine which of these scenarios seems to be the cause.

Rabbits have a good evolutionary reason for cannibalizing their young. If the rabbit feels threatened, then she can't take the chance of being killed or endangering the whole group by having babies who attract attention or babies who take her strength raising them. In addition, if enough food isn't available, like several other species of animals that live in groups, the lower level in the society of females destroys their litters so that the group can survive.

Another possibility is that the rabbit aborted her litter early and ate it, or that her body *reabsorbed* them (they disappeared within your rabbit's uterus before being born). These are all situations that can occur in pregnant rabbits, and can be caused by any number of reasons. Consult your veterinarian if you suspect these conditions in your rabbit.

Stress

Stress can create problems for both humans and rabbits, and does who are pregnant and perpetually upset can be driven to eat their young as soon as the kits are born.

To determine if this is the reason your doe has taken to destroying her babies, examine her lifestyle.

- Is she getting enough exercise?
- Does she have privacy and a secure nest box where she can raise her babies?
- Is her environment quiet and comfortable?
- Is she being properly and infrequently handled?

If you answer "no" any of these questions, stress could be your doe's problem.

If you think your rabbit cannibalized her litter because of stress, change the situation that caused her stress and wait several months before breeding her again. If she cannibalizes her litter a second time, it's time to give up.

Genetics

If your doe's diet seems adequate and stress is not a factor, you can assume her propensity to eat her young is genetic. This behavior appears to run in families, and rabbits can pass this behavior down through the generations.

Rabbits who eat their young for genetic reasons will never make good mothers. Rabbits who have exhibited this behavior in the past should not be bred.

Naming them Annie: Orphaned kits

In the event that your doe dies after giving birth or rejects the babies, you must hand-feed them, keep them warm, and clean up after them. In essence, you're the mother rabbit's replacement.

First off, be aware that hand-raising orphaned rabbits isn't easy. Even those most skilled in this practice lose babies all the time.

Warming babies

If you decide to tackle this, keep the babies in the kindling box, preferably with some of the mother rabbit's fur to keep them warm. If you don't have any of her fur, you can snip some from another, healthy rabbit. Use cotton rags or tissue in a pinch.

Litters of three or more babies means that each baby can probably warm the other in the kindling box. However, if you only have one or two babies, you need to provide heat. Keep the temperature in the room where the babies are kept around 70 degrees Fahrenheit. If you can't keep the room that warm, you can place a heating pad set on low on one side of the nest box.

Be careful not to put the pad directly under the entire box because it will get too hot and harm the babies.

Feeding by hand

The hardest aspect to raising orphaned kits is feeding them. Hand-feeding can be done in three ways:

- **Bottle:** Tiny plastic bottles designed for feeding baby animals can be purchased at pet supply stores. For the inexperienced, bottle-feeding is the safest. With this method, the formula is less likely to end up in the baby rabbit's lungs.

- **Syringe:** Without the needle.

✔ **Tube-feeding:** Inserting a feeding tube into the esophagus. (This should only be done a veterinarian or veterinary technician; the tube could be inserted into the windpipe by mistake if done by someone else.

You can buy bottles, usually designed for puppies and kittens, at a pet supply store. Make sure the hole in the nipple permits a fine spray of milk to come out when you squeeze it. If drops (big or tiny) come out, the hole isn't the right size. If you opt to use the syringe, you can get a few from your veterinarian as well as instructions on how to use them

Baby bunnies do well on *kitten milk replacer* (a canned commercial formula designed to replace mother cat's milk), which you can also buy at pet supply stores. They can also be fed with goat's milk. Both should be given at room temperature. Feed the babies twice a day — once in the morning and once in the evening. Table 13-1 gives the feeding amounts for all ages. If the babies you're feeding are of a small breed, you can give them a bit less than this. If they're a giant breed, they need more.

Table 13-1	How much milk per feeding?
Age	*How much?*
Newborn to 1 week	2 ml
1–2 weeks	5–7 ml
2–3 weeks	7–13 ml
3–6 weeks	13–15 ml

You can tell if your babies aren't getting enough to eat because they cry and their abdomens appear sunken rather then round.

When the kits eyes open, you can start offering them solid food, such as hay and greens, in addition to their milk feedings. They'll probably nibble at it. Don't expect them to be entirely on solid food until they reach about 6 weeks of age.

If you are having any trouble feeding your baby rabbits, contact a veterinarian right away. The vet can help provide you with tips on feeding and can show you the proper way to do it if you are unsure.

Cleaning up

One of the mother rabbit's jobs is to clean her babies' bottoms. This helps keep the nest box sanitary and also stimulates the babies to go to the bathroom. Because you're functioning as a substitute mother rabbit, this task is now yours!

Using clean cotton balls moistened with warm water, wash the babies' bottoms after every feeding. Keep stroking until you see urine and/or stool being passed. You can also wash their faces with a clean, moistened cotton ball after eating because they'll probably have formula around their mouths. Avoid getting the babies too wet during this process because a wet baby can develop hypothermia quickly and go into shock.

As for the nest box itself, be diligent about keeping it clean. Remove soiled bedding several times a day to prevent harmful bacteria from building up around the babies. (Keep the babies in a traveling crate while you are cleaning up the nesting box.)

Offering body heat: Chilled kits

Baby rabbits need to stay warm to survive. If a kit wanders away from his siblings, gets wet, or if the entire litter is subjected to cold temperature, you have *chilled kits* on your hands — literally!

The best way to warm up a chilled kit is to cup the baby in both your hands, using your own body warmth to heat him up. After the little one starts to move around, he's warming up. You can then place him with the other kits, assuming they've all been warmed up, too.

If the kit doesn't respond to the warmth of your hand, the baby may be too far gone. You can rush the baby to an emergency veterinary facility to see if they can help the kit, taking care to keep the baby warm during the car trip. However, be aware that newborn baby rabbits are delicate creatures, and after their body temperature drops dangerously low, bringing them back is difficult.

If your entire litter is chilled, the room temperature they've been exposed to is much too low. Don't let the temperature drop below 65 degrees Fahrenheit at night. If you can't keep the room warmer than this, use a heating pad. Place the pad on one side of the nesting box and put it on a low setting.

Make sure the babies can crawl away from the pad if they find that they're getting too hot. Excessive heat is just as dangerous as the cold to baby rabbits.

Fighting Female Trouble

Unspayed female rabbits can develop a variety of problems. The ailments listed here can happen before, during or after a pregnancy and some occur even if you never breed your rabbit. Knowing how to recognize these problems increases your doe's chances of survival. Chapter 9 gives good information about choosing a vet.

Keep in mind that spaying your doe eliminates the possibility of all these conditions developing in your rabbit.

Mammary gland disorders

Nursing mother rabbits are prone to a number of problems that affect the *mammary glands,* or breast tissue. Each requires help from a veterinarian. Rabbits have four pairs of mammary glands, making eight nipples available to the babies. Disease can strike one or more of these glands.

The mammary glands may become swollen and painful and the doe will refuse to nurse the kits. If the glands appear to be a normal color and normal in temperature with no nipple discharge, then she's likely suffering from an overabundance of milk. She should still be eating and acting otherwise normal. In this case, apply a warm compress to her abdomen and reduce the amount of food you feed her for 24 to 48 hours.

If the swollen glands are discolored (red or blue), hot to the touch, or if there is any discharge from the nipples, then your doe is suffering from a more serious condition called mastitis. *Mastitis* is an inflammation or infection of the breast tissue and can be caused by trauma due to abrasive bedding or rough edges on the nest box opening. It can also be caused by bacteria entering the breast tissue from a dirty cage.

Mastitis is a serious and potentially fatal condition and your doe should be seen by a veterinarian as soon as possible. In addition, the kits may become ill if they nurse from infected mammary glands. Remove them and hand feed until the situation is resolved.

Does with mastitis are put on antibiotics. The kits aren't allowed to nurse while she is being medicated because some medications may be dangerous for the kits to ingest. In addition, mastitis is a painful condition and nursing only adds to the discomfort. Warm compresses can be used to soothe the inflamed tissue. If the condition is advanced, surgical removal of the affected breast tissue may be the only treatment that can save the doe.

If left untreated, mastitis can result in

- Depression
- Loss of appetite
- Swollen and painful nipples

- Discolored breast tissue
- Death of the doe and kits

Pregnancy toxemia

Pregnancy toxemia occurs in the last few days of pregnancy or the first days after giving birth. This is a metabolic disease that results in a type of poisoning of the rabbit's system. It usually strikes obese rabbits, so an obvious prevention is to feed your rabbit a healthy diet before and during pregnancy.

The disease also can be brought on when the doe doesn't take in sufficient amounts of calories in the late stages of her pregnancy or when there are extreme environmental stresses during this same period.

Does with pregnancy toxemia can develop

- Depression
- Loss of appetite
- Weakness
- Seizures
- Rapid or difficult breathing
- Incoordination (clumsiness)
- Coma and death

If you see any of these signs in your rabbit, this is an emergency situation. Seek veterinary attention immediately. Pregnancy toxemia is a difficult condition to treat, and the prognosis is grave.

Taking some preventive measures to ward off the development of the condition in the first place is much easier:

- Don't allow your rabbit to become obese.
- Feed your rabbit a healthy diet *before* and during the pregnancy.
- Avoid excessive stress during pregnancy.

Endometritis and pyometra

Endometritis is an inflammatory disease of the lining of the uterus, and *pyometra* is an accumulation of pus in the uterus accompanying the inflammation. This condition can occur in both does that have never been bred and breeding does. With mild disease there may be few signs other than an inability to breed. However, as the disease progresses, she may develop

- ✔ A distended abdomen
- ✔ Loss of appetite
- ✔ Weakness
- ✔ White, smelly vulvar discharge

Take your rabbit to a veterinarian immediately if you notice this problem. It's difficult to treat this condition medically. Surgical removal of the uterus and ovaries is usually performed to save the doe's life.

Uterine adenocarcinoma

Uterine adenocarcinoma is a form of cancer of the uterus and is the most common cancer seen in female rabbits. Although it's a slow-growing tumor, if left untreated it can *metastasize,* or spread, through the body attacking the lungs, liver, bones, skin, and other organs. Eventually it can result in death.

Uterine adenocarcinoma is seen most often in aging does, particularly those over 2 years of age, regardless of whether they've ever been bred. Early in the disease there are very few outward signs. As the disease progresses, however, you may see the following develop:

- ✔ Blood at the end of urination
- ✔ Infertility
- ✔ Loss of appetite
- ✔ Difficulty breathing
- ✔ Weakness

A key sign of uterine disease is blood within the urine pool. In this case blood collects in the vaginal area and when she urinates, the collected blood is expressed at the end. This leads to a distinct puddle or spot of blood within the pool of urine, rather than being mixed completely with the urine. This is most often visible on a sheet of smooth bedding or on the floor. If you see this, you need to have your doe examined by a veterinarian as soon as possible.

If you have an intact female rabbit, have her examined at least annually by your veterinarian. Early disease of the uterus can be found when the vet *palpates* (feels for) abnormalities in the abdomen. Further diagnosis is done with an X-ray of the abdomen. If cancer of the uterus is detected, your veterinarian will X-ray your bunny's chest to make sure the disease hasn't spread to the lungs.

If the cancer has not spread to other areas of the body, treatment is the complete removal of the uterus and ovaries. If the cancer has spread extensively, it's best to consider euthanasia before the disease becomes painful and debilitating. (Chapter 14 can help you deal with this decision.) If you're not going to breed your rabbit, avoid this common disease by spaying her before her second birthday.

Uterine aneurysm

Uterine aneurysm is a noninfectious disease that results from the rupture of one or more large veins in the uterus. These veins can rupture, heal, and rupture several times. The blood loss may be gradual or sudden. What causes this condition in the rabbit is unknown. The signs can mimic uterine cancer with blood being passed at the end of urination. If the blood loss is excessive, the results can be fatal. The treatment for this disorder is the removal of the uterus and ovaries. Surgery can be successful if the rabbit hasn't lost excessive amounts of blood. However, the best prevention is spaying your rabbit before it develops this disorder as mentioned under *uterine adenocarcinoma*.

Bunny genetics

So you want to breed bunnies? Then you need a basic lesson in bunny genetics. Knowledge of how rabbit genes work can help you make the best decision about which doe to put with which buck.

If you think back to high school biology, you'll remember cells and DNA and all that stuff. Well, rabbit cells contain 22 pairs of chromosomes. The DNA in each of these chromosomes holds the information that determines what the rabbit looks like. When two rabbits are bred, each bunny contributes a half copy of DNA strands. In other words, the doe contributes 11 pairs of chromosomes, and the buck gives 11. Each of these pairs contains the respective DNA of the contributing rabbit. As a breeder, you're hoping that the best traits of the doe and the best traits of the buck were passed along in those 11 chromosomes.

Of course, you can't know what's going to happen for sure with all that DNA until after the baby bunnies are born. This is what makes animal breeding such a gamble. Many people see it as an art and a science as well, since nature can be unpredictable in what she doles out as far as DNA is concerned. Remember that not only are breed and personality characteristics passed along when rabbits are bred to each other, but also recessive genes that can cause genetic problems. For example, *malocclusion*, improper teeth alignment, can be a genetic problem passed from one rabbit to another.

If your doe or your buck has an undesirable physical trait or health problem, chances are that this trait will be passed along to its offspring. Responsible breeders decline to breed a rabbit in this situation for the betterment of the breed.

Chapter 14

Saying Goodbye

· ·

In This Chapter

▶ Making the decision to euthanize

▶ Burying your pet in a pet cemetery

▶ Having a good cry is healthy

▶ Bringing home a new bundle of fur

· ·

The hardest part of having a rabbit in your life is saying goodbye when your pet's final moment comes. Rabbits have a way of hopping into your heart and then you feel a tremendous sense of loss when you no longer have your bunny to hug and hold.

When your rabbit is ready to pass on, you may suddenly have to make an incredibly difficult decision. Whether to keep your rabbit alive or euthanize your pet to spare her more suffering is one of the hardest decisions you will ever have to make. Whether their death is untimely or the result of old age, letting go of your rabbit so you can go on to love again in their memory is important.

Letting Go: Euthanasia

If you're lucky, your beloved rabbit will live to a ripe old age and won't leave until it's truly her time to go. However, illness or injury may take a rabbit away from her human companions prematurely. If your rabbit is ill and struggling with illness and/or incapacity, you may be forced to consider euthanizing your rabbit. If so, then consider the following:

✔ Find out more about what euthanasia is and what it involves.

✔ Consider your rabbit's quality of life.

✔ Talk with your vet.

Hearing about the humane option

Understanding exactly what euthanasia is can help you decide whether to take this route with your pet. Basically, *euthanasia* is the humane process of taking an animal's life. Veterinarians use a *barbiturate* (a drug that depresses the nervous system), which they inject in large quantities into a rabbit's bloodstream. The drug ceases brain function almost immediately; thus the rabbit loses consciousness, stops breathing, and her heartbeat ceases.

If you ever had a dog or cat euthanized, it may be helpful to know that the process is somewhat different for rabbits. For dogs and cats, a *catheter* (a needle that can be attached to a tube or syringe) is usually placed in the animal's vein while the dog or cat is still awake. The euthanasia solution is then administered. For rabbits and other small exotic pets, the catheter can't be placed unless the animal is heavily sedated. In rabbits that are sick or small, it can be difficult to place the catheter at all.

For this reason, veterinarians opt to sedate the rabbit first with a small injection in the muscle or with an *inhalant anesthesia* (an inhaled gas that sedates the rabbit). When the pet is no longer conscious, the euthanasia solution is administered via another injection. If the animal is sick or small, injecting the solution into the vein may not be possible. In these cases, the injection may have to be given directly into the heart or abdomen.

Although the thought of this can be upsetting, remember that the rabbit is already sedated and therefore can't feel anything. The rabbit isn't even aware of the injection. Rabbits feel no pain during the euthanasia process. From what scientists now know, rabbits don't experience fear when they're slipping away either, but instead, just a quiet sense of falling into a deep sleep.

If you find yourself in the position of asking a veterinarian to euthanize your rabbit, you can ask for sedation if the vet doesn't normally provide it. The sedative reduces any fear that your rabbit may have of being handled by the veterinarian and will result in a more peaceful euthanizing process.

House calls

Some people prefer the option of having their pet euthanized at home, particularly if it is difficult for them or their pet to travel. Check with your veterinarian to see if he offers an at-home euthanasia service or call a veterinarian who specializes in house-call service.

Considering her quality of life

If you find yourself struggling with this difficult decision, remember that euthanasia can be a great gift to a rabbit who is suffering and beyond help. Without you to make the decision to let your rabbit go painlessly, your rabbit would suffer needlessly.

Think about your rabbit's quality of life and whether it is fair to keep her alive in her condition. Do you think that she would welcome a peaceful, quiet death? Getting advice from your veterinarian can make this difficult decision a bit easier.

Consider the following questions to help determine your rabbit's quality of life:

- ✔ Is she able to move around comfortably?
- ✔ Does she still enjoy eating?
- ✔ Can she comfortably relieve herself?
- ✔ Does she respond to you when you try to interact with her or does she seem tired or withdrawn?
- ✔ Can she still take part in the activities that she enjoys?
- ✔ Does she experience more pleasure than pain in her life?

If your answer is no to a number of these questions, you have to come to terms with the fact that your bunny's quality of life isn't what it used to be.

Making the decision to euthanize a pet is extremely difficult. After you do, you'll probably experience all kinds of unpleasant emotions and plenty of doubt, too. You can read more about emotions and how to deal with them in the "Grieving is Good for You" section of this chapter. Most people aren't often in the position of making life and death decisions and having to decide to have their rabbit euthanized.

Asking a pro

When it comes to making a decision about whether to put down your ailing rabbit, your veterinarian is a valuable resource. She can give you a good idea of how much pain your rabbit is experiencing and what the likelihood of curing or managing your rabbit's condition may be. After hearing your vet's opinion, you're then able to make an educated decision about how to handle your pet's future.

TIP

Should you stay?

When you make the decision to euthanize your rabbit (whether you take him to the vet or the vet comes to your home), your vet may ask you if you'd like to stay with your pet during the process. Choosing whether to be with your pet in her final hour is a personal decision, and one that only you can make. If your rabbit is sedated (which is highly recommended), your bunny won't even know that you're present. However, being at your pet's side at his final moment may provide you with comfort.

However, if you feel that you can't handle being present when your rabbit dies, you aren't obligated to stay nor do you need to feel guilty about leaving the room. Remembering to take care of your own feelings is important when you're in this situation. Do what feels right for you.

If you're uncertain about the medical aspects of the decision, getting a second opinion from another veterinarian is also helpful. You can get a second opinion from a vet in the same practice or in another clinic.

REMEMBER

The decision is ultimately yours; do whatever makes you the most comfortable in the long run. Don't let anyone push you into a decision that you don't feel right about or that you aren't ready to make. Take a few days to think it over before you decide. Don't feel that you have to make a rush to judgment. If your pet is uncomfortable, ask your vet for suggestions on how to make her more comfortable, including using pain medication.

In the event that your decision needs to be made immediately, take a few minutes to sit by yourself and think about the situation or talk to a supportive loved one or friend. Feeling right about your decision is important, even if it has to be made sooner than you'd like.

Finding a Place of Rest

TIP

Everyone has different feelings about how to handle the remains of their beloved rabbit. Planning what you'll do with your pet's remains well in advance is a good idea, so you don't have to make this sometimes difficult decision when you're feeling badly about just having lost your pet.

You have several options when it comes to dealing with your bunny's remains:

✔ **Individual burial.** You probably heard of pet cemeteries and may have even seen one as you're driving. For a fee of several hundred dollars, your bunny may be interred at a pet cemetery. A headstone or grave marker is usually included in the fee. By giving your pet a marked grave, you can visit your bunny whenever you like.

✔ **Communal burial.** Most pet cemeteries provide the option of a communal burial, which is more affordable. With this method, your rabbit is interred with other pets (sometimes cremated) at the pet cemetery in an unmarked grave.

✔ **Individual cremation.** Some rabbit owners choose the option of individual cremation. Then they place their bunny's cremated remains in a container for burial or in an urn that they keep at home. Keeping your pet's ashes at home is less expensive than a burial.

✔ **Group cremation.** For a lesser fee, your rabbit may be cremated with other deceased pets and buried in a communal grave at the cemetery.

✔ **Disposal by a veterinarian.** All vets offer to dispose of your pet's body after euthanasia. Depending on the clinic, group cremation or other means of disposal are used.

✔ **Burial at home.** If your county or municipality allows it, you can bury your rabbit at home on your property. Consult your local zoning laws before you take this route to make sure that burying your pet on your own property is legal where you live.

Grieving Is Good for You

People who haven't loved and lost a rabbit are often shocked at how devastated they feel when their bunny dies. They hadn't imagined they could feel such grief over an animal. Many people who have lost pets say that the level of their sadness matches feelings they had when they lost a family member or loved one. The intense grief that someone may feel at the loss of a pet doesn't diminish the value of the beloved family member but instead makes a rabbit owner realize just how much attachment she had for her rabbit.

Your thinking processes won't be rational while you're grieving the loss of your pet. If you had your rabbit euthanized, you may feel as if you did something terrible; if she died naturally, you may feel as if you *let* her go. All those who grieve go through stages.

All of grief is a stage

When you lose someone you love, whether you lose a loved one or a pet, you experience a number of emotions. Grieving is a process with several distinct stages:

- ✔ **Denial:** "I can't believe it."
- ✔ **Bargaining:** "If I had only done this or that, she'd have lived."
- ✔ **Anger:** "This is so unfair!"
- ✔ **Depression:** "I'm never going to have a pet again. No more pets."
- ✔ **Acceptance:** "I did the right thing. It was her time to go, and I loved my rabbit while she was here."

These feelings can come in any order, at any time, and can often repeat themselves in a period of an hour, a day, or a week. You may also feel other sentiments. The grieving process is unique to each person and there is no "right" way to grieve. It's important to

- ✔ Understand that these emotions and more are part of the normal grieving process.
- ✔ Be aware of why you're feeling these things.
- ✔ Talk to someone who's sympathetic. The Appendix in this book has grief resources.
- ✔ Know that in time, if you allow yourself to go through this process, the intensity of the emotions and pain lessen and you'll enjoy life again. Avoiding and ignoring your feelings won't stop the process, but only delay it and make it more difficult to recover.

Finding support

Sometimes, finding a sympathetic ear when you're grieving the loss of your pet is difficult. People who don't care much for rabbits or who never had a pet tell you to just "Get over it," or "Go buy a new one," or ask you "What's the big deal?"

At this time of grieving, try surrounding yourself with other like-minded people who understand what you're going through. Limit your discussions of sadness over your pet's loss to friends and family members who can relate to what you're feeling. Keep in mind that everyone grieves differently. Don't expect members of your family to act and feel the same way that you do over your rabbit's death.

If you can't find anyone sympathetic to talk to, help is available. Over the past several years, a number of veterinary schools have set up grief counseling hotlines for rabbit lovers and other pet owners who have lost a beloved animal. See the Appendix for a listing of these hotlines. Make use of these services and contact other rabbit owner groups. They'll help you work through the grieving process and help you recover from your loss. Local pet loss support groups meet regularly in many areas. Your veterinarian can provide information on local groups.

In Memory of Fluffy

One way of feeling better after losing a beloved rabbit is to honor your pet's memory. You can do this in any number of ways, such as those that follow.

✔ **Make a donation.** One of the nicest ways to honor your rabbit's memory is to make a donation to a rabbit rescue group. You don't have to make a huge donation. An organization that works hard to provide homes to unwanted bunnies will appreciate the $5 or $10 that you sent. Contact your veterinarian, local animal shelter, or House Rabbit Society (see the Appendix for contact info) to locate a rabbit rescue group in your area. Be sure to include a note with your check, stating that the donation is in honor of your rabbit's memory.

✔ **Discuss your rabbit.** A number of Web sites are set up to help grieving pet owners talk about their feelings and honor their pet's memories with poems, essays, and photos. See the Appendix and Chapter 19.

✔ **Create something.** Writing your feelings about your rabbit on paper can help you work through the grief while also honoring your rabbit's memory. You don't have to show your words to anyone. They can be just for you and your rabbit, or you can choose to share them with other rabbit owners on the Internet or through a rabbit club. If you're artistic in some way, you may find it more comfortable to express your feelings through drawing, painting, sculpting, or through another type of art. Perhaps you'd like to paint a portrait of your deceased pet from a photograph. Consider making a photo album for your pet, too. A great way to honor your rabbit's memory, making a photo album is a helpful way to cope during the grieving process.

✔ **Volunteer.** Rabbit rescue organizations need plenty of help. Consider donating your time, energy, or special services to one of these groups in your pet's honor. (See the Appendix for more information on volunteer rabbit groups.)

✔ **Adopt a bunny.** It may sound a bit strange at first, and it's certainly not for everyone, but a wonderful way to honor your rabbit's memory is to provide a home for a bunny in desperate need of love. Knowing that your rabbit's passing provided an opportunity for a rabbit who really needed a home can help you overcome your grief, putting your rabbit's life in a truly positive light.

Bonding with a New Bunny

Just after losing your rabbit, the last thing you want to do is get another. The pain is too strong. You need time to heal.

After going through the initial loss, some people find that opening their home to a new rabbit can help with healing. Doing so is scary because it feels like you're setting yourself up for more pain in the future. However, if you are ready for this step, providing a good home to a rabbit in need can return your thoughts to the joys of rabbit companionship again. The affection that you shared with your first rabbit was so wonderful, that you're anxious to feel that warmth again — this time with your new bunny.

If you feel like getting a new bunny, consider it. If not, don't feel obligated or pressured to get another rabbit or any other pet. The decision is purely yours. Your new rabbit won't be a replacement of your old pet but a new companion to enjoy. For some people, giving a home to a rabbit in need is a wonderful way to honor their deceased pet.

Part IV
Enjoying Your Fun Bunny

The 5th Wave   By Rich Tennant

"Oh see, now that was what I was afraid of. We didn't give him enough toys to play with so he started making his own mischief. Morris! Come and see what bunny made in the broom closet!"

In this part . . .

This part exposes all the fun stuff you can do with your rabbit: play, enjoy watching him romp around on his own, and make toys for him. You also discover the safest way to travel with your rabbit. A close-up look at rabbit shows and the new sport of rabbit hopping help you get even more involved with your pet, while discussions of rabbit rescue and organizations give you ideas for volunteer jobs.

Chapter 15

Playing Around

In This Chapter

▶ Choosing the best toys

▶ Playing interactive games

▶ Watching rabbits have fun

Whoever coined the phrase, "Jump for joy," must've had rabbits in mind. Bunnies love to run, jump, and play probably as much or more than any other creature. Seeing a rabbit play is one of the most delightful scenes to watch.

Play is a natural behavior for rabbits, even in the wild. When a rabbit plays, he cavorts, running, leaping and batting around inanimate objects. The amount of play any rabbit engages in depends on his personality (some are more playful than others) and the opportunities he has for playing.

As a rabbit owner, you have a couple of options when it comes to appreciating your rabbit's propensity for play (and helping him get the required daily exercise he needs). You can choose to share in your rabbit's playful moments by providing toys for your pet (some interactive), or you can sit back and delight in the rabbit's goofiness.

Toying Around

It comes as a surprise to many people that rabbits love to play with toys. People typically think of cats and dogs as being the only critters who like to bat a ball around or carry something in their mouths, but rabbits are right up there with animals who like to amuse themselves with a variety of inanimate objects.

Some common toys for rabbits include household items like empty toilet paper rolls, cardboard boxes, and plastic cups. Store-bought toys often enjoyed include items commonly sold for cats: small balls, catnip mice (rabbits don't get turned on by catnip, but they like the shape of the toy), and string-equipped toys you can drag around.

Of course not every rabbit likes every toy. Rabbits are individuals, and while one toy may make one rabbit crazy, the same toy can bore another. Trial and error is key to discovering what your rabbit likes to play with. Donate the toys he doesn't like to an animal shelter or swap them with your rabbit-owning friends.

In the case of rabbits, toys are a great way to

- ✔ **Help your rabbit focus his energies.** House rabbits deprived of toys play with furniture, electrical cords, and other interesting items. (Although if you read Chapter 5, you know how to help prevent these catastrophes from occurring.) By providing your rabbit with suitable toys to play with, you help him to be a good, nondestructive member of the household.

- ✔ **Encourage regular exercise and prevent boredom.** By providing your rabbit with a toy and space to play, you give him the opportunity to remain physically active and mentally alert. And of course, exercise means a healthier rabbit, who's less likely to develop health problems, such as obesity, weak bones and muscles, and digestive maladies (which you can read more about in Chapter 9).

- ✔ **Bond with your bunny.** While using toys to play with and even interact with your bunny, you enrich the relationship between you and your bunny and build trust in the heart of your rabbit. (Another great way to bond is through grooming, which is discussed in Chapter 8.)

Whether you give your rabbit toys that are homemade, commercially made, or a combination of the two, safety is important. The list that follows tells you what to look out for:

- ✔ **Rabbits like to chew on just about everything.** Be certain that all products that you give your rabbit are nontoxic.

- ✔ **If you see your bunny chomping on a toy that's not meant to be chewed — a towel, rubber ball, a shoe, or stuffed sock — take the toy away.** Otherwise, your rabbit is likely to swallow some of the material and end up with a gastrointestinal (GI) blockage. Chapter 12 has more information about how to reckon with an ornery rabbit.

- ✔ **Keep an eye out for toys with small parts that can be pulled or fall off and be easily swallowed.** Look out for string, plastic eyes, and other toy parts that can end up in your rabbit's stomach, causing a blockage.

Going prefab

If you like shopping for your rabbit, then you'll enjoy going to the pet supply store and buying toys for your pet.

See the following list of commercially made toys that rabbits often like:

- Assorted toys and bells made for parrots
- Hard plastic toys made for human babies
- *Sisal* (a type of rope) toys made for rabbits
- Small cat or dog houses made of cloth that look like tents
- Small plastic or wire balls with bells inside made for cats
- Straw or bamboo balls made for hamsters
- Stuffed socks made for cats
- Unfinished (no stain or lacquer applied) wicker, straw, or woven grass baskets of all sizes
- Unfinished wicker tunnels for rabbits
- Wooden chew toys made for rabbits or rodents

You can also search the Internet for rabbit toy manufacturers. See the Appendix for a list of online rabbit supply retailers.

Made from scratch

If your budget is tight, go the homemade route with your rabbit. Or if you're like most rabbit owners, you may want to combine homemade rabbit toys with store-bought items. (Keep in mind that rabbits can sometimes be destructive with their toys. Don't share anything with bunny that you don't want teeth marks in!)

Check out this listing of homemade toys that rabbits enjoy:

- Box of shredded white paper
- Cardboard box of any size (Make sure all staples, tape, and other non-cardboard items are off the box before the rabbit gets ahold of it.)
- Cardboard toilet paper and paper towel rolls
- Dried pine cones (Make sure they're *untreated*. Some pine cones are sold painted or varnished.)
- Large PVC pipes for tunnels or large cardboard tubes
- Newspapers
- Oatmeal boxes with the ends cut off
- Old phone book
- Paper cups (without coating and no Styrofoam)

- ✔ Paper grocery bags
- ✔ Metal rings from canning jars
- ✔ Soda can with a pebble inside (Be careful about any sharp edges.)
- ✔ Straw baskets
- ✔ Straw whisk broom
- ✔ Tree branches for your rabbit to gnaw on and drag around (fresh or dried — *not* fruit or elderberry)

Reindeer games aren't nearly as fun

You can get interactive with your pet and make it a game for two. Rabbits have been known to initiate games of tag with humans, to bat the ball, and to chase toys dragged around in a circle.

If you want to play interactive games with your rabbit, keep in mind that the game is best left up to the rabbit. Because of the rabbit's wary nature, chasing your pet isn't a good idea. If you initiate a game of chase, you'll usually frighten a rabbit, who may suddenly feel like he's being preyed upon. However, if your rabbit starts to chase you, he wants you to leave the area, or he's prodding you for a game of tag.

Table 15-1 shows some games that you can play with your rabbit.

Table 15-1	Rabbit Games: Fun for the Whole Family		
Game	*How to Initiate*	*What Happens*	*Possible Concerns*
Towel drag-and-chase	Drag a towel across your rabbit's body and then in front on your rabbit.	Your rabbit may start to give chase! Drag the towel around the room with your rabbit chasing it or over and around your bunny as he tries to pounce on it.	Your rabbit may feel attacked. Be cautious and watch your rabbit's reaction. If he's fearful, he may become aggressive or spend more time hiding.
Hanging clothes	Hang some strips of newspaper or paper towel from a clothesline within your rabbit's reach.	Your pet may find it amusing to grab these items with his teeth or paws and tug on them.	

Game	How to Initiate	What Happens	Possible Concerns
Hide and seek	Hide in a spot where your rabbit can easily find you. With a favorite treat in hand, call your bunny and when he discovers you, give him the treat. Then hide again with another treat.	It won't take long before you won't have to use the treat. Some rabbit owners have even discovered their bunnies will take turns hiding with them.	
Tag	You don't initiate this game: He does. If your rabbit is in a playful mood and starts to chase after you, he's initiating a game of tag.	Let him catch you and then sprint off again.	Avoid chasing and tagging the rabbit because this frightens bunnies.
Toy pull	Buy a cat toy attached to a string and a pole. Pull it around in front of your rabbit.	Your bunny may start to chase after it. You can pull this toy all around the house, with your rabbit in hot pursuit.	

Watching Your Wacky Wabbit

One of the greatest joys of rabbit ownership is watching your bunny play in a rabbit-proofed room or backyard (See Chapters 5 and 6 for details on rabbit proofing.) Rabbits can be incredibly silly and goofy, and their antics can leave you rolling on the floor laughing.

Much like their wild ancestors, pet rabbits also like to play. Rabbits have been known to play with dogs and cats, as well as with other rabbits. Solitary play is also a popular pastime of rabbits, who love to find ways to amuse themselves.

Making like The Pointer Sisters: Jumping

Nature gave the rabbit strong hindquarters and leg muscles to escape from predators, but rabbits also use these assets for jumping in play. Playful rabbits can be seen leaping up in the air, springing forward, or even straight up for the sheer joy of it.

In the wild, jumping helps a rabbit change direction quickly when running from a predator. When a rabbit leaps, her body twists in the air and usually lands facing a different direction, usually a 180-degrees turn.

When two rabbits play together, they often run together, one chasing the other. The bunny being pursued sometimes leaps into the air, twists around, lands, and takes off again. The goal of the pursuing rabbit is to switch directions just as fast as the bunny she's chasing.

Tiny Chariots of Fire

Another defense mechanism that rabbits use for amusement when they feel safe and relaxed in their environment is running at top speed. This ability comes in handy for avoiding predators, but a speedy run is also a terrific way to have a good time, especially with other rabbits.

If you have a single rabbit, your bunny may simply run through the house or yard just for the fun of it. If you have more than one rabbit, running and chasing will be a favorite pastime among the two.

Watching your rabbit run playfully at full speed is loads of fun. The speed at which bunnies run is amazing. If you blink, you can literally miss your pet going by.

Various and sundry other hijinks

When it comes to funny antics, rabbits have a slew of tricks up their proverbial sleeves, such as those that follow:

- **Binki:** A rabbit may hop quietly along and then suddenly leap straight up for no apparent reason and then land again. Then the bunny continues to mosey along as if nothing happened.

- **Digging:** Another favorite and funny pastime of rabbits is digging. Give a bunny a good box or corner of sand, fine gravel, or soft dirt, and watch it fly. You can buy bags of sandbox sand at home-improvement stores and nurseries (the plant kind of nursery, not the baby kind). (Giving your rabbit a box to dig in is also a good way to keep him from doing it to the carpet.)

- **Tunneling:** Rabbits love tunnels, and you'll see your bunny go in one end of a box or tube and come out the other, over and over again. Some owners buy play tunnels meant for cats and hook them together with built-in snaps to create elaborate tunnel systems for a playful bunny.

A rabbit and her friends

In the wild, rabbits are playful creatures who love to engage their fellow rabbits in games. In his book *The Private Life of the Rabbit,* R.M. Lockley writes about wild rabbits chasing each other, running in circles, jumping into the air, and rolling in the grass. In the situations Lockley observed, the only reason for this behavior appeared to be that the rabbits felt good and wanted to show it.

Chapter 16

Hitting the Road with Your Rabbit

You don't have to live with a rabbit for too long before you find yourself completely bonded with your pet. Pretty soon, you won't even want to leave your rabbit for extended lengths of time, even when you go on vacation! You'll think that maybe he'd enjoy seeing the Grand Canyon. You'll tell yourself that he's yearning for a look at Mount Rushmore, or maybe your aunt and uncle in Paris would like to meet him.

Well, don't let your affection carry you away. The truth is that rabbits aren't the greatest of travelers. Take your rabbit only if the trip is absolutely necessary for him: trips to the veterinarian, relocations with you to a new home, and the like. When there's just no getting around it and you have to hit the road together, you can reduce your pet's stress and keep him safe and sound.

Pleasure jaunts aren't necessary or even healthy for most rabbits. (Sorry, but you'll have to satisfy your urge to share your travels with your rabbit by showing him your vacation slides.) The reason rabbits don't travel well is simple: They're easily prone to stress, and being exposed to new environments stresses them out. They prefer the safety and comfort of familiar surroundings. Also, rabbits who travel are at risk of being exposed to diseases and parasites — another reason why bunny is best off at home.

Buckling Up and Heading Out

If you find that you have to travel with your rabbit, do it in a way that's safe and comfortable for your pet.

Options for rabbit travel are usually limited: cars and airplanes are the vehicles where rabbits are usually welcome. Whatever mode of transport you choose, the situation must be handled carefully to keep your bunny in good health —physical and mental — during the trip.

You'll also need to pack for your bunny. (I've yet to meet a rabbit who could close his own suitcase.) Packing the right items is vital to keeping bunny comfy while on the road. First off, keep in mind these general dos and don'ts when it comes to bunny globe-trotting.

Travel dos

Before taking your pet on a trip, bear the following tips in mind: These bits of advice can make the difference between smooth travel and a cumbersome ride.

✔ **Plan ahead.** Think about the circumstances of the journey and how to best make your rabbit comfortable. (See the "Carrier comfy" sidebar in this chapter.) If you're flying with your pet, you need to contact the airline to make advance reservations for your rabbit. For overnight road trips, plan ahead by making reservations at pet-friendly hotels.

✔ **Get veterinarian information at your destination.** Before your trip, get the name and phone numbers of rabbit veterinarians in the towns where you'll be staying. If your rabbit gets sick, the last thing that you want to do is struggle to find a qualified veterinarian.

✔ **Consider the weather.** Think about how hot or cold it will be. Rabbits can tolerate cold much better than heat. If you're traveling by car during the summer, be sure your air conditioning is working. If you're traveling by plane, consider rescheduling your trip. Your rabbit can be exposed to extreme heat during loading and while in the cargo hold, and when it comes to rabbits, heat kills.

✔ **Use a travel carrier.** Airline carriers, the best traveling case for a rabbit, come in different styles. (See what a travel carrier looks like in Figure 16-1.)

Travel don'ts

Make sure that you do follow these "don'ts." Your rabbit and you will be far better off if you

✔ **Never leave your rabbit alone in a car, even for a few minutes.** A hot car is a death trap for a rabbit. Even if the windows are rolled down, the temperature in a sun-baked car can rise at a fast and deadly rate. Leaving a rabbit alone in a car (whatever the weather) can put the rabbit at risk for being stolen.

✔ **Don't skimp on a carrier.** Don't carry your bunny in a box or bag but only in travel crates or carriers designed for small animals. Plastic-and-wire airline crates are an excellent choice, although some owners prefer soft nylon carriers.

✔ **Don't fly.** Avoid taking your rabbit on airplane trips if at all possible. Airplane trips should be reserved for relocation situations only. Most airlines don't allow rabbits to fly in the cabin of an airplane, which is the preferred way for a rabbit to fly. Rabbits who do not fly in the cabin are relegated to the cargo area, where they're exposed to life-threatening stressors, such as heat, barking dogs, and rough handling. Avoid flying with your rabbit in cargo if you can help it.

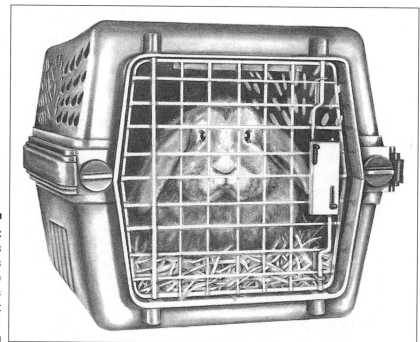

Figure 16-1:
Why did this rabbit cross the road? To get to this great carrier!

Packing a mean bag

If you're planning an overnight trip, you pack all these items for your traveling bunny. You need some of this stuff while you're traveling (if your trip is longer than an hour or so) and after you get to your destination.

You can put all this fun stuff in a plastic grocery bag or a canvas tote bag. Or you can go all out and get your bunny his own Samsonite. If you travel often with your pet and have some money to spend (not as much as you'll need if you were to buy a piece of serious luggage), you can purchase a nylon pet travel bag or knapsack at a pet supply store. These bags are actually made for dogs, but Bunny never has to know.

- **Food:** If you won't be traveling through an area where hay and fresh vegetables are readily available, you need to pack these items for your trip. Bring a cooler, fill it with ice and the fresh, washed food your rabbit needs. Bring hay in a plastic bag to help keep it fresh.

- **Water:** Don't upset your bunny's digestive system by giving him strange water. Pack some bottled water and give that to him on your trip.

- **Litter box and litter:** If your rabbit is trained to use the litter box, bring his litter box along. He'll take comfort in being able to use his familiar commode when nature calls.

- **Bedding:** Bring fresh bedding (whatever you use at home) for your rabbit if you're staying overnight. He needs his bedding changed every day. See Chapter 5 for information on rabbit bedding.

- **Chew items:** Your bunny takes comfort in gnawing on some favorite item while he's traveling.

- **A toy or two:** When your bunny gets to where he's going, help him acclimate to his new environment with a familiar toy.

- **Harness and leash:** Bring your rabbit's harness and leash with you so you can take him out of the carrier when necessary and still have complete control over him. Chapter 11 tells you about the harness and how to use it.

- **Grooming tools:** If you'll be gone for a week or more, bring your rabbit's brush and nail clippers. If you have a longhaired rabbit, even an overnight trip requires that you groom your pet during your trip, so bring along your grooming tools. Chapter 8 tells you all about grooming and its required tools.

- **Rabbit vets contact information at your destination:** If you planned ahead, you'll have this when it's time to go.

✔ **Identification:** Equip your rabbit's carrier with an ID tag bearing your name, address, and phone number. Include the phone number of your destination. This is in the event that your rabbit becomes separated from you during the trip.

✔ **Paper towel rolls:** For cleanup of cage or hotel room if needed.

✔ **Carpet cleaner:** For cleaning up the hotel carpet in case of an accident.

✔ **First-Aid kit.** Bring along your bunny's first-aid kit so you'll be equipped should he become sick or injured. (See the Cheat Sheet for information on putting together a first-aid kit.)

Your rabbit's carrier is his home away from home. You don't need to bring your pet's entire cage with you. Think of his carrier as his traveling cage.

Bunny you can drive my car

If your rabbit is just taking a short trip to the vet, you'll mostly likely be traveling with him by car. That's a no-brainer unless, of course, you live in a big city and don't have a car, instead relying on public transportation. If that's the case, call a car service or hail a taxi for a ride to the vet. Avoid subways and buses with your rabbit if you can. The noise and commotion will scare him and is best avoided. (Check ahead before taking your rabbit on public transportation. Some cities don't allow pets on trains and buses, even if they are in a carrier.)

Another reason why you may be traveling by car with your rabbit is to move to a new home. This is an excellent reason to take your rabbit on a car trip. If you move, your rabbit moves with you.

Keep the following points in mind when traveling by car with your rabbit:

✔ **Keep your rabbit in a carrier while in the car.** This is for your safety as well as the safety of your rabbit. In the event of an accident, your rabbit is safer in a carrier. Also, a loose rabbit can be distracting to a driver and can actually be the cause of an accident. Be sure to get your rabbit used to his carrier before taking him on a trip. (See the "Carrier comfy" sidebar in this chapter.)

✔ **Protect your rabbit from heat.**

• Use the air conditioner if you're driving in hot weather.

• Make sure your rabbit's carrier is not in direct sun. Move the carrier to the other side of the car's seat or put a towel over the area of the crate that's exposed to the sun. (Be sure to leave some open areas for ventilation.)

✔ **Provide healthy air.** If you get stuck in traffic, keep the windows rolled up and the air vent closed, preferably with the air conditioner turned on.

✔ **Take breaks on long trips.** If you're driving for a long time (more than a couple of hours), stop and give your rabbit a break. Park in the shade if the weather is hot and let him hop around inside your parked car, making sure you block off any areas in the car where the rabbit can become wedged or hide. and use his litter box while you're inside the car to supervise. Make sure he has fresh water in his carrier, and clean up any accidents that may have occurred while he was confined.

Carrier comfy

Before taking your rabbit on a trip, help him get used to his carrier. The more comfortable he feels in his travel carrier, the less stressed out he'll be when he travels. This whole process can take up to a month, so be sure to start way ahead of your scheduled departure time.

First off, make sure that you have a good carrier for your bunny. The best ones for rabbits are the small airline approved plastic-and-wire carriers normally used for cats. Rabbits find these cozy because they're enclosed, and the construction helps protect the four-legged occupants in the event of an accident. You can also opt for a soft nylon pet carrier bag, although these don't provide as much protection during car travel and rabbits can more easily chew through them.

Take the following steps to familiarize your rabbit with his carrier:

1. During your bunny's exercise time, place the carrier in the area where he runs around. Leave the door open. Put some clean straw in the carrier, or your rabbit's sleeping blanket inside. Leave the door open, and place some treats inside. After your rabbit eats the treats, add more goodies about half an hour later.

2. After a few days of eating treats in his carrier, your rabbit is ready for you to close the door while he's inside. Keep the door shut for just a minute or two at a time and then let him come out if he wants to. Gradually increase the amount of time the door is closed until your rabbit is confined for at least half an hour.

If your rabbit shows distress at being confined, you're moving too fast. Back up and start up over by putting treats in the carrier and leaving the door open. Gradually begin to close the door for short periods of time until you work up to a comfortable confinement time for your rabbit.

3. After your bunny is okay with being inside his carrier with the door closed, it's time to take him on some short car trips. When he first feels the car moving, he may become distressed. If this happens, have someone else drive while you sit in the backseat with him. Feed him some of his favorite treats through the carrier door and talk softly to him. Keep the trips short and gradually work up to longer car rides as he becomes more comfortable.

When your rabbit is completely comfortable confined to his carrier and traveling in the car, you're ready for your trip. Your carrier (or car) should be equipped with the things mentioned in this chapter's "Packing a mean bag."

Seating rows 20 through 10

Traveling by plane is the least favorable way to get your rabbit from one place to another. Between the crowds, the extensive security, and the reluctance of airlines to allow rabbits to travel in cabins, rabbits are better off traveling by car or staying home completely. Also, rabbits who have to travel in the plant's cargo hold (where they keep the checked bags) can be exposed to heat if the plane gets trapped on the runway for an extended period of time. They're also likely to encounter cold temperatures and lack human attention during the flight.

If your rabbit must fly by plane, certain precautions can help your pet survive the stress of the trip. Follow these guidelines if you're planning a plane ride for your pet:

- **Fly *with* your rabbit.** Avoid sending your rabbit alone on a plane. Without you on board, the rabbit has no one to watch out for him. If the plane gets trapped on the runway for hours on end, your rabbit could die of heat exhaustion.

- **Book a direct flight to reduce the amount of handling your rabbit has to endure.** A connecting flight increases the chances of circumstances going awry in your pet's journey. More than one dog or cat has been incorrectly routed and ended up in the wrong city. Also, ask for your rabbit to be loaded last, after all the checked bags have been placed in the cargo hold. If your rabbit goes in last, he'll be unloaded first when he arrives at his destination.

- **Get your rabbit a place in the cabin.** Most airlines allow two pets to fly in the cabin of the plane, as long as the pet's carrier fits under the passenger's seat. Not all airlines allow rabbits in the cabin, however. Call ahead to find out. In order to secure a place in the cabin for your rabbit, make your reservations way ahead of time.

- **Do not sedate your rabbit for the flight.** In the event of heat or another problem with your pet's flight environment, tranquilizers can send your rabbit over the edge.

- **Prepare your rabbit for the flight by making sure he's completely comfortable in his carrier.** Follow the steps in the "Carrier comfy" sidebar in this chapter to get your rabbit used to being confined in an airline carrier weeks before you take your flight.

- **Prepare your rabbit's crate so your bunny has everything he needs during the flight.** If your rabbit is flying in the cargo hold, equip his crate with his favorite towel or blanket, a gravity water bottle (see Chapter 5 for more on this) attached on the inside of the crate door filled with fresh water, and a good amount of fresh hay. (See Chapter 7 for more on what to put in his cage.)

- ✔ **Clearly mark the outside of the crate with contact information.** Put more than one person's information in case of an emergency and friendly information such as, "Hi, my name is Thumper, and I'm a lop-eared rabbit. I'm traveling for the first time, so please treat me gently." This catches the attention of the handlers. Also put a tag on your pet's crate with your name, address, and phone number, along with care instructions in the event your pet becomes separated from you.

- ✔ **Make sure you have appropriate health certificates.** All airlines and state health officials require a USDA (United States Department of Agriculture) health certificate issued by a licensed veterinarian prior to travel. The exam needs to be done within 10 days of air travel.

- ✔ **If you absolutely have to put your rabbit on a plane without you, book your pet's flight in the cooler weather for his safety.**

- ✔ **Use a professional pet shipper if necessary.** You may have to book your rabbit's flight through a professional pet shipper if the airline doesn't allow pet owners to make pet reservations.

Being a law-abiding bunny

If you're taking your rabbit out of state or the country or flying on a plane, call the agricultural authorities where you're going at least six weeks in advance to find out the regulations regarding rabbits in that area. You may need a USDA health certificate issued by a licensed veterinarian before you can bring a rabbit into the area, or you may find that rabbits can't be brought into the area at all.

You can go online to `www.aphis.usda.gov/oa/pubs/pettravel.html` for more information on government regulations on interstate and international travel with pets. You can also contact APHIS (Animal and Plant Health Inspection Service) for this same information at 301-734-4981.

Some places, such as Hawaii and the United Kingdom, have strict *quarantine* restrictions, requiring that rabbits spend considerable amounts of time in a quarantine facility when they're first brought into the area. This ensures that they are free of illness before mingling with the rest of the rabbit population. Find out if the place you're going has these kinds of rules and what following them entails.

Staying at a Five-Carrot Hotel

These days, hotels have cable and pay-per-view movies and room service and internet access. What else do you need? Your rabbit! Who cares if a mint is on your pillow if you can't stay there with your pet? If you have to stay somewhere overnight, you need to find a bunny-friendly hotel along your route. Not to worry — plenty of them are out there.

Be prepared to pay a pet deposit, which is refunded if your room is void of pet-related damage after you leave. You may also have to pay a small fee (usually $5 to $15 per night) for the privilege of keeping your pet with you for the night.

Booking a reservation

The best way to find the right hotel or motel is to use a pet-friendly hotel/motel guide. A number of these books have been published for hotels and motels around the US. Although not labeled specifically for rabbit owners (some even refer only to dog-friendly places), the pets-okay policies at these lodges are often applicable to rabbits as well. (Refer to the guides listed in the Appendix.)

If you don't want to go to your bookstore and purchase a guide, you can do some research on the internet. By simply typing **pet-friendly hotel** in any search engine, you get a list of Web sites to the kinds of places you're looking for.

After you find the listing, call the hotel to make sure that rabbits are indeed allowed. Don't count on that hotel or motel having available rooms on the night you plan to stay. Book while you're on the phone to make sure that you have a place to stay — don't just show up with bunny in tow!

Being a good guest

When you stay at a pet-friendly hotel or motel with your rabbit, be a good guest. The impression you leave on the manager and staff is vital because it determines whether future rabbit owners will be allowed to bring their pets to this facility in the future.

Follow these guidelines when staying in a hotel or motel with your rabbit:

- **Control your pet.** Don't let your rabbit run amuck in a hotel room. Rabbits are inclined to dig carpet, poop and pee under the bed, and chew on the wooden furniture if left to their own devices. By all means, give your rabbit some exercise but keep a close eye on him to make sure he doesn't damage the room.

- **Clean up after your pet.** If your rabbit has an accident on the rug, clean it thoroughly. Scoop up any hay or litter that spills out of your pet's carrier. Avoid using room towels to clean up pet messes. If you didn't bring paper towels along with you as suggested earlier in this chapter (tsk, tsk!), run to the store and buy some if you need them or get a bunch of paper napkins from the hotel restaurant. (Chapter 5 tells you how to get rid of urine on the floor.)

✔ **Confine your rabbit.** This one is for the safety of the room and your pet's safety, too. Whenever you aren't in the room, keep your rabbit in his carrier. You don't want the maid to accidentally let your pet out of the room, and you certainly don't want your rabbit destroying carpet or furniture or disappearing into the box spring or some other nook or cranny.

Keeping Him at Home

Because traveling with your rabbit is a last resort, your first resort is to keep your pet at home. Rabbits take great comfort in familiar surroundings, and leaving your rabbit in his usual place with a responsible person (either someone whom you trust or a pet sitter) to care for him is your best option. If you can't find someone to care for your rabbit at home, you can also board him. Although leaving your rabbit in your house is better, boarding is an option if you absolutely can't find anyone to care for him.

The most crucial aspect of keeping your rabbit at home while you travel is finding the right person to care for your pet. Get someone who is responsible beyond question because your rabbit's life literally depends on this person while you're away. If you have a friend or neighbor who you trust implicitly with your rabbit, you can go this route. If the person you're considering is under the age of 12, make sure a parent is overseeing your rabbit's care.

Consider your

✔ Boyfriend or girlfriend

✔ Friend

✔ In-laws (no outlaws)

✔ Parents or adult children

✔ Spouse

✔ Trusted co-member at rabbit club

✔ Professional pet sitter

Preparing your pet sitter

After you hire someone to take care of your rabbit, you need to prepare your home and your pet for your absence.

- ✔ **Go over your rabbit's needs with the sitter.** Invite your sitter over for a visit before you're scheduled to leave. If it is someone you know well and she can't come before you leave, give specific instructions over the phone. When she's there, give a run-through of all duties so she can ask questions.

- ✔ **Create a how-to list of all the rabbit chores and dos and don'ts.** Even though you'll have verbally instructed your rabbit's caretaker on what she needs to do, it can't hurt to write it all down and leave it in a place where your sitter can see it. Also let the caretaker know what she should do — or shouldn't: Don't let the rabbit run loose throughout the house, do give her supervised exercise in a rabbit-proofed room, and so on.

- ✔ **Stock up on supplies.** Make sure your rabbit's caretaker has everything she needs to care for your rabbit properly and knows where you keep this stuff. Have a supply of hay on hand so your caretaker won't need to scramble to find some, and have some fresh vegetables chopped up and ready to go in the refrigerator. Make sure you have enough litter for your rabbit's litter box if your bunny uses one and have plenty of fresh bedding on hand.

- ✔ **Make a list of foods.** If you are going to be gone for an extended period of time, your caretaker needs to go to the store to pick up fresh foods for your rabbit. Leave behind some cash or payment instructions for the caretaker, along with a list of foods that your rabbit can eat.

- ✔ **Instructions for veterinary care.** Post the phone number and address of your rabbit's veterinarian in a prominent place, with a 24-hour emergency clinic number and address alongside. Leave a signed note stating that you authorize the rabbit's caretaker to seek veterinary attention for your rabbit in your absence and provide a means for the caretaker to pay for veterinary care. (If you don't feel comfortable leaving cash or a credit card, simply call your vet's office and work out an arrangement in the event that your rabbit gets sick while you're away.)

- ✔ **Your contact information.** Leave phone numbers and addresses where you can be reached while you are away. Also leave the number of a local friend who's willing to be responsible for your rabbit if you're unreachable. If you have a cell phone, bring that with you in case your caretaker needs to reach you in an emergency. And don't forget to include that phone number in your contact info.

Sitting for a living

Another route you can take is to hire a professional pet sitter. A *professional pet sitter* comes to your home to take care of your rabbit every day. That means she'll feed your rabbit, give her fresh water, let her out of her cage for supervised exercise and clean up after her. If you have other pets, you can have the pet sitter care for these critters, too. (If that's the case, let your sitter know whether your rabbit can safely be with your other pets.)

To find a reputable pet sitter, get a referral from another rabbit owner or your veterinarian. If you're unable to get the name of a pet sitter in your area from either one of these sources, contact Pet Sitters International or the National Association of Pet Sitters, listed in the "Resources" chapter, for a listing of pet sitters near you. These organizations have standards that its members must meet. For example, they must be insured and bonded (see explanation in following bulleted list), have experience caring for animals, and be able to provide references, to name just a few requirements.

Before you hire a pet sitter, you need to interview her and ask some important questions. Most pet sitters want to come to your home to meet you and your pet, and this is the time to pose the following questions:

- ✔ **What is your experience with rabbits? Have you cared for rabbits before?** If you can't find a sitter who has rabbit experience, then get one who interacts calmly with your pet and seems to have a natural feel for being around these sensitive pets.

- ✔ **How much do you charge to care for a rabbit? Do you charge per day, per visit?**

- ✔ **How many times a day will you come see my rabbit? At what times of the day will you come? What services are available?** For example, in addition to feeding and giving fresh water, will the pet sitter sit with your rabbit during exercise time? Will the pet sitter groom your rabbit? How much extra does the pet sitter charge for these additional services?

- ✔ **May I see references?** Preferably get several and from other rabbit owners. Call each one of these people to find out if they were happy with the pet sitter's work. Ask if the pet sitter is responsible, if she took good care of the animals in question, and if the pet owner would recommend this pet sitter to others.

- ✔ **Are you bonded?** If a professional pet sitter is *bonded,* you as the customer are financially protected against theft of your property perpetrated by the pet sitter. In other words, if the pet sitter steals something from your house, you'll be reimbursed for it. Most professional pet sitters will also ask you to sign an agreement as to the services that will be rendered. A liability waiver may also be included in the agreement, holding the pet sitter free from certain responsibilities if anything happens to your pet or your home while the pet sitter is in charge. Read any agreement carefully before you sign it, and make sure you have no problem with the stipulations that the pet sitter has put forth.

Feeling board?

Another option for your rabbit while you're away is boarding in a private home. Some people, for a fee, take in others' pets for short-term boarding.

Home-boarding is preferable to placing your rabbit in a boarding kennel, the kind that regularly services cats and dogs. Boarding kennels are generally not hospitable for rabbits because of the close proximity of all those barking dogs.

You can locate one of these rabbit-friendly boarding homes through a rabbit club in your area. Contact the House Rabbit Society (see the Appendix for contact information) and ask for a reference to a House Rabbit Society chapter in your area. Your local club should be able to recommend someone in your area. In addition, contact your rabbit-experienced veterinarian's office; they often have a list of qualified people who can board your pet.

When choosing a private boarding situation, make sure

- ✔ To visit the home before you commit to leaving your rabbit in the proprietor's care.

- ✔ The home is clean.

- ✔ The rabbit's quarters are secure, have all the comforts of home, and are safe from predators.

- ✔ To ask for references of other rabbit owners who have used the services of this home-boarder, and call them. Find out if they had a pleasant experience in the situation, and if their rabbits came back happy and healthy.

Chapter 17

Getting Hoppy with Your House Rabbit

· ·

In This Chapter

▶ Flocking together with other rabbit lovers

▶ Saving bunnies from going down the gutter

▶ Leaping into rabbit hopping

▶ Competing against other purebreds

· ·

Most people get enough joy from their rabbits by just having them as companions. If you're more laid-back or have little time to spare, you can have plenty of fun playing at home with your rabbit (see Chapter 15). But if you're the type of person who likes to really get involved with your pets and has the time and money, you may want to consider participating in any of one several activities available for rabbit owners.

Whether showing your rabbit, hopping alongside your pet, participating in a rabbit club, or rescuing homeless rabbits, you get much more from your relationship with your rabbit if you take advantage of some of what's out there for rabbits.

Who Needs Social Butterflies? Rabbit Clubs

If you love rabbits, you want to be around other people who love rabbits, too. Being with other rabbit lovers is where rabbit clubs come in. You can find all kinds of rabbit clubs, designed for various tastes:

✔ **Regional show clubs:** For people who show their rabbits.

✔ **Rescue groups:** If you want to help rabbits in need.

✔ **Youth rabbit clubs:** Will do the trick if you want to get involved with kids and rabbits.

Regional show clubs

People are much like rabbits. They like to be with their own kind. That's why regional rabbit clubs are growing in popularity. Geared toward rabbit owners who live within a specific geographical area, regional rabbit clubs are locally based. Not every city and town in the country has a regional rabbit club, of course, but plenty of them do. If you live in a place that doesn't have one, consider starting one.

In the United States, most regional rabbit clubs are geared toward adults who are showing purebred rabbits, but some groups do include pet owner and youth programs. The purebred groups are usually chartered with the American Rabbit Breeders Association, Inc. (ARBA) and include all breeds. In some cases, a regional club specializes only in one breed.

By joining a regional rabbit club, you can attend meetings and local shows, and you'll subsequently find out much more about caring for your rabbit. If you're interested in showing and breeding, you'll gain invaluable knowledge on these subjects from fellow members. Beginners in the rabbit-showing world do themselves a favor when they join a regional rabbit club.

To locate the regional rabbit club in your area, contact the American Rabbit Breeders Association, Inc. (ARBA). Links to ARBA chartered clubs can be found on the group's Web site www.arba.net or by asking your local rabbit veterinarian if a regional club exists in your area. (If you are outside the US, see the Appendix for contact information on international rabbit associations.)

Feeling philanthropic? House Rabbit Society

If you want to devote your rabbit-oriented energies to helping bunnies in need, as well as helping to educate others about rabbit care, you may want to consider joining a local House Rabbit Society chapter. The House Rabbit Society is a national organization that works to improve the quality of life for rabbits everywhere. The members at local chapters host regular meetings, volunteer at shelters, house abandoned rabbits in foster homes, and set up booths at community events to promote responsible rabbit ownership.

To find a House Rabbit Society chapter near you, see the Appendix for a listing. For more information about fostering, see Chapter 4 and the "Throwing out a Life Preserver: Rescuing" section, later in this chapter.

Getting choosy: Specific breeds

If you're serious about showing, breeding, or finding out more about your rabbit's breed, join your breed's national club. (See the Appendix for a listing of national breed clubs.) For more info on showing, look at the "Showing off" section, later in this chapter. For more breeding information, see Chapter 13.

Each recognized ARBA breed (see Chapter 4) has a national breed club. New breeds not yet recognized by ARBA also have national clubs.

By joining your breed's national club, you gain access to plenty of information about the kind of rabbit that you own. Most national breed clubs offer networking opportunities (meeting other rabbit owners who can help you learn more about rabbit showing) and a newsletter to their members, as well as information about the particular breed, national shows, and contests.

Including the kids

So your daughter begged you for a rabbit, and now, you're the one cleaning his litter box. Or maybe you bought the rabbit that your son wanted and he just can't get enough of his pet. Either way, getting your child more involved is a good idea. Your best bets are

- **4-H:** By getting involved in a 4-H rabbit project, your child can find out about rabbit care and handling. She can also show her rabbit, even if the bunny isn't a purebred.

    Parents have plenty of opportunities to get involved with their child's 4-H rabbit project, too. Clubs are always looking for leaders, chaperones, and other volunteers. You can also help your kid with the rabbit's daily maintenance, which is a must. You want to be sure that the rabbit is being properly cared for. Find out more about 4-H in the "Taking the 4-H route" section, later in this chapter.
- **House Rabbit Society**
- **Local kid-focused groups**

Throwing out a Life Preserver: Rescuing

If you want to go beyond being a responsible rabbit owner, you can get more involved by joining a local rabbit *rescue club,* a group devoted to the rescue and re-homing of unwanted rabbits. The problem of homeless rabbits is a serious one, and people who love rabbits are needed to volunteer at rescue organizations around the country. Chapter 4 offers more specific shelter and rescue group information, including why this problem exists and how each works from the adoption perspective.

The House Rabbit Society has local chapters around the United States, and each is involved in rabbit rescue and welfare. By getting involved with a House Rabbit Society chapter or another rabbit rescue organization, you can do wonders to help rabbits in need. (You'll find a list of House Rabbit Society local chapters and other rescue organizations in the Appendix.)

Among the type of volunteer opportunities available for rabbit lovers:

- ✔ Passing out fliers in front of pet stores about rabbits needing homes.
- ✔ Providing rabbit food to a rabbit foster home in your area.
- ✔ Providing a foster home for a rabbit. (See the "Halfway there: Fostering" section, later in this chapter, for more on this topic.)
- ✔ Start a local chapter of the House Rabbit Society if one doesn't exist already.

Being proactive

Your heart aches for homeless bunnies, but what can you do about it? Plenty.

- ✔ **Consider adopting one from a shelter or a rabbit rescue group.** That is, when the time comes to acquire a rabbit, take in a homeless rabbit.
- ✔ **Be a responsible rabbit owner.** This means spaying or neutering your pet rabbit and refraining from breeding your pet if you don't plan to get involved with showing.
- ✔ **Educate fellow rabbit owners about the plight of homeless rabbits.** Encourage them to spay and neuter their pets and advise them not to breed their pets or turn them loose for a life of so-called freedom.

  Give them information on local rabbit organizations and give them printed information on the proper care of rabbits (available from the House Rabbit Society) Be honest about the pros and cons of owning a rabbit when asked and have people read in advance about rabbits for pets . . . books like this one!.

- ✔ **Be an advocate for responsible rabbit ownership.** If you come across a friend or relative who is thinking about getting a rabbit, encourage them to consider their decision seriously. Owning a rabbit is a big commitment and shouldn't be taken lightly. Maybe you could loan this book to him.

> ✔ **When you meet someone who has just acquired a rabbit, offer to help with the new pet.** Provide the new pet owner with literature on how to properly feed and care for a rabbit and explain the importance of responsible ownership. Remind new rabbit owners that if they want to get rid of their pet, they should take it to a shelter or rabbit rescue group — *not* turn it loose to fend for itself.

Halfway there: Fostering

If you have a big heart and want to help homeless rabbits, you may want to consider providing a foster home for a bunny in need. Foster homes for rabbits are halfway houses of sorts, providing homeless bunnies with a temporary place to live and adjust to normal life while a permanent home is sought.

As a foster parent to a rabbit, you keep the bunny until a home is found. You'll probably be asked to evaluate the rabbit's temperament and behavior, so people seeking to adopt a rabbit have a sense of what the bunny is like.

Instead of shelters, foster homes are used by a variety of rabbit rescue groups throughout the country. In the case of the House Rabbit Society, the organization has local chapters and a network of foster homes within each chapter. (A list of House Rabbit Society chapters can be found in the Appendix.)

A call to your local House Rabbit Society chapter can start you on the road to becoming a foster parent. Providing a foster home for a rabbit is a rewarding experience, and one that really makes a difference for the animal. Of course, when you foster a rabbit, you may fall in love with the bunny and want to keep it. Many foster parents do.

Hopping to It

Some people think that showing rabbits is fun, but they ain't seen nothin' 'til they've gone rabbit hopping. What the heck is *rabbit hopping?* Similar to dog agility and horse show jumping, rabbit hopping is a competitive activity that involves both rabbit owners and their rabbits negotiating various obstacles on a course.

In the United States, the sport of rabbit hopping is managed by the Rabbit Hopping Organization of America, or RHOA (see the Appendix for contact information). According to rabbit owners who participate in this sport, the rabbits enjoy it as much as the owners. The obstacles are varied but most of them are jumps. The following jumps are typically seen in the rabbit hopping arena:

- **Broad:** Two horizontal poles with a set of boards laid on the ground between them.
- **Pole:** Two horizontal poles with one or more raised vertical poles between them.
- **Water:** An obstacle consisting of a small body of water, usually with bushes on either side

For the safety of your rabbit, do not try these obstacles at home! Both you and your rabbit need training to participate safely in rabbit hopping. Get involved in the RHOA to safely learn this sport. See the Appendix for contact information.

Getting up to speed (and height)

Just as the hopping course has hurdles, so does the preparation process.

1. **Become a member of your national rabbit hopping organization.**

   In the US, contact the RHOA. Outside the US? See the Appendix for rabbit-hopping organizations in your country. Not all countries have one of these groups.

2. **Train your rabbit.**

   Putting your rabbit into practice involves careful work with the rabbit's safety and emotional well-being in mind. Keep in mind that training must be positive and gentle. Training is described in depth in Chapter 11. You'll use a structured groundwork technique, which shows you how to train your rabbit to negotiate a rabbit hopping course.

   Conditioning, another important aspect of training, requires you to slowly build your rabbit up to the point where he has the physical agility and endurance to negotiate a rabbit hopping course.

Jumping right in

Horse show jumping was the inspiration for rabbit hopping, and many of the first rules and ideas for rabbit hopping came from horse show jumping. Rabbit hopping started in Sweden in the 1970s and quickly spread to other parts of Europe. The sport is popular in Norway and Denmark and is growing in Germany and the United States.

Putting on the sweatsuit: Training

Before you can participate in a rabbit hopping event, you need to train your rabbit. This involves careful work with the rabbit's safety and emotional well being in mind. Keep in mind that rabbits are timid creatures, and training must be positive and gentle! A structured ground work technique is used in training rabbits for this sport. Conditioning is another important aspect of training, and requires that you slowly build your rabbit up to the point where he can negotiate a rabbit hopping course.

For help on training your rabbit for rabbit hopping, contact the Rabbit Hopping Association of America. For the price of membership, the organization provides detailed information on how to train a rabbit for competition, along with other kids of information on the sport of rabbit hopping.

For help on training your rabbit for rabbit hopping, contact the local chapter of your national rabbit hopping association. If you live in the United States, contact the RHOA.

3. **Become familiar with the rules.**

   Designed for the safety of the rabbit in large part, the rules for rabbit hopping are more complicated than you may think:

   - Any rabbit over the age of 4 months can participate.

   - Rabbits must wear a harness and leash during the hopping competition.

   - Handlers must give rabbits enough room to move around the jumps if they're so inclined and jump freely through the course.

4. **Memorize the course in advance.**

   Walking through the course several times will help you remember the order of the obstacles when it's time to do your *run*. The obstacles tend to be laid out in a logical order — the obstacle you first see upon completing a step is usually the one you are supposed to take next.

Taking the plunge

If rabbit hopping sounds like fun to you, and you'd like to try it, contact your national rabbit hopping association. Because the sport is just getting started in the United States, not too many clubs have been created throughout the country. However, you can start your own rabbit hopping club.

Membership in a rabbit-hopping organization usually includes a packet with rules and guidelines, detailed information on choosing the right rabbit for hopping, training information, directions to and descriptions of the hopping courses available, diagrams on how to build jumps and judge's score sheets for hopping events.

Showing Off

Probably one of the oldest of all rabbit activities is the sport of showing. Although no bunny show parallels the Westminster Dog Show broadcast on TV every year, you can still take your rabbit in front of an American Rabbit Breeders Association (ARBA) judge for evaluation.

To participate in the *conformation* part of ARBA rabbit shows (the part of showing where your rabbit is judged on his appearance as opposed to you being judged on your handling skills), you need a special show rabbit, one that you have purchased specifically for this reason.

Showing is a fun activity for the entire family. Beware though: Once you start showing your pet rabbit, you'll probably become heavily involved in the rabbit "game" and will no longer want to get more bunnies.

What it is

ARBA rabbit shows are basically bunny beauty contests. Rabbits are judged in categories according to their breed and are compared to their breed *standard,* a blueprint of the ideal rabbit of that breed, which describes what the rabbit's body should look like in great detail. Judges give points to each of the rabbit's body areas described in the standard.

Picking up the rabbit and looking over his physical qualities, judges examine the rabbit. A rabbit is *not* judged on the basis of his behavior — only his appearance. The rabbit exhibited in a given show within his breed class who most represents the breed standard that day is the rabbit who wins the blue ribbon.

Owners who show their rabbits are responsible for grooming the bunny before the show, transporting him to the event, and getting him to the judging arena in time for the rabbit's class.

Only unneutered and unspayed purebred rabbits can be shown in the beauty contest aspect of rabbit shows. (See Chapter 12 for information on problems relating to rabbits who are not spayed or neutered.) Showmanship classes for youngsters that evaluate the child's *presentation* of a rabbit (the way the child presents the rabbit to the judge for evaluation) don't require an unspayed or unneutered purebred bunny.

Considering pros and cons

Before you embark on a show career with your rabbit, consider the pros and cons of participating in this activity with your pet.

Pros

- ✔ Showing your rabbit can be plenty of fun. You'll not only enjoy the excitement of the game, but you'll meet other rabbit owners and find yourself becoming part of a whole new world of rabbit lovers.
- ✔ You'll find out more about rabbits by showing them.
- ✔ Because of the grooming and special care that show rabbits require (see Chapter 8 for details on grooming), you're likely to bond more closely with your bunny if you show him.

Cons

- ✔ Showing puts plenty of pressure, both physical and emotional, on your rabbit because of extensive handling and transporting. He's also more likely to come in contact with a contagious disease from another rabbit at a show.
- ✔ For a rabbit to be shown at some events, he must be tattooed. (See the "Getting some ink: Tattooing" section, later in this chapter, the "Tattoo you" sidebar in this chapter, and the color insert of this book for a picture of a rabbit with a tattoo.) Some rabbit owners don't like tattooing because a tattoo leaves a permanent mark on the rabbit's ear, and the tattooing process causes some temporary pain to the rabbit.

Attending your first show

What can you expect when you attend your first rabbit show? The experience can be a bit daunting if you don't know what's going on. However, if you have a sense of the process, you'll be less confused and intimidated, and you may actually have fun your first time around.

Preparing

Before you even set foot at the show venue, prepare yourself and your rabbit in the following way:

- ✔ **Go to a show.** Before you enter your first show, attend a rabbit show as a spectator. Being a spectator at a show is the best way to prepare for entry in another show. Attending gives you a good idea of what to expect, and knowing what to expect can make the difference between a nervous rookie and a confident pro. Arrive at the show in the morning and spend the entire day walking around and watching how things work. Don't forget to ask questions if you don't understand what you're seeing. Rabbit people are a friendly lot, and most are happy to answer your questions.

- ✔ **Study the breed standard.** Before you even select your first show rabbit, familiarize yourself with your rabbit's breed standard. Write to ARBA or visit the organization's Web site to order a copy of *Standard of Perfection* — a booklet that contains descriptions of all ARBA-recognized breeds of rabbits. Judges use these breed standards to evaluate rabbits that come before them at shows. After you study the standard, take a good look at your rabbit to get a sense of how much your bunny exemplifies the breed's standard. You can even ask another expert in your rabbit's breed for an opinion.

- ✔ **Have your rabbit tattooed.** Before you show your rabbit, you must have someone place a permanent tattoo in his left ear that will be registered with ARBA. You can see an example of such a tattoo in this book's color insert.(See the "Tattoo you" sidebar in this chapter and the "Getting some ink: Tattooing" section, later in this chapter.)

- ✔ **Groom your rabbit.** The quality of your rabbit's coat has a strong impact on the judge's decision at a rabbit show. The judge wants to see a coat that's proper for the breed (according to the breed standard) and that looks healthy and well cared for. (See Chapter 8 for details on grooming your rabbit, which is a common part of every rabbit's life, not just show rabbits. Chapter 4 can tell you more about rabbit coats.)

- ✔ **Condition your rabbit.** Rabbit show judges not only look for rabbits with good fur but also in good "flesh." The term *flesh* refers to the rabbit's overall body condition. Rabbits who are underfed or poorly fed won't be in good flesh, and a judge is likely to mark down your show rabbit. (See Chapter 7 for details on how to properly feed your rabbit.)

- ✔ **Psyche up your rabbit.** No, you don't need to teach your rabbit to meditate before he goes into the competition ring, but you do need to get him ready for the way that the judge will handle him. Practice handling him the way the judge will.

Judges usually pose a rabbit in his *proper position,* the designated proper position each breed must be shown in. Then judge then turns the rabbit over on his back to check the teeth, toenails, and straightness of legs, eye color, and tail. The rabbit is returned to his proper pose and checked for *body conformation* (the way your rabbit is put together) and condition of the flesh and fur.

Keep in mind that not all rabbit breeds are posed the same way, so determine the proper posing for the breed that you're showing. (Do this by studying the breed standard and watching the judging of your breed while at a show.) Spend about 10 to 15 minutes a day practicing this with your rabbit and remember to be patient with your pet.

Making your checklist

Glance at this checklist the night before the show and make sure everything is packed before you head out:

✔ **Entry forms and judge's card.** Pack your filled-out entry cards (that you have picked up at another show) and judge's comments cards, assuming you have done this ahead of time. (If you didn't, don't worry. You can get the forms and fill them out when you get to the show.) Figure 17-1 shows a judge's card.

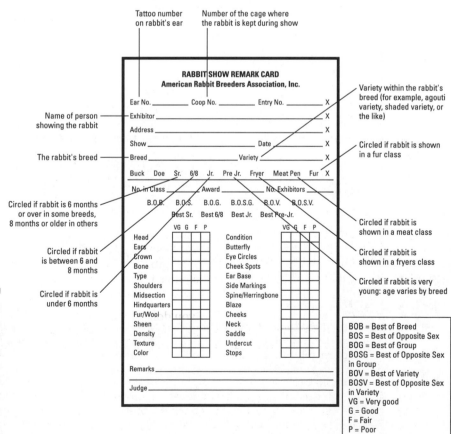

Figure 17-1:
You can complete this judge's card before you get to the show or when you arrive.

✔ **Pedigree.** If you plan to register your rabbit at the show, bring your rabbit's three-generation *pedigree* (your rabbit's genealogy) with you.

✔ **Rabbit eats.** Your bunny needs food and familiar water during the time he's at the show. Bring chopped-up vegetables, hay, and timothy pellets, if he eats those. Use a cooler to keep the produce fresh and bring a bottle of water from home.

✔ **Grooming tools.** Don't forget to bring a brush for last-minute fur brushing. (More about these tools in Chapter 8.)

✔ **Disinfectant.** Bring a hand disinfectant to clean your hands after handling rabbits other than you own. You can also buy wipes of the same type to wipe off a table or other items touched by another rabbit. These products are alcohol based and should contain 60 to 70 percent alcohol to be effective. You may also want to bring a spray disinfectant and paper towels to clean up any accidents your pet may have outside of his cage.

✔ **Clothing and shoes.** Consider bringing a smock or another shirt you can put on over your regular clothes if you are going to handle rabbits other than your own. Remove that shirt before going back and handling your rabbit; this minimizes spread of disease. If rabbits are allowed to run around the floor at the show, consider wearing washable shoes that can be removed before you return home.

✔ **Your other stuff.** Bring a chair to sit on, something to drink, your lunch, and whatever else you may need. Don't forget the directions to the show and something to read. (If you had to travel far to get to the show, bring your overnight bag. See Chapter 16 for information on how to pack your rabbit's suitcase, too.) Remember, most of your day is spent waiting for your rabbit to be judged, so you want to be comfortable.

✔ **Your good sportsmanship.** Whether you win or lose, remember to always be a good sport. Be polite to the judge and to the other exhibitors. And have fun!

The big day

On the day of the show, you'll have a number of responsibilities. Following these guidelines will help you feel more confident and may even improve your chances of winning.

1. **Travel well.**

   You need to get your rabbit to the show, and you'll probably be doing this by way of automobile. Believe it or not, the way that you transport your rabbit that day can make a big difference in how well you do at the show. This is because rabbits are easily stressed.

You can help reduce the chance of this happening by

> Keeping your rabbit in a secure, comfortable carrier that contains your rabbit's favorite bedding.

> Making sure that water and food are available to your rabbit at all times during the trip.

> When placing your rabbit's carrier in the vehicle, face the carrier to the side instead of from front to back of the car. This way, if you have a sudden stop or take off, your rabbit is less likely to be thrown forward into the carrier door, where she may break a tooth.

> Try padding under the carrier to reduce the bumpiness of the ride for your rabbit. Chapter 16 has in-depth traveling information.

Showgrounds and parking areas are usually well marked with large signs that say "This way to rabbit show!" Be prepared to have to pay for parking, although this depends on the venue.

2. **Check in with the show secretary.**

   There you also

   - Pay for your entries (for each class your rabbit enters, usually a fairly small fee per class).

   - Fill out *entry cards* (your rabbit's name and breed, your name and address, and so on) and *show remarks cards* (the card that the judge writes her comments on after judging your rabbit) if you haven't already done this at home.

3. **Register.**

   If you haven't already registered your rabbit with ARBA and you want to do so, you can do it if you have time before your first class. Take the rabbit to the registrar seated at an ARBA table at the show. Show your three-generation pedigree to the registrar. (See the "The ARBA Way" section, later in this chapter, for more on how such shows are organized and what's required.)

4. **Find the judging.**

   Locate the table where your breed is being judged and pick a place close by to set up your rabbit's carrying cage and your chair. Be sure to find a shady spot if the show is being held outdoors because direct sun and heat can hurt your rabbit.

5. **Pay attention.**

   You'll soon find yourself visiting with other rabbit owners and getting distracted looking at all the cute bunnies. Don't forget to pay attention to when your class is called, so you can be sure to bring your rabbit to the judging table.

Taking the 4-H route

If your kids are interested in rabbit activities, you may want to join a 4-H club in your area. 4-H is an organization created to help children learn about how to care for and exhibit livestock.

To obtain information on a local 4-H rabbit project, contact your local Cooperative Extension Office listed in your local telephone book under County Government. For general information about 4-H, contact the National 4-H Council listed in Chapter 23.

Working with 4-H

4-H is open to children from age 9 through 19, and sometimes younger, depending on the individual club. Typical 4-H rabbit projects feature hands-on work with rabbits. Children are taught how to feed, care for, handle, groom, and show their rabbits, and often bring their rabbits to weekly meetings.

Volunteers, usually parents whose children have been involved with the program for some time, run 4-H clubs. Individual 4-H projects, such as rabbits, have leaders as well. These people are usually parents and are often breeders or former breeders who have spent a substantial amount of time showing rabbits.

Shows specifically for 4-H rabbit owners are held around the country and follow the rules and breed standards established by ARBA. Typically, 4-H members exhibit their rabbits at county fairs because 4-H often has a strong presence at these events.

Aside from valuable hands-on experience, members of 4-H rabbit projects can also earn awards. Although actual awards and requirements vary from club to club, typical activities, such as displaying a winning rabbit-related project in the local 4-H fair, or successfully exhibiting a rabbit at a show, can earn participants medals, ribbons, or certificates.

Welcoming mixed breeds

Don't get the impression that your kid can't participate in 4-H if she has a mixed breed rabbit. If your bunny isn't a purebred, your child can still show the animal in the 4-H showmanship class. In showmanship, the exhibitor presents the rabbit to a judge, demonstrating an understanding of rabbit care and anatomy as well as proper handling. Children are graded on their ability to present the animal properly and to understand their pet's overall health. The breed of the rabbit is irrelevant.

No relation to the Swedish band: ARBA

When it comes to the big time in rabbit showing, the American Rabbit Breeders Association, Inc. (ARBA) is the governing body. ARBA began in the early part of the twentieth century and is the official organization for rabbit showing and registration in the United States. ARBA sponsors rabbit shows, put on by regional rabbit clubs, around the country. Rabbit fanciers, serious about showing, attend these shows, which are usually for all breeds of rabbits but are sometimes only open to one breed.

ARBA maintains a list of rules and regulations for rabbit shows, and each sanctioned show operates by these rules. Officiating the ARBA shows, judges evaluate the rabbits using the breed standards published by ARBA. Rabbits that are exhibited at ARBA shows may be registered with the organization, but this isn't absolutely necessary.

The ARBA Way

Rabbits at ARBA shows are judged in classes organized by breed. Within the breed classification, rabbits are then divided up by age before they're judged. Awards are given to individual class winners, as well as the best of

- ✔ Breed
- ✔ Opposite Sex (given to the best rabbit of the opposite sex of the Best of Breed winner)
- ✔ Show
- ✔ Variety or Group

Class winners usually receive a ribbon; Best of Variety or Group, a *rosette* (a type of ribbon); Best of Breed, a trophy; and Best In Show, a large trophy. Small cash awards are also given to some of the winners.

When competing in ARBA shows, rabbits can also earn legs toward their Grand Championship. Three legs qualify a rabbit as a Grand Champion, which is a distinctive title in the rabbit world.

Registering

Registering a rabbit isn't necessary in order to show it. However, many people choose to do so because having a registered rabbit assures that the animal's pedigree is true and that the rabbit meets all the requirements of its breed. (It's interesting to note that you don't need any solid proof that a rabbit is a purebred to show it. If the rabbit looks purebred, it's assumed that the rabbit is purebred.)

Tattoo you

Before you can show your rabbit, your bunny must be given a permanent tattoo containing an identification number. According to ARBA rules, the tattoo must appear in the left ear and can be a personal identification number, letters, or a series of both — it's up to you. Your rabbit's tattoo allows you and the judge to properly identify the bunny.

A few different methods are out there for choosing the number or letters that make up your rabbit's tattoo. Some owners with more than one rabbit use odd numbers to identify bucks and even numbers to identify does. To place the tattoo in the rabbit's ear, the most common way is the *ear clamp method.* In this procedure, the letters or numbers are placed into a tattoo clamp. The clamp is placed around the rabbit's ear and squeezed together. The ear is punctured with the numbers or letters chosen, and ink is placed into the holes.

Another method involves using electric tattoo needles. With this method, the number or letters are written into the ear with a stylus. Electric tattoos are usually more expensive but do permit more versatility in design than the clamp method.

To register your rabbit in the purebred classification, your bunny needs a *three-generation pedigree* (a genealogy showing your rabbit's last three generations of ancestors). An official ARBA registrar must examine your rabbit and determine if your bunny is eligible for registration. The rabbit must be 6 months or older and meet the senior weight limits for its breed. It must also be free from disqualifications or eliminations as defined by its breed standard.

Getting some ink: Tattooing

If you've been to a rabbit show, you probably noticed that some rabbits have tattoos in one of their ears. You may also see a registrar actually tattooing rabbits at the show.

For a rabbit to be shown, he must have an identifying number tattooed into its ear for many shows. The registrar tattoos the rabbit's registration number in its ear at the time of examination. Many breeders do their own tattooing, using a system of letters and numbers that they've created for their own record-keeping purposes.

Unless you're an experienced tattooer, don't attempt to tattoo your own rabbit. Instead, take your rabbit to a rabbit show and have the show registrar apply the tattoo for you. (Your rabbit doesn't need to be entered in the show for you to have his number tattooed at the event.) You can also ask your rabbit's breeder to do it for you. Keep in mind that the procedure is painful for the rabbit, but an experienced tattooer can do it quickly.

Part V
Part of Tens

The 5th Wave   By Rich Tennant

"Let me guess — the vet's analysis of the rabbit's fleas showed them to be of the 100 percent fresh ground Colombian decaf variety."

In this part . . .

This part is a hodgepodge of information. These chapters tackle knowing when you should take your rabbit to the vet, pronto. On the fun side, ten of the best rabbit Web sites are listed.

Chapter 18

Ten Signs That Require Emergency Action

. . . .

In This Chapter

▶ Coping with a pet emergency

▶ Knowing when to rush to the vet

▶ Discovering the signs of a sick rabbit

. . . .

*J*ust like other pets (and people, too) rabbits can require emergency treatment. An illness or injury may mean that your rabbit needs immediate help, even before you take him to a veterinarian. Of course, everyone knows an ounce of prevention is worth a pound of cure. So if you want to do right by your rabbit, check out Chapters 2, 8, and 9 for more health information and some preventive medicine.

Suddenly seeing that your bunny is sick or injured can be pretty scary. Thinking straight in these kinds of situations is often difficult. Before taking any other action:

✔ **Stay calm.**

✔ **Check the address for the vet clinic.** Record this information on the sheet provided in the front of this book; then tear out the sheet and put it by your phone.

One way to keep calm is to prepare in advance for an emergency. Read through this chapter to figure out how to handle the most common rabbit emergencies; read Chapter 9 so you know about interacting with your vet; read Chapter 16 so you know how to travel with your rabbit. If you ever find that your rabbit needs emergency care, you may be surprised at how well your memory serves you.

Blood in Urine

Red blood in the urine is a serious sign of disease. Causes include uterine disease (in females), bladder stones, bladder cancer, and trauma to the bladder. Blood that appears at the end of urination and as a separate puddle is most likely caused by a uterine problem. Excess blood loss can be a life-threatening condition. Bloody urine should be reported to your veterinarian immediately, particularly if it is associated with

- ✔ Straining to urinate
- ✔ Frequent urination
- ✔ Weakness
- ✔ Depression

Normal rabbit urine can range in color from yellow to rusty orange due to pigments produced in the bladder and from the plants the rabbit eats. However, blood in the urine is distinctly red. If you are in doubt about your rabbit's urine color, take a sample to your veterinarian for evaluation.

Diarrhea

True diarrhea in the rabbit is characterized by stool that is

- ✔ Profuse
- ✔ Watery
- ✔ Sometimes bloody stool in the absence of normal stool

It's most often caused by a serious disruption of the flora normally in your rabbit's gastrointestinal tract. In addition, the pet will become dehydrated and go into shock. If your rabbit has diarrhea, don't attempt to treat it yourself. Take your bunny to a veterinarian as soon as possible. A serious disease of the GI tract — not a change in diet — causes diarrhea.

Rabbits can also develop soft, pudding-like stools often mixed with normal hard, round droppings. This is not true diarrhea and although it does represent a disease of the gastrointestinal tract that should be addressed, it's not a dire emergency. This condition is most often related to diet.

Excessive Salivation

Dental disease is the most common cause of excessive salivation. If the rabbit is drooling because of dental disease, it means he's in pain and the condition should be attended to as soon as possible. Signs of excessive salivation include

- Not eating well
- Quickly losing weight
- Constantly wet fur around the mouth and neck

Excessive salivation can also be caused by certain types of poisons and if this condition is accompanied by generalized weakness you need to seek veterinary attention immediately.

Head Tilting to Side

If your rabbit is holding her head to the side, she may be suffering from an inner ear infection, trauma to the head, or a problem in the brain due to infection, parasitic disease, or other disease.

A veterinarian should see your rabbit right away. The problem may be treatable, depending on the cause.

Heatstroke

Rabbits are susceptible to heatstroke and can tolerate cold weather better than hot. A hot and humid day can be all it takes to send a rabbit into heat exhaustion. Chapters 5 and 6 give further information about how to prevent this problem. Signs of heatstroke include labored breathing, extreme lethargy, and an elevated body temperature.

If your rabbit has been exposed to high temperatures and you suspect she's suffering from heatstroke, do the following to help her cool down:

1. Get her out of the heat and into an air conditioned or shady area.

2. Wrap her ears in a cool, wet towel.

3. Rush her to a veterinarian immediately.

Labored Breathing

A variety of serious problems can cause *labored breathing* (visible difficulty moving air in and out of the lungs) in rabbits. Anything from pneumonia to shock to heatstroke can cause labored breathing.

Labored breathing in a rabbit is a serious emergency. Rush your pet to a veterinarian as soon as possible. If it's hot outside, run the car air conditioner first because hot air is difficult for the rabbit to breath and will cause further difficulties.

No Stool

If a rabbit doesn't produce any stool for 24 hours, particularly if any of the following signs accompany it, he's in need of immediate medical attention. The most common cause is a complete or partial obstruction to the gastrointestinal (GI) tract or a complete shutdown of the GI tract caused by a chronic GI motility problem.

- ✔ Bloated abdomen (May feel tight or like it's filled with fluid, like a water balloon)
- ✔ Constant tooth grinding
- ✔ Dull appearance to the eyes
- ✔ Hunched posture
- ✔ Loss of appetite
- ✔ Reluctance to move
- ✔ Weakness

This is a dire emergency and medical attention should be sought immediately. These conditions are fatal within 48 hours if left untreated. If an obstruction is present, emergency surgery needs to be performed.

Pain

If your rabbit is in pain, he should be rushed to a vet immediately so the cause of the pain can be determined.

The following are signs of pain in a rabbit:

- Depression
- Excessive salivation
- Frequent grinding of the teeth (Occasional tooth grinding can be normal.)
- Inability to sleep
- Loss of appetite
- Rapid or labored breathing
- Reluctance to move
- Sitting in a hunched posture all the time (particularly with dull, half-closed eyes)
- Unexplained aggression
- Unusual body posture

Signs of Injury

Rabbits can get hurt in a variety of ways. Other animals attack them. When being handled improperly, rabbits are often hurt, and when really frightened, they'll do anything to escape — including injure themselves. (Chapter 8 helps you understand how to properly handle your rabbit.) If you didn't see the injury occur, you may not be certain as to what's wrong. Look for the following signs of injury.

Bleeding

Bleeding can result from a predatory attack or from catching the skin on a sharp surface.

If your rabbit is bleeding profusely, put pressure on the wound using your hand or finger with a clean gauze pad or small towel. Try to stop or slow the bleeding.

If the blood is coming out in a steady flow, the injury is less serious. If the blood spurts out in rhythm, your rabbit has a damaged artery. In the latter case, stopping the blood flow is difficult, and more pressure and time is required. Meanwhile, try to get your rabbit to an emergency veterinary facility.

Broken bone

Broken bones occur from some type of trauma. The fracture causes pain and if it occurs in the legs, the rabbit might drag or hold his leg up. If the fracture is in the spine, you'll see dragging (usually the hind legs) or difficulty standing. Most fractures occur under the skin, but sometimes the bone can protrude through the skin causing bleeding and increasing the possibility of infection.

All fractures should be seen by a veterinarian as soon as possible, because your pet is in great pain with this condition. Prepare a small deep box or carrier with thick blankets or towels padding the bottom and gently place your pet inside. Try not to jostle the rabbit's body unless absolutely necessary. Doing so may cause further injury. Do not splint or immobilize the fractured leg because the rabbit may struggle with pain and more damage may be done. The rabbit will get himself in the position that is most comfortable for the ride.

Paralysis

An inability to move two or more legs can be paralysis — the result of a spinal injury. If your rabbit is conscious but unable to move part or all of her body, gently place your rabbit on a folded towel and blanket. Then carefully place all, with your bunny still lying on the towel and blanket, in a large carrier or open box.

Seizures

Seizures can be frightening to see. A rabbit who is having a seizure lays on his side, jerking and twitching uncontrollably. Remembering that the rabbit is unconscious during these moments and isn't feeling any pain may help even though it appears that she's struggling. Try covering the head and body of the bunny loosely with a lightweight towel to cut out visual stimulus and light. This may help to shorten the seizure. Gently lift the rabbit and place her in a large carrier or open box that's been fitted with a blanket, towel, or other soft material.

Do not restrain the rabbit while she's convulsing because this may cause further injury. Do not put your hands near her mouth.

Sudden Weakness

Any number of problems, all serious, can cause sudden weakness. Heatstroke, blood loss, shock, overwhelming infection, neurological disorder, intestinal obstruction, poisoning, trauma to the spine or legs, and metabolic diseases are just a few of the conditions that result in weakness.

If your rabbit can't stand up, don't try to force him. Instead, to make him comfortable, place him on a towel or blanket and take him to the veterinarian immediately.

Chapter 19

Ten Great Rabbit Web Sites

Rabbits have a huge presence on the Internet. And why not? Everything else does. What's great about computer-literate rabbit aficionados is that they enjoy welcoming newcomers to the world of rabbits. Most are dedicated to providing novice rabbit owners with all the information that they need, so their new pets get the best possible care.

The Web sites listed in this chapter, which are just a sampling of what's on the Internet, aren't intended as an endorsement. The Internet isn't regulated, so people can put up any information they like and call it fact. Use discretion and check more than one source for information.

The following Web sites contain a plethora of information that may help you to understand and care for your rabbit. If you visit any of these sites on a regular basis, your bunny's life may be enriched.

Check out the links on these sites to be transported deeper into the rabbit web.

www.acrs.cjb.net

Rabbits aren't only popular pets in North America, but in the Land Down Under, too. Proof? The **Australian Companion Rabbit Society** Web site contains tons of great rabbit information — terrific information to help you care for and live with your rabbit. You can also participate in live chats with Aussie bunny owners, if you like. And you can buy stuff from the site, if you and the webmasters can work out shipping arrangements. Don't forget the Gallery section, featuring photos of adorable Australian bunnies and "Ask Fuzzy," an e-mail link to a rabbit expert who can help you with an assortment of rabbit problems.

Don't let the fact that this Web site is generated from the other side of the planet scare you off. You won't need to spend much time here before you discover that love of bunnies is universal.

www.arba.net

In the world of American rabbit shows, **The American Rabbit Breeders Association, Inc.** (ARBA) is the grand overseer. The organization registers 45 different purebred rabbit breeds, manages the standards of each breed, and sanctions rabbit shows around the country.

If you're into purebred rabbits and even rabbit shows (see Chapter 13 for more info on breeding), you must pay a visit to the ARBA Web site. This site provides a window into the organization and provides loads of information on purebred rabbits. Take for example the "Breed Photos" area: A photograph of each recognized breed is pictured, along with a hot link that takes you to that breed's national club Web site. If one is available, that is. Not all national clubs have sites up yet.

This is where you can find information on all the national rabbit breed clubs, including contact names, addresses, phone numbers, and e-mail addresses. You can get a listing of all the upcoming rabbit shows around the country. You can also shop online for fun things like bumper stickers . . .

Be aware that ARBA promotes *all* uses of rabbits, including commercial fur production and food production. Read their statement at the top of their page.

www.bunnyheaven.com

If you're like many rabbit people, you like to buy paraphernalia that bears the likeness of rabbits. That means T-shirts with rabbits on them, rabbit jewelry, and even bunny-decorated home furnishings. That's why **Bunny Heaven** exists: to sell you loads of this stuff.

The Bunny Heaven Web site features links to a slew of items, all featuring a bunny theme. Apparel, crafts, home décor: You name it, they have it — with a bunny on it, of course. For example, a tapestry pillow featuring a lounging bunny and the words, "Home is where the rabbit is." Or a bathrobe with an appliqué featuring a sleeping bunny floating on a cloud. Or even a set of heart-shaped rabbit breed plates.

Besides spending money on your habit, you can also find out about rabbits on this site, too. Links to various rabbit-oriented sites on the Web are found on the opening page.

www.rabbitnetwork.org

The **House Rabbit Network** offers information on rabbit adoption as well as a listing of veterinarians in the northeastern United States. Hailing from Massachusetts, New Hampshire, and Connecticut, this excellent and complete Web site offers many solid educational articles regarding rabbit health — from weight watching to eye care. You can also make your own bunny e-card on this site, too.

www.rabbit.org

The **House Rabbit Society** (HRS) is an all-volunteer, nonprofit organization devoted to the rescue of rabbits and the education of the public on rabbit care. The HRS not only has chapters all over the country and even the world, but it also has an impressive presence on the Internet.

The House Rabbit Society home page is a veritable feast of information for rabbit lovers. You could literally spend hours browsing through all the information provided on this wonderful site. Start your exploration with the goodies listed in the center of your screen. The FAQS section provides details on litter-box training, diet, housing, chewing, and aggression. This section also provides you with helpful care links to topics such as how to safely change your rabbit's diet, how to figure out your rabbit's breed, and how to care for your rabbit in hot weather.

You can also get a list of all the HRS chapters in the United States and how to contact the one nearest you. And then there's the section on kids and rabbits, links to other rabbit sites, and a page of adorable bunny shots. Truth is, if you have a thing for rabbits, you just might get lost in the HRS site and never come out. They have veterinary referral lists as well.

www.spacerad.com/lara/rabbit.html

Larissa's Bunny Guide opens with this proclamation: "The purpose of this rabbit page is to educate people about rabbit care, behavior, and companionship." It's simple, but it says it. And the Web site's creator lives up to her purpose.

On the site, she provides an abundance of information on basic care, bunny behavior (including an answer to the age-old question "Why doesn't my bunny cuddle with me?") and taxonomy (dedicated to the scientific study of rabbits). She also has a section called "Foo Foo's Movie reviews." I'm not sure if these reviews are from a rabbit's point of view, but they very well could be. Don't forget to check out the "Pictures" link if you want to see the Webmaster's adorable bunnies and see the "Q & A" link for a bunch of bunny FAQs.

www.veterinarypartners.com

Veterinary Partners hosts hundreds of articles and links to information on all species of animals. This large library of rabbits information includes lots of disease info, behavior, and more.

www.oxbowhay.com

Oxbow Pet Products, one of the best and largest suppliers of healthy diets for rabbits, has a high level of integrity. They have sincerely supported the change to a healthy rabbit diet for years and continue to be sensitive to the needs of this community. They've changed and improved their products over the years and continue to do so. You can order all kinds of *fresh* grass hays in any quantity over the Internet and have it delivered instead of trying to locate this food in local stores. Also, their pellets are healthier than many if you have to feed pellets.

www.therabbitcharity.freeserve.co.uk

The Rabbit Charity, based in the United Kingdom, is an international charity that's dedicated to rescuing homeless rabbits, educating the public about rabbits, and preventing cruelty to rabbits. The organization publishes a quality newsletter by veterinarians for veterinarians, and their educational and diverse Web site has many links and carries articles on rabbit health topics — from aging to urinary tract infections, from arthritis to respiratory disease. This site tends to keep up with current topics and issues. The Rabbit Charity also organizes International Rabbit Day.

www.geocities.com/Petsburgh/6989/main.html

The Rabbit Ring is the rabbit ring. Just about everything on the Web has its own ring. For those readers who aren't computer-addicted and don't know what I'm talking about, a *ring* in Web-ese is a group of sites all linked together. These sites feature the same general topic.

Go to this site to find yourself hooked into a whole slew of rabbit Web sites from around the world. The Rabbit Ring home page features links to more than 300 sites, covering everything rabbit related, from pet rabbit sites to breeders to rescue groups.

The downside of surfing the bunny 'Net via a Web ring home page, such as The Rabbit Ring, is that the links aren't organized, and you don't know what you're going to get next. But if that doesn't bother you, go to The Rabbit Ring home page, find the link that says "Random" and click on it. You'll be transported to one of the sites on the ring. From there, you can do the same — you'll find the "Random," "Next," and "Previous" buttons at the bottom of the site, usually, and you'll be whisked to yet another rabbit Web site.

If you really feel like surfing the 'Net and just seeing all the cool bunny sites out there, try this approach. It's plenty of fun!

www.rabbitweb.net

Rabbit fanatics love the **Rabbit Web** for good reason. When you sign on to this site, you feel as if you have become part of an interactive community of rabbit lovers. And truth be told, you have.

The opening page of the Rabbit Web features news items and different timely items of interest to rabbit owners. Links at the side of the opening page take you to bulletin board discussions, live chats with other rabbit people, a gallery of bunny photos, classified ads, and a section featuring rabbit products for sale. A click on the Zine link brings you to an online magazine featuring a number of articles on a flurry of bunny topics, including how to buy your first rabbit, how to build a hutch, and how to litter train a rabbit.

You can even get free e-mail here. Imagine: your own rabbit-y e-mail address!

www.rainbowsbridge.com

Although not exclusively a rabbit Web site, I opted to include the **Rainbow Bridge** in this list because it's an important place on the Internet for rabbit owners — and pet owners of any kind.

The Rainbow Bridge is a site where grieving bunny owners can go to find solace and support as they try to cope with the loss of their pet. Plain and simple: If you lose your pet bunny, spend some time here. You'll find it a healing place. When visiting the Rainbow Bridge, you can look at the names of deceased bunnies and read their owners' sentiments or add your own. You can also participate in an online grief loss support group and chat and even post your pet's story or a poem in honor of your bunny on the site.

The Rainbow Bridge is both a sad and a happy site. It's sad because it contains the names of bunnies and other pets that have passed on, as well as the sentiments of grieving owners — some that will break your heart to read. On the other hand, it's a happy place because it shows just how much people really love their rabbits. It is also a place where you can honor the memory of your pet by writing about your memories. For many rabbit owners, the Rainbow Bridge site is the only place they can go to be understood in their moment of grief. For that reason, this site is worth its weight in gold.

Appendix

Rabbit Resources

· ·

*T*hese resources are worth scoping out. Many of these clubs and associations can provide invaluable information to help you become a better rabbit owner.

Educational Organizations

House Rabbit Society
148 Broadway
Richmond, CA 94804
(510) 970-7575

Ontario Rabbit Education Organization
PO Box 903, Station B, 515 Richmond Street
London, Ontario
CANADA N6A 4Z3
ontariorabbits@rogers.com

The Rabbit Charity
PO Box 23698
London N8 OWS
U.K.
www.therabbitcharity.freeserve.co.uk

Activity Clubs

Rabbit Hopping Organization of America

Linda J. Hoover

P.O. Box 184

Veneta, OR 97487

www.geocities.com/kaninhop2002/

National 4-H Headquarters

Families, 4-H & Nutrition

CSREES/USDA

1400 Independence Ave. SW

Washington DC 20250-2225

www.reeusda.gov/4h

Rabbit Rescue Groups

House Rabbit Network

P.O. Box 2602

Woburn, MA 01888-1102

781-431-1211

www.rabbitnetwork.org

Rabbit Rescue, Inc.

P.O. Box 452105

Sunrise, FL 33345

(954) 749-1367

http://fig.cox.miami.edu/Faculty/Dana/RR.html

House Rabbit Resource Network

P.O. Box 152432

Austin, TX 78715

(512) 444-3277

www.geocities.com/Heartland/Ranch/8093

Brambley Hedge Rabbit Rescue

P.O. BOX 54506

Phoenix, AZ 85078-4506

(480) 443-3990

www.nivoloc.com/RabbitRescue.html

Rabbit Rescue of Utah

P.O Box 613

Draper, Utah 84020-0613

www.mediaplan.com/people/wendy/rr

Zooh Corner Rabbit Rescue

P.O. Box 836

Claremont, CA 91711

www.mybunny.org

Rabbit Publications

Rabbits U.S.A. (Annual publication)

P.O. Box 6050

Mission Viejo, CA 92690

(949) 855-8822

www.animalnetwork.com

Rabbits Only (Bimonthly magazine)

P.O. Box 207

Holbrook, NY 11741

(516) 737-0763

www.rabbits.com

Critters (Annual publication)

P.O. Box 6050

Mission Viejo, CA 92690

(949) 855-8822

www.animalnetwork.com

Rabbit Tracks (Free quarterly publication)

P.O. Box 2602

Woburn, MA 01888-1102

www.rabbitnetwork.org/tracks.shtml

Rabbit Specialty Supply Outlets

Oxbow Pet Products, Inc.

29012 Mill Rd.

Murdock, NE 68407

(800) 249-0366

www.oxbowhay.com

(Many varieties of hays and healthy foods)

Thumpers Hollow

3089-C Clairemont Dr. PMB #202

San Diego, CA. 92117

(619) 276-4022

www.thumpershollow.com

The Ferret Store

P.O. Box 2346

Wilkes-Barre, PA 18703-2346

(888) 833-7738

customercare@neeps-inc.com

Bass Equipment

P.O. Box 352

Monett, MO 65708

(417)235-7557

ePetPals

3660 Soquel Dr.

Soquel, CA 95073-2035

800-604-2263

Leith Petworks

1276 Old Capital Pike

Bloomington, IN 47403

(800) 956-3576

www.leithpetwerks.com

PetMarket.com

PO BOX 523

Laurel, DE 19956

(888) PET-MRKT or (302) 875-7111

store.yahoo.com/petmarket/rabbitsupplies.html

Best Little Rabbit, Rodent & Ferret House

14325 Lake City Way NE

Seattle, WA 98125

Pet Loss Hotlines

University of California, Davis: 530-752-4200

Tufts University School of Veterinary Medicine (Massachusetts):
508-839-7966

Virginia-Maryland Regional College of Veterinary Medicine: 540-231-8038

Michigan State University College of Veterinary Medicine: 517-432-2696

Washington State University College of Veterinary Medicine:
509-335-5704

Chicago Veterinary Medical Association: 630-325-1600

Travel Guides

On the Internet you can go to www.petswelcome.com, a Web site featuring hotel listings for pet owners. However, the rest of the guides in this section are actual printed materials. Bon voyage with your bunny!

North America

AAA. *Traveling with Your Pet: The AAA Petbook*. Edited and published by American Automobile Association, June 2002.

Arden, Andrea. *Fodor's Road Guide USA: Where to Stay with Your Pet*. Fodor, June 2001.

Barish, Eileen. *Vacationing with Your Pet: Eileen's Directory of Pet-Friendly Lodging in the United States and Canada*. Pet Friendly Publications, Inc., August 2001.

United Kingdom

Farm Holiday Guides Publications. FHG, January 2003. www.HolidayGuides.com

AA Pet Friendly Places to Stay 2002. AA Publishing, November 2001. www.theaa.com/aboutaa/features/newfea038.html

Rabbit Registries

American Rabbit Breeders Association, Inc. (ARBA)

P.O. Box 426

Bloomington, IL 61702

(309) 664-7500

www.arba.net

British Rabbit Council

Purefoy House

7 Kirkgate, Newark,

Notts NG24 1AD England

www.thebrc.org

Australian Show Rabbit Council Inc.

PO Box 138

Rouse Hill NSW 2155

AustraliaShowRabbitCouncil@rabbits.au.com

www.rabbits.au.com

National Specialty Breed Clubs

American Belgian Hare Club
Frank Zaloudek
90206 N Harrington Rd
West Richland, WA 99353
509-967-3688
www.nmia.com/~arba/natclubinfo/natinfo.htm

American Beveren Rabbit Club
Pat Vezino
PO Box 65
Sunfield, MI 48890
517-566-8218

American Blue & White Rabbit Club
Charles Osborn
255 East Line Rd
Ballston Lake, NY 12019
518-899-2788

American Britannia Petite Rabbit Society
Janet Forrest
4092 King Dr
West Richland, WA 99353-9331
509-967-2134

American Checkered Giant Rabbit Club, Inc.
Carol M. Edwards
542 Aspen St NW
Toledo, OR 97391
541-336-2543
www.americancheckeredgiantrabbit.com

American Chinchilla Rabbit Breeders Association
Darlene Doyle
1017 S. Hillcrest
Springfield, MO 65802-5113
417-866-3908

American Dutch Rabbit Club, Inc.
Doreen Bengtson
Rt 1 Box 95
Lewiston, MN 55952
507-864-2103
www.geocities.com/EnchantedForest/6949/dutch.html

American Dwarf Hotot Rabbit Club
Sharon Toon
4061 Tremont Ave
Egg Harbor Township, NJ 08234-9421
609-641-8839
www.angelfire.com/mi3/buns4u/youthstand.htm

American English Spot Rabbit Club
Rosalie Berry
513 E Kent Rd
Lubbock, TX 79403-1609
806-762-1918
www.englishspots.8m.com

American Federation of New Zealand Rabbit Breeders
Susan Estes
23628 S Hwy 211
Colton, OR 97017
503-630-6193
www.geocities.com/newzealandrba/

American Fuzzy Lop Rabbit Club

Muriel Keyes

14255 SE Stephens

Portland, OR 97233

503-254-2902

http://forum.heartland.net/community/fuzzylop

American Harlequin Rabbit Club

Judy Bustle

1299 Josie Lane

Conover, NC 28613-8302

828-466-2274

www.geocities.com/~harlies/default.html

American Himalayan Rabbit Association

Errean Kratochvil

7715 Callan Court

New Port Richey, FL 34654

727-847-1001

http://ahra.homestead.com/

American Netherland Dwarf Rabbit Club

Sue Travis

326 Travis Lane

Rockwall, TX 75032

972-771-4394

www.andrc.com

American Polish Rabbit Club

Betty Strathman

417 Washington Ave

Terrace Park, OH 45174

513-831-3176

http://home.att.net/~polish/

American Sable Rabbit Society

Richard King

3360 Graham Rd

Rising Sun, OH 43457

419-288-3296

rnking@woh.rr

American Satin Rabbit Breeders Association

Edythe Weih

1895 Wilson Ave

Wilton, IA 52778

319-785-6365

http://titan.spaceports.com/~satins//

American Standard Chinchilla Rabbit Association

Robert Bowman

7905 Thompson Twp Rd 81

Bellevue, OH 44811

419-483-1009

American Tan Rabbit Club

Virginia Akin

718 CR 216,

Sweetwater, TX 79556

915-236-4032

http://crpud.net/~nwrs/atrsc/

Californian Rabbit Specialty Club

C. Eunita Boatman

22162 S Hunter Rd

Colton, OR 97017

503-824-2138

http://home.woh.rr.com/crsc/

Champagne d'Argent Rabbit Federation
Wayne Cleer
1704 Heisel Ave
Pekin, IL 61554
309-347-1347
cleerchamp@gallatinriver.net
http://hometown.aol.com/cdrgentfedration/CDRF.html

Cinnamon Rabbit Breeders Association
Barbara Hall
PO Box 571
Mexico, MO 65265-0571
573-594-2468
cinnamonrabbit@netscape.net

Créme d'Argent Rabbit Federation
Travis West
2293 Factory Rd
Albany, OH 45710
740-698-7285
west@cybermail.net
www.expage.com/page/cremedargent

Florida White Rabbit Breeders Association
Pat Fossler
21411 LA Hwy 1032
Denham Springs, LA 70726-7326
225-664-9791
http://members.tripod.com/~aliene22/index.htm

Giant Chinchilla Rabbit Association
Larry Miley
4195 County Rd 115
Mt Gilead, OH 43338
419-864-7936

Havana Rabbit Breeders Association

Joyce Walker

PO Drawer O

Cortez, CO 81321

970-565-2768

www.geocities.com/Heartland/Flats/1530

Holland Lop Rabbit Specialty Club

Pandora Allen

2633 Seven Eleven Rd

Chesapeake, VA 23322

757-421-9607

www.hlrsc.com

Hotot Rabbit Breeders International

Matthew Fischesser

4921 Cass Union Rd

Rising Sun, IN 47040

812-438-4227

Lop Rabbit Club of America

Jeanne Welch

PO Box 8367

Fremont, CA 94537-8367

510-793-4977

www.pettals.com/lrca.html

Mini Lop Rabbit Club of America

Pennie Grotheer

PO Box 17

Pittsburg, KS 66762

417-842-3317

www.tiadon.com/minilop/minilop.htm

National Angora Rabbit Breeders Club

Vicki Johnston

2380 Co. Rd. 9 NE

Nelson, MN 56355

320-762-0376

http://narbc.tripod.com

National Federation of Flemish Giant Rabbit Breeders

Allen Bush

2259 Barbara Dr

Camarillo, CA 93012

805-491-2029

bushflem@gte.net

www.nffgrb.com/

National Jersey Wooly Rabbit Club

Nancy Hinkston

1311 Poe Lane

San Jose, CA 95130

408-241-038

www.njwrc.bizland.com

National Lilac Rabbit Club of America

Bob Koch

N3650 Oak Ridge Rd

Waupaca, WI 54981-8707

715-258-3106

bobkoch@execpc

National Mini Rex Rabbit Club

Karen Heintz

1105 20th Ave.

Pipestone, MN 56164

507-825-3641

www.nmrrc.com

National Rex Rabbit Club

Bill Lorenz

21840 S 116th Ave

New Lenox, IL 60451

815-469-5150

http://members.tripod.com/rexrabbit

National Silver Rabbit Club

Laura Atkins

1030 SW KK Hwy

Holden, MO 64040-8221

816-732-6208

www.nationalsilverfoxrabbitclub.org

National Silver Fox Rabbit Club

Judith Oldenburg-Graf

PO Box 31

Lockridge, IA 52635

319-696-2604

www.nationalsilverfoxrabbitclub.org

Palomino Rabbit Co-Breeders Association

Deb Morrison

396202 W 4000 Rd

Skiatook, OK 74070

918-396-3587

www.geocities.com/Petsburgh/Park/4198/

Rhinelander Rabbit Club of America

Linda Carter

1560 Vine St.

El Centro, CA 92243

760-352-652

http://hop.to/rhinelanders

Silver Marten Rabbit Club

Leslie Tucker

2113 Sommer St

Napa, CA 94559

707-255-2821

rabbitld@napa.net

www.silvermarten.com

Pet-Sitting Associations

National Association of Pet Sitters

17000 Commerce Parkway, Suite C

Mt. Laurel, NJ 08054

856-439-0324

www.petsitters.org

Pet Sitters International

201 East King Street

King, NC 27021-9161

336-983-9222

www.petsit.com

Index

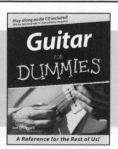

FOR DUMMIES®

A world of resources to help you grow

TRAVEL

0-7645-5453-0

0-7645-5438-7

0-7645-5444-1

Also available:

America's National Parks For Dummies
(0-7645-6204-5)

Caribbean For Dummies
(0-7645-5445-X)

Cruise Vacations For Dummies 2003
(0-7645-5459-X)

Europe For Dummies
(0-7645-5456-5)

Ireland For Dummies
(0-7645-6199-5)

France For Dummies
(0-7645-6292-4)

Las Vegas For Dummies
(0-7645-5448-4)

London For Dummies
(0-7645-5416-6)

Mexico's Beach Resorts For Dummies
(0-7645-6262-2)

Paris For Dummies
(0-7645-5494-8)

RV Vacations For Dummies
(0-7645-5443-3)

EDUCATION & TEST PREPARATION

0-7645-5194-9

0-7645-5325-9

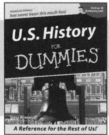

0-7645-5249-X

Also available:

The ACT For Dummies
(0-7645-5210-4)

Chemistry For Dummies
(0-7645-5430-1)

English Grammar For Dummies
(0-7645-5322-4)

French For Dummies
(0-7645-5193-0)

GMAT For Dummies
(0-7645-5251-1)

Inglés Para Dummies
(0-7645-5427-1)

Italian For Dummies
(0-7645-5196-5)

Research Papers For Dummies
(0-7645-5426-3)

SAT I For Dummies
(0-7645-5472-7)

U.S. History For Dummies
(0-7645-5249-X)

World History For Dummies
(0-7645-5242-2)

HEALTH, SELF-HELP & SPIRITUALITY

0-7645-5154-X

0-7645-5302-X

0-7645-5418-2

Also available:

The Bible For Dummies
(0-7645-5296-1)

Controlling Cholesterol For Dummies
(0-7645-5440-9)

Dating For Dummies
(0-7645-5072-1)

Dieting For Dummies
(0-7645-5126-4)

High Blood Pressure For Dummies
(0-7645-5424-7)

Judaism For Dummies
(0-7645-5299-6)

Menopause For Dummies
(0-7645-5458-1)

Nutrition For Dummies
(0-7645-5180-9)

Potty Training For Dummies
(0-7645-5417-4)

Pregnancy For Dummies
(0-7645-5074-8)

Rekindling Romance For Dummies
(0-7645-5303-8)

Religion For Dummies
(0-7645-5264-3)

Available wherever books are sold. Go to www.dummies.com or call 1-877-762-2974 to order direct

FOR DUMMIES®

Plain-English solutions for everyday challenges

HOME & BUSINESS COMPUTER BASICS

0-7645-0838-5

0-7645-1663-9

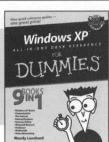

0-7645-1548-9

Also available:

Excel 2002 All-in-One Desk Reference For Dummies (0-7645-1794-5)

Office XP 9-in-1 Desk Reference For Dummies (0-7645-0819-9)

PCs All-in-One Desk Reference For Dummies (0-7645-0791-5)

Troubleshooting Your PC For Dummies (0-7645-1669-8)

Upgrading & Fixing PCs For Dummies (0-7645-1665-5)

Windows XP For Dummies (0-7645-0893-8)

Windows XP For Dummies Quick Reference (0-7645-0897-0)

Word 2002 For Dummies (0-7645-0839-3)

INTERNET & DIGITAL MEDIA

0-7645-0894-6

0-7645-1642-6

0-7645-1664-7

Also available:

CD and DVD Recording For Dummies (0-7645-1627-2)

Digital Photography All-in-One Desk Reference For Dummies (0-7645-1800-3)

eBay For Dummies (0-7645-1642-6)

Genealogy Online For Dummies (0-7645-0807-5)

Internet All-in-One Desk Reference For Dummies (0-7645-1659-0)

Internet For Dummies Quick Reference (0-7645-1645-0)

Internet Privacy For Dummies (0-7645-0846-6)

Paint Shop Pro For Dummies (0-7645-2440-2)

Photo Retouching & Restoration For Dummies (0-7645-1662-0)

Photoshop Elements For Dummies (0-7645-1675-2)

Scanners For Dummies (0-7645-0783-4)

Get smart! Visit www.dummies.com

- **Find listings of even more Dummies titles**

- **Browse online articles, excerpts, and how-to's**

- **Sign up for daily or weekly e-mail tips**

- **Check out Dummies fitness videos and other products**

- **Order from our online bookstore**

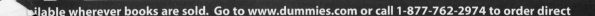